THE MATRIMONIAL IMPEDIMENT OF PUBLIC PROPRIETY

A Historical Synopsis and a Commentary

The Catholic University of America
Canon Law Studies
No. 304

The Matrimonial Impediment of Public Propriety

A Historical Synopsis and a Canonical Commentary

A DISSERTATION

SUBMITTED TO THE FACULTY OF THE SCHOOL OF CANON LAW
OF THE CATHOLIC UNIVERSITY OF AMERICA IN PARTIAL
FULFILLMENT OF THE REQUIREMENTS FOR THE
DEGREE OF DOCTOR OF CANON LAW

BY
JOHN F. GALLAGHER, J.C.L.
Priest of the Diocese of San Diego

The Catholic University of America Press
Washington, D. C.
1952

NIHIL OBSTAT:

JOANNES ROGG SCHMIDT, J.C.D.

Censor Deputatus

Washingtonii, D. C., die 10 Februarii, 1952

IMPRIMATUR:

✠ CAROLUS FRANCISCUS BUDDY

Episcopus Sancti Didaci

Sancti Didaci, die 1 Februarii, 1952

Copyright 1952
THE CATHOLIC UNIVERSITY OF AMERICA PRESS, INC

MURRAY & HEISTER
WASHINGTON, D. C.

PRINTED BY
TIMES AND NEWS PUBLISHING CO.
GETTYSBURG, PA., U.S.A.

To Mary
Immaculate Mother of God

TABLE OF CONTENTS

TABLE OF CONTENTS (Continued)

TABLE OF CONTENTS (Continued)

FOREWORD

The promulgation of the Code of Canon Law marked a radical and all but complete change in the impediment of public propriety. Hence a work purporting to treat of the impediment naturally falls into two sections. The first section, leading up to the Code, has little more than a historical interest. Yet, because of certain points of contact between the present law and the former legislation both on public propriety and affinity, a brief historical outline may serve to furnish a background against which the impediment of public propriety in the Code law may be better seen in perspective.

The second section of this dissertation is a canonical study of the impediment of public propriety in the present Church legislation. The impediment, as set forth in canon 1078, is true to its historical antecedent in that it is a celebrated subject of controversy. It is no exaggeration to say that a commentary on the present law consists, for the most part, in an attempt to resolve a series of doubts as reflected in the commentaries. In trying to arrive at a solution of the various problems presented the writer has drawn heavily on the numerous commentators of the Code law on matrimony, although frequent reference is made to the classical commentators on the pre-Code law on marriage.

It is a pleasant duty to give expression to the heartfelt gratitude of the writer towards His Excellency, The Most Reverend Charles F. Buddy, Bishop of San Diego, California, for the opportunity of pursuing advanced studies; towards the Faculty of the School of Canon Law for their unfailing assistance; and towards his family and many friends, who by their prayers and encouragement have fortified the years of study and research.

PART I

Historical Synopsis

CHAPTER I

The Impediment of Public Propriety in the Civil Law Systems

ARTICLE 1. IN ROMAN LAW

. Betrothal, in one form or another, is such a natural prelude to marriage that it is not surprising that it found a place in the Roman legal system. Betrothal, or *sponsalia,* as it was called, gave rise to the marriage impediment of quasi-affinity in Roman law.[1] The derivation of the word *sponsalia* is given by Ulpian (ca. 170-228).[2] According to Ulpian, *sponsalia* or betrothal in the pre-classical period had taken the form of *sponsiones*—promises—between the intending husband or his *paterfamilias* and the *paterfamilias* or tutor of the woman. Florentinus (180) gave in succinct form the concept of betrothal in Roman law when he said that betrothal was the mutual promise of a future marriage.[3]

Betrothal was considered a verbal contract in Roman law.[4] However, it differed from the usual verbal contract inasmuch as there was no available judicial action to compel marriage, at least in classical times. Freedom from such action to compel marriage came

---

[1] Jolowicz, *Historical Introduction To The Study Of Roman Law* (Cambridge: University Press, 1932), p. 242, n. 3. The title *iustitia publicae proprietatis* or simply *publica proprietas*—public propriety—was later in common use among canonists for designating in Church legislation the impediment to marriage which arose from *sponsalia*—betrothal—and a non-consummated marriage. Cf. Scherer, *Handbuch des Kirchenrechtes* (2 vols., Graz, 1886-1898), II, 347 (hereafter cited Scherer); Freisen, *Geschischte des canonischen Eherechts bis zum Verfall der Glossenlitteratur* (2. Ausgabe, Paderborn, 1893), p. 497 (hereafter cited Freisen); Esmein, *Le Mariage en Droit Canonique* (2 ed., 2 vols., par R. Genestal et J. Dauvillier, Paris: Recueil Sirey, 1929-1935), I, 159 (hereafter cited Esmein); Feije, *De Impedimentis et Dispensationibus Matrimonialibus* (2 ed., Lovanii, 1874), n. 387 (hereafter cited Feije).

[2] D. (23.1) 2-3.

[3] D. (23.1) 1. "Sponsalia sunt mentio et repromissio nuptiarum futurarum."

[4] D (15.17) 185.

to be regarded as a matter affecting the public good. Paulus (+210) in his *Responsa*[5] declared that even an indirect enforcement of the promise to marry was not in the public interest.

This expression of Roman jurisprudence is reflected in the Decretal Collection of Pope Gregory IX (1234)[6] and in the *Ne temere* decree of the Sacred Congregation of the Council, which obtained the force of law on Easter Sunday, April 19, 1908,[7] as well as in the present Code of Canon Law,[8] all of which deny judicial action as arising from betrothal, if the action is to be invoked for the purpose of enforcing the contracting of marriage.

In the classical period of Roman Law no specified form was required for betrothal. Ulpian is authority for the statement that consent alone was all that was necessary.[9] However, betrothal retained its many legal effects. Ulpian further stated that a man was forbidden to marry the *sponsa* of his father, and similarly a *sponsa* was forbidden to marry the father of her *sponsus*. Paulus made mention of a decision in a case in which a man was forbidden to marry the mother of his *sponsa* because she was looked upon as his mother-in-law.[10]

A party to a betrothal could not be betrothed to two persons at the same time, nor could such a party while betrothed to one party marry another. Such action entailed praetorian infamy.[11] By a law attributed to Emperor Septimius Severus (193-211), legal action was given to the *sponsus* for infidelity in the *sponsa*. If she was found guilty, she was liable to the penalty set down for adultery in the *Lex Iulia de Adulteriis*.[12] Justinian (527-565) accepted in principle the law of Severus that immorality in a betrothed woman was equivalent to adultery.[13] Justinian also incorporated in his Code the provisions of the Theodosian Code (3. 6), which set

---

[5] D (45.1) 134.

[6] C. 17, X, *de sponsalibus et matrimoniis*, IV, 1.

[7] *Acta Sanctae Sedis* (41 vols., Romae, 1865-1908), XL (1907), 525 (hereafter cited *ASS*).

[8] Canon 1017, § 3.

[9] "Sufficit nudus consensus."—D. (23.1) 4.

[10] D. (23.2) (14.4).

[11] D. (3.2) (13.1-4).

[12] D. (48.5) (13.3).

[13] C. (4.13) 1; cf. N. 143 (*De raptis mulieribus et quae raptoribus nubunt*), praefatio.

forth that when an official, if charged with the administration of a province and therefore in a position to influence decisions, contracted betrothals, the parents of the woman, or the woman herself, could recant without incurring any penalty. Moreover, if they wished to keep the sponsal gift they could do so. The law was also extended to the children, the relatives, and the subordinates of such officials.[14] The Roman law and especially the legislation of Justinian, when it was in accordance with the tenets of the Christian faith, acquired special influence in church matters.[15] With the exception of Lombardy, Justinian law was received generally throughout Italy. In the regions of Central Italy subject to the Oriental Empire, the law of the land, the *ius terrae,* was the Justinian law promulgated in the West by the *Pragmatic Sanction* on the petition of Pope Vigilius, August 13, 554.[16]

In Southern Italy, subject to the Oriental Emperors up to the time when it became occupied by the Normans, the law of Justinian, somewhat modified however by the later law of the Byzantine Emperors, held sway as the law of the land. The Theodosian Code (438), especially as adopted in the Breviary of Alaric (506), was extended to Spain and Gaul. It was admitted as the personal law of the clergy and as the law of the Church by the bishops of the region in accordance with Constitution 58 of the Ripuarian Law, *Ecclesia vivit lege Romana.*[17]

---

[14] C. (5.2) 1.

[15] Cf. Kurtscheid, *Historia Iuris Canonici, Historia Institutorum,* Vol. I (ab Ecclesiae fundatione usque ad Gratianum), (Romae: Officium Libri Catholici, 1941), pp. 184-185 (hereafter cited Kurtscheid); Cicognani, Canon Law (2. ed., authorized English version by J. O'Hara and F. Brennan, Philadelphia: Dolphin Press, 1935), pp. 47-54 (hereafter cited Cicognani).

[16] Jaffé, *Regesta Pontificum Romanorum ab condita Ecclesia ad annum post Christum natum MCXCVIII* (2. ed., correctam et auctam auspiciis Gulielmi Wattenbach curaverunt F. Kaltenbrunner, P. Ewald, S. Loẅenfeld, 2 vols. in I, Lipsiae, 1885-1888), n. 137 (hereafter cited Jaffé).

[17] *Monumenta Germaniae Historica,* 188 vols. incomplete, Hannoverae, 1826-; *Leges* (5 vols., Vols. I-IV, ed. G. Pertz; Vol. V, ed. G. Pertz-G. Waitz-H. Brunner, Hannoverae, 1835-1889), V, 242 (hereafter cited *MGH, Leges*); Mansi, *Sacrorum Conciliorum Nova et Amplissima Collectio* (53 vols. in 60, Parisiis, 1901-1927), XVIIB, 41 (hereafter cited Mansi); cf. Van Hove, *Commentarium Lovaniense in Codicem Iuris Canonici,* Vol. I, Tom. I, *Prolegomena ad Codicem Iuris Canonici* (2 ed., Mechliniae-Romae: H. Dessain, 1945), pp. 220-221 (hereafter cited *Prolegomena*).

ARTICLE 2. IN GERMANIC LAW

Among the Germanic peoples the institution of betrothal or *sponsalia* had its separate juridical development. The simple marriage act which obtained in the Germanic period became divided in the Frankish period into two distinct legal acts. These two acts combined were essential for the creation of the marriage relation.[18]

Betrothal was looked upon rather as the initial stage of marriage than as a commitment for marriage at some future date.[19] Accordingly, the obligations imposed by betrothal were viewed with utmost seriousness. A Lombard law under King Rotharius (636-652) set forth that, if a betrothed woman had been accused by her betrothed of carnal intercourse with another, the sin was to be considered adultery.[20]

However, it was permissible for the parents to purify such a one with certain rites of purification and, in that case, the betrothed man was compelled to marry her or suffer a penalty to the extent of double the sponsal gift. But if the parents could not purify her, the sponsal gift had to be returned to the man, and the woman was subjected to the penalty for adultery.[21]

A penalty of double the amount of the sponsal gift was imposed on parents who had betrothed their daughter to one man and later fraudulently, with or without her consent, married her off to another.[22] A similar law in Burgundian territory, as adopted from the Theodosian Code (3. 5), compelled the parents to return to the betrothed man thus defrauded four times the amount of the sponsal gift.[23]

By a law of Emperor Lothaire I (840-855) in the *Lex Alamanorum* a man who took the betrothed of another was bound to re-

---

[18] Huebner, *A History of Germanic Private Law;* translated by Francis S. Philbrick (Boston: Little Brown and Company, 1918), p. 597 (hereafter cited Huebner); Hörmann, *Quasiaffinität* (2 vols., Innsbruck: Verlag der Wagner'schen *Universitätsbuchhandlung,* 1897-1906), II, 467.

[19] Joyce, *Christian Marriage* (New York: Sheed and Ward, 1933), p. 48 (hereafter cited Joyce); Huebner, p. 601; Hormann, *Quasiaffinität,* II, 554.

[20] *MGH, Leges,* tom. IV (ed. G. H. Pertz, 1868), 46, n. 192.

[21] *MGH, Leges, loc. cit.*

[22] *MGH, Leges, loc. cit.*

[23] *MGH, Leges,* tom. III (ed. G. H. Pertz, 1863), 612, n. 1.

turn her and pay a fine of two hundred *solidi.*[24] A man who violently carried off the betrothed of another or deceitfully led her into marrying him was compelled to return her and pay a fine of eighty *solidi.*[25] The capitularies of Louis II (843-875) and Lothaire I appealed to Pope Siricius (384-399) as authority to show that a man may not take as his wife the betrothed of another.[26]

It seems that the oldest Germanic law which specifically mentioned as an impediment to marriage the relationship between a man and the betrothed of his blood relative is to be found in a constitution of Emperor Henry II (1002-1024).[27] In this constitution it seems that the Emperor attributed to betrothals an effect equal to the effect deriving from marriage.

The consequence of dividing the marriage ceremony into two distinct acts in the German law territories was that neither act alone sufficed to establish the marriage relation. The betrothal was followed, when the designated day arrived, by the delivery of the bride from her guardian (the holder of the *mundium*) to the bridegroom (the newly constituted *mundoaldus*). This was the *traditio puellae* (Anglo-Saxon *gifta*). It was performed as a public and solemn rite in the bride's home in the presence of the kindred of both parties, and was accompanied with the marriage feast. The final act was the festive leading of the bride home to the bridegroom's house—the *traditio in domum.*

The law books of the middle ages emphasized, more frequently and with greater stress than did the Frankish sources, the importance of marital cohabitation as the act most decisive for the consummation of the legal consequences of marriage. However, that betrothals and nuptials were equally necessary preconditions for the creation of a legally valid marriage, and continued also to constitute one act legally, is shown by the generally prevalent custom of performing in connection with each the formalities that were usual in the other.[28]

---

[24] *MGH, Leges,* III, 62.

[25] *MGH, Leges,* III, 301.

[26] *MGH, Leges,* tom. I (ed. G. H. Pertz, 1835), 278; cf. *infra,* p. 25.

[27] "Ut quicumque . . . uxorem duxerit vel desponsaverit, si morte praeventus fuerit, nulli propinquorum suorum liceat viduam vel desponsatam illius uxorem ducere."—*MGH, Leges,* IV, 585; cf. Hörmann, *Quasiaffinität,* II, 313.

[28] Huebner, pp. 601-602; Hörmann, *Quasiaffinität,* II, 467; Joyce, p. 50.

This also is the explanation of the fact that expressions as used in designation of betrothed persons were employed also with reference to married people—*Ehegespons, promessi, sponsi, eponser, to espouse, to wed, vermählen.*[29] It is furthermore worthy of note that an essential part of the ceremony in both cases, at least in the Lombard law territories, was the handing over of the bride, but in the betrothal ceremony the man immediately handed the bride back again to the mundium holder.[30]

During the later Carolingian period there was a lack of civil law enactments on betrothals because of the growing recognition of the Church in such matters. According to Huebner, "this had the further effect that the formal requisites of secular law, particularly the old division of the ceremony into betrothal and nuptials, were displaced."[31]

ARTICLE 3. THE INFLUENCE OF THE CIVIL LAW ON CHURCH LAW

In order to evaluate the influence of civil law on the institution of betrothal and on the impediment of public propriety it will be helpful to review briefly the relationship that existed between canon law and civil law. While the Church never admitted that the civil rulers had a right to legislate for purely spiritual matters, it is not to be thought that civil law had no influence in church affairs. The civil law, in some instances, applied also to ecclesiastical affairs, but only in so far as it was accepted by proper ecclesiastical authority.[32]

Although it was not accorded the honored place that has been given to Roman Law in the Church, the Germanic law had a definite influence, especially on the legal institutions regarding property and benefices. The so called barbarian laws, *leges barbarorum,* were rarely received into the canonical collections, although the *capitularies* of the German and Frankish kings and the privileges granted by them to the Church quite frequently found a place in these collections.[33]

---

[29] Cf. Huebner, p. 602; Joyce, p. 50.

[30] Huebner, p. 602.

[31] *A History of Germanic Private Law,* p. 602.

[32] Van Hove, *Prolegomena,* p. 226.

[33] Van Hove, *Prolegomena,* p. 262.

Charlemagne (800-814) exercised power not only in civil affairs but also in ecclesiastical matters, and so issued many *capitularies* on matters dealing with the Church.[34] In the beginning of the tenth century Regino of Prüm (+ 915) in his work *De Synodalibus Causis* (906) incorporated two hundred and sixty-five texts from *capitularies,* and in doing so seemed not to doubt the power of the secular princes to make laws for the Church.[35]

On the other hand, while Burchard of Worms (+ 1025) incorporated in his *Decretum* (1012) eighty-nine texts from *capitularies* of secular rulers, he ascribed them to Church authorities, thereby showing that although he did not wish to publicize their secular origin he approved the reforms they introduced. Burchard treated the provisions of Roman law in a similar manner.[36]

Gratian (+ ca. 1157) incorporated in his *Decretum* (ca. 1140) many capitularies taken especially from Charlemagne. Some of them were not given textually, but they were often proposed by Gratian as sources of law, especially when they favored the Church and tended to the emendation of morals or the reforming of marriage regulations. Gratian did not state that these capitularies had a supplementary force in canon law. Many of them however were received by the Church.[37]

From the foregoing it may be seen that the Germanic law had no small influence on Church legislation. It was, however, to the Roman law that the popes more frequently appealed in support of canon law, particularly from the ninth century onward. From that time, one may say, Roman law was accorded in the Church a position of influence subordinate only to the canon law itself. Pope Eugene II (824-827) in a decretal letter to the Bishop of Vienne in France recommended to him all that he found approved by the popes in the law of Justinian.[38]

---

[34] *MGH, Leges,* I, 161.

[35] Migne, *Patrologiae Cursus Completus, Series Latina* (221 vols., Parisiis, 1844-1864), CXXXII, 175-455 (hereafter cited *MPL*). The edition by F. W. H. Wasserschleben, *Reginonis abbatis libri duo de synodalibus causis et disciplinis ecclesiasticis,* Lipsiae, 1840, was not available to the writer.

[36] *MPL,* CXXXX, 537-1090; cf. Van Hove, *Prolegomena,* p. 263.

[37] Van Hove, *Prolegomena,* p. 265; cf. c. 4, C. XV, q. 3; *Dictum* of Gratian to cc. 6, 7, D. X.

[38] Mansi, XIV, 414; Jaffé, n. 2563.

It is clear from this letter that Pope Eugene attributed to Justinian law a subsidiary legal force in the Church. Pope John VIII (872-882) was very explicit in invoking the Roman law as an auxiliary legal system for the Church. In the year 878 this pope declared, erroneously however, that the Roman laws concerning spurious children were made with the sanction of Pope John (II) (533-535) as well as the Emperor Justinian.[39]

In 867 Pope Nicholas I (858-867) requested from King Charles the Bald (840-877) that a new trial be granted in the cause of the divorce of Charles' nephew, King Lothaire II (855-869), and directed that a place for the trial be selected in accordance with the sacred canons and the venerable Roman laws.[40]

In the tenth century Pope Benedict VI (973-974), speaking of marriages that were prohibited, stated that not even the civil laws prohibited marriage between a man and a woman whose sister he had previously betrothed.[41] Pope Urban II, in 1088, declared that neither the civil laws nor the Church admitted betrothal if the consent of the parents and the consent of the betrothed were not both present.[42]

Hincmar of Rheims (806-882) very frequently appealed to the Theodosian Code in his writings, but only inasmuch as it was also received as the law of the Church by the popes. Speaking of the Roman law, Hincmar stated that these Christian laws were often promulgated by the emperors and kings at the request of the popes, and that the provisions of Roman law as well as the canon law were used in court trials with the sanction of the popes. He mentioned particularly Popes Damasus I (366-384), Leo I

---

[39] ". . . sanctientibus Ioanne Papa Romano et Iustiniano Imperatore."—Mansi, XVII, 112; Jaffé, n. 3167.

[40] ". . . ubi nulla sit vis multitudinis formidanda et non sit difficile testes producere vel ceteras personas, quae tam a sanctis canonibus quam a memorandis romanis legibus in huiusmodi controversiis requiruntur."—Mansi, XV, 318-321; Jaffé, n. 2872.

[41] Mansi, IX, 863; Jaffé, n. 3773; cf. c. 18, C. XXVII, q. 2; there is much doubt about the authenticity of this letter. Cf. *infra*, pp. 36-37.

[42] *MPL*, CLI, 534; Jaffé, n. 5382.

(440-461), and Gregory the Great (590-604) as sanctioning the use of Roman law.[43]

Certain councils of France, especially those held under Archbishop Hincmar (845-882) based some of their decisions on Roman law. The Council of Soissons (853), appealing to the Roman law, decreed that a judicial sentence that was not issued in writing was void.[44] The Council of Reims (991), which reflects many of Hincmar's ideas, quoted his dictum that the Church, at least in some instances, approved and observed the law of Justinian.[45]

---

[43] "Leges saeculi christianae, quas etiam in ecclesiasticis necessitatibus promulgari saepe soleat ab Imperatoribus et regibus, ecclesia postulante, quarumque sententiis in suis judicibus simul cum sententiis canonum episcopalis auctoritas frequentius utatur et in tantum acceptet, ut Damasus et Leo atque sanctus Gregorius, legum sententias fecerint esse canonicas." *MPL,* CXXVI, 274; cf. Van Hove, *Prolegomena,* pp. 237-238.

[44] Mansi, XIV, 182.

[45] "Iustiniani catholici Imperatoris lex, quam probat et servat Ecclesia."—Mansi, XIX, 165; cf. Van Hove, *Prolegomena,* p. 238.

CHAPTER II

IDENTITY OF BETROTHAL AND NON-CONSUMMATED MARRIAGE IN CHURCH LEGISLATION

ARTICLE 1. REASON FOR THE ABSENCE OF CHURCH LEGISLATION REGARDING THE IMPEDIMENT OF PUBLIC PROPRIETY TILL ABOUT THE TWELFTH CENTURY

In Roman law the marriage impediment of quasi-affinity or public propriety had its origin in betrothal—the Roman law *sponsalia.*[1] For many centuries after the introduction of Christianity into the Empire, Church legislation was silent regarding the impediment. It was not until the eleventh or twelfth centuries that the impediment of public propriety as arising from betrothal found a place in Church legislation.[2]

Yet, many authors maintain, with good reason, that the impediment of public propriety as it existed in canon law derived from the Roman law.[3] That the impediment of public propriety

---

[1] Cf. *supra*, p. 3.

[2] Freisen, p. 500; Wernz, *Ius Decretalium* (3. ed., 6 vols., Prati, 1913-1915), Lib. IV, tit. XIX, n. 448 (hereafter cited Wernz); De Smet, *De Sponsalibus et Matrimonio* (4. ed., Brugis: Charles Beyaert, 1927), n. 635 (hereafter cited De Smet); Cappello, *Tractatus Canonico-moralis de Sacramentis* (3 vols., in 6, Vol. III, Partes I et II, *De Matrimonio* 4. ed., Romae: Marietti, 1939), III, n. 555 (hereafter cited *De Matrimonio*); Chelodi, *Ius Matrimoniale iuxta Codicem* (3 ed., Tridenti, 1921), n. 103 (hereafter cited Chelodi, *Ius Matrimoniale*).

[3] Esmein, I, 159; Hörmann, *Quasiaffinität,* II, 13; Devoti, *Institionum Canonicarum Libri IV* (4. ed., 3 vols., Venetiis, 1827), II, 213 (hereafter cited *Institiones Canonicae*); Rosset, *De Sacramento Matrimonii Tractatus Dogmaticus, Moralis, Canonicus, Liturgicus et Iudiciarius* (6 vols., Parisiis, 1895-1896), III, n. 1984 (hereafter cited Rosset).

Freisen (1853-1932) denied that any connection existed between the impediment of public propriety as it existed in Roman law and church law.—*Geschichte des Canonischen Eherechts bis zum Verfall der Glossenlitteratur,* p. 449; Gasparri (1852-1934) (*Tractatus Canonicus de Matrimonio* [3. ed., 2 vols., Parisiis, 1904], n. 801) suggested that the impediment of public

in Church law derived from the Roman law seems all the more probable because of the fact that in both laws the same reason was given for the existence of the impediment, namely, when there was question of marriage not only what was lawful but also what was proper had to be taken into account.[4]

In view of the great probability that the impediment of public propriety as it later existed in canon law really derived from the Roman law, the question why the impediment had not been made the subject of ecclesiastical legislation naturally presents itself. In the early centuries of Christianity the absence of such legislation could well be understood. It was not till the fourth century that the Church was no longer faced with open persecution, and for some time afterwards disciplinary legislation could hardly be regarded as a primary consideration. Moreover, after the conversion of Emperor Constantine the Great (306-337) the Roman law obtained a growing influence and many of its provisions were tacitly accepted by the Church.[5]

The absence of such legislation from about the fifth or sixth centuries onward would not be so readily explained however. The most probable reason for this absence is that which according to Joyce (1864-1943)[6] was first given by Hörmann (1865-1946)[7]

---

propriety may have been gradually introduced into Church law through custom arising from the decent mores of a Christian civilization (hereafter cited *De Matrimonio* [1904]).

[4] Compare D. (23.2) 42 with c. 3, X, *de sponsalibus et matrimoniis,* IV, 1. Regarding this chapter in the Decretals Panormitanus (1386-1453) stated: "Scias quod hoc impedimentum non causatur ex consanguinitate, nec ex affinitate: quia ante consummationem matrimonii, seu carnis commixtionem non est orta affinitas: sed oritur ex consensu praestito in sponsalibus, et fuit inductum hoc impedimentum ab Ecclesia propter honestatem, dumtaxat: quia quandoque oriebantur graves inimicitiae inter consanguineos, cum uni desponsatam alius consanguineorum quaerebat ducere in uxorem, et appellavit Ecclesia illud impedimentum publicam honestatem: quia non poterat dari congruentius nomen, cum non posset attribui alicui ex cognationibus, scilicet legali, vel spirituali, vel carnali: nam triplex est cognatio; istud ergo impedimentum est per se ex sola honestate ab Ecclesia inductum."—*Commentaria in Quinque Libros Decretalium* (5 vols. in 7, Venetiis, 1588), Lib. IV, tit. 1, n. 3 (hereafter cited *Commentaria*); cf. Esmein, I, 148.

[5] Van Hove, *Prolegomena,* pp. 198-199; Kurtscheid, p. 313.

[6] Cf. Joyce, pp. 46-47 and 84.

[7] Cf. Hörmann, *Quasiaffinität,* II, 217-223, also pp. 454 and 568-569.

namely, that there developed in the Church a practice which combined betrothal and marriage into one act. This combined act was called *pactio coniugalis* or simply *desponsatio.*[8] When betrothal and marriage were combined into one act there was no place for the impediment of public propriety, for the *desponsatio,* since it already constituted a valid marriage, would have given rise, as it did in Roman law and in early Church law, to the impediment of affinity proper.

In the early centuries the matrimonial impediment of affinity as recognized by the Church was adopted from the Mosaic law and from the Roman law. In both those legal systems affinity arose, not from carnal union, but from valid marriage, whether consummated or not.[9] Hence it was natural to expect that this same concept of affinity would have been admitted by the Church. That such was actually the case seems well established.[10]

It was several centuries before the Church used its power to legislate with regard to the impediment of affinity, but when it did so, its legislation reflected the Mosaic and Roman law concept of affinity. The first ecclesiastical legislation on the impediment of affinity is to be found in canon 61 of the Council of Elvira (300/306).[11] Two councils held in Rome, one in the year 402[12] and one in 721,[13] contain further legislation respecting the impediment of

---

[8] Cf. Esmein, I, 112-113; Huebner, p. 604; Hörmann, *Quasiaffinität,* II, 218.

[9] Joyce, p. 522; De Becker, *De Matrimonio Praelectiones Canonicae* (ed. nova, Lovanii; Fr. Ceuterick, 1931), p. 189; Wahl, *The Matrimonial Impediments of Consanguinity and Affinity,* The Catholic University of America Canon Law Studies, n. 90 (Washington, D. C.: The Catholic University of America, 1934), pp. 67-68; Heinlein, "Affinity in the Bible," *Catholic Encyclopedia,* I, 178.

[10] Joyce, pp. 535, 537 and 638; Cappello, *De Matrimonio,* n. 540; Freisen, p. 449; Scherer, II, 333; De Smet, n. 624; Wernz, IV, n. 429, note 31.

[11] Mansi, II, 15; Bruns, Canones *Apostolorum et Conciliorum Saeculorum IV, V, VI, VII* (2 vols., Berolini, 1839), II, 10 (hereafter cited Bruns); Joyce, *loc. cit.;* Wahl, p. 70.

[12] Mansi, III, 1137.

[13] Mansi, XII, 264; Hardouin, *Acta Conciliorum et Epistolae Decretales ac Constitutiones Summorum Pontificum* (12 vols., Parisiis, 1714-1715), III, 1865.

affinity.[14] The introduction of the idea of carnal union as the basis for the impediment of affinity came only at a later date.

In the Oriental Church St. Basil (+ 379) in his letter to Diodorus of Tarsus (378-ca. 393)[15] was the first to use the words of Genesis (2. 24), *"Et erunt duo in carne una,"* as one of the reasons justifying the rule against marriage with a deceased wife's sister. This method of reasoning paved the way for the later doctrine which asserted that the physical union of a man and a woman was the foundation of the impediment of affinity in law.[16]

In the West St. Augustine (+ 430) in a similar manner invoked this same reason to show the gravity of the sin involved in the union of Juda and Thamar (Genesis, 38. 13-18). Yet there is no evidence to show that St. Augustine regarded carnal union as the real basis for all prohibitions that concerned affinity.[17]

The first papal document in which carnal union appears to be considered as the actual basis for the prohibition of marriage with *affines* is a response of somewhat doubtful origin. This response allegedly was sent by Pope St. Gregory (590-604) to St. Augustine of Canterbury (+ 604).[18]

The time of the introduction of the doctrine which regarded affinity as arising from carnal copulation alone and apart from a valid marriage is not known with any degree of exactitude. Michiels[19] holds that the introduction of the doctrine is traceable to the pseudo-Isidorian Decretals in the ninth century. This author

---

[14] Oesterle, *Consultationes de Jure Matrimoniali* (Romae: Officium Libri Catholici, 1942), p. 266; cf. *infra,* p. 22.

[15] *Ep. CLX,* c. 7, n. 5—*MPG,* XXXII, 627; cf. Hörmann, II, 324, n. 1.

[16] Oesterle, *loc. cit.;* Hörmann, *loc. cit.;* Joyce, p. 535.

[17] *Contra Faustum Manichaeum,* Lib. XXII, c. 61—*MPL,* XLI, 538; *Questiones ad Heptateuchum,* Lib. III, n. 58—*MPL,* XXXIV, 704; cf. Esmein, I, 418-419.

[18] Venerabilis Beda, *Historia Ecclesiastica,* Lib. I, c. 27—*MPL,* XCV, 59; Hörmann, *op. cit.,* II, 237-242; Joyce, p. 536. For a brief discussion of the authenticity of the *Responsum* of Pope Saint Gregory to Saint Augustine of Canterbury see Eidenschenk, *The Election of Bishops in the Letters of Pope Gregory the Great,* The Catholic University of America Canon Law Studies, n. 215 (Washington, D. C.: The Catholic University of America Press, 1945), p. 61, note 158.

[19] *Principia Generalia de Personis in Ecclesia* (Lublin: Universitas Catholica, 1932), p. 215.

maintains that an apocryphal rescript of Pope Gregory the Great to Felix, Bishop of Messina, which is found in the Isidorian Decretals,[20] influenced the tract of Hincmar of Reims *De Nuptiis Stephani,*[21] in which it is alleged that carnal copulation alone constituted an impediment to marriage. Stephen would not consummate his marriage with the daughter of Count Reginald, for he claimed that the marriage was invalid for the reason that he had previously indulged in illicit carnal relations with a near-relative of the bride.[22]

Other authors,[23] however, maintain that the doctrine regarding affinity as deriving from illicit copulation had been received in the Frankish Church before the appearance of the pseudo-Isidorian Decretals. The canons of the Council of Compiegne (753) support this view.[24]

According to Scherer (1845-1918),[25] the origin of the doctrine which made affinity to derive from illicit carnal intercourse is to be traced to the penal discipline of the Church. At first the prohibition to marry was imposed as a temporary penance on public sinners. Later the persons who had been guilty of rather serious crimes were declared disqualified for contracting marriage or for continuing on in a marriage already contracted. This penalty was imposed in the graver cases of incest or adultery. Ordinarily only a marriage partner who committed incestuous adultery with a close blood relative of the innocent partner, that is, one related in the first degree, incurred the penalty of absolute incapacity for conjugal life.[26]

---

[20] "Nec eam quam quis ex propria consanguinitate conjugem habuit vel aliqua illicita pollutione maculavit in conjugem ducere ulli profecto christianorum licet vel licebit."—Hinschius, *Decretales Pseudo-Isidorianae et Capitula Angrilramni* (Lipsiae, 1863), p. 751; cf. c. 10, C. XXXV, q. 2 & 3.

[21] *MPL,* CXXVI, 132-153.

[22] Cf. Joyce, p. 54.

[23] Freisen, pp. 450-457; Wernz, *loc. cit.;* Joyce, p. 538.

[24] C. 7—"Si quis, uxore accepta, invenit eam fratre suo contaminatam, ipsam dimittens accepit aliam. . . ."—Hardouin, III, 2005.

[25] *Handbuch des Kirchenrechtes,* II, 333-336.

[26] Cf. Council of Verberie, c. 12—Hardouin, III, 1990 (c. 30, C, XXVII, q. 2, and *dictum* of Gratian to this canon); Council of Tribur (895), c. 43—Mansi, XVIII, 152 (c. 6, C. XXXIV, q. 1 & 2); Council of Compiegne, c. 14—Hardouin, III, 2006 (c. 9, C. XXXIV, q. 1 & 2; c. 5, C. XXXV, q. 2 & 3); Joyce, p. 588.

An unmarried person who indulged in carnal relations with a relative in the first degree was punished by relative incompetency to marry and sometimes, by way of exception, by being declared absolutely incompetent to marry. Certain canons, which were later received as ancient documents testifying that affinity resulted from illicit copulation, were occasioned by the fact that conjugal life with the close relative of a person with whom one previously had carnal relations was looked upon as criminal.[27] These particular statutes which referred to persons who were blood relatives in the first degree were extended by the pseudo-Isidorian Decretals to all blood relatives of the person with whom the candidate for marriage had had carnal relations.[28]

In this way the penal character of the prohibition to marry became amplified, and an absolute marriage impediment of affinity which arose from illicit carnal copulation was introduced. This doctrine, in time, passed from the German territory into the Roman territory, in view probably of the influence of Anselm of Lucca's collection which was introduced into the Roman Church about the end of the eleventh century.[29] It was not till the twelfth century that final approbation was given by Pope Alexander III (1159-1181) to the doctrine which had made affinity to derive from illicit carnal copulation.[30]

In the early Church, then, the impediment of affinity arose from a valid marriage, whether consummated or not, just as that rule had obtained in Roman law. It was only about the eleventh century that it was generally accepted as the doctrine of the Church that affinity was based solely on carnal copulation. It was more than mere coincidence that the impediment of public propriety appeared in Church legislation about the same time.[31] The doctrine which

---

[27] Council of Compiegne, c. 13—Hardouin, *loc. cit.* (c. 32, C. XXVII, q. 2); Council of Tribur, c. 24—Mansi, *loc. cit.* (c. 6, C. XXXV, q. 2 & 3); cf. Scherer, *loc. cit.*

[28] Cf. Hinschius, *loc. cit.;* c. 10, C. XXXV, q. 2 & 3; Oesterle, *loc. cit.*

[29] *Collectio Canonica,* Lib. X, c. 45—*MPL,* CIL, 523; cf. Oesterle, *loc. cit.;* Knecht, *Handbuch des katholischen Eherechts* (Freiburg im Breisgau: Herder, 1928), p. 509; Hörmann, *Quasiaffinität,* II, 283-293; Joyce, p. 538.

[30] Cf. c. 2, X, *de eo qui cognovit consanguineam vel affinam,* IV, 13; Oesterle, *loc. cit.;* Wahl, p. 73.

[31] Cf. *infra,* p. 31.

had come to recognize physical carnal union as the sole basis for affinity deprived a valid non-consummated marriage of the power to beget the impediment of affinity as it had in the early centuries of the Church, and thus created a void in the law which was filled by means of the introduction of the impediment of public propriety.[32]

Furthermore, as already indicated and as will appear more fully from what immediately follows, non-consummated marriage and betrothal in the early centuries of the Church were identified in one act of espousal—*desponsatio.* Only later, about the twelfth century, when non-consummated marriage and betrothal had been definitely set apart by the clarifying distinction of Peter Lombard (+ 1160) into *sponsalia de praesenti* and *sponsalia de futuro,*[33] were both recognized as giving rise to the impediment of public propriety. In this way the silence of the writers before Gratian concerning the impediment of public propriety, otherwise difficult if not impossible to explain, finds a logical explanation. Neither the pseudo-Isidorian Decretals (847-852), nor Regino of Prüm (906), nor the *Decretaum* of Burchard of Worms (1008-1012), nor Anselm of Lucca (1083) so much as mentioned the impediment.[34]

ARTICLE 2. EVIDENCE FROM CHURCH CANONS AND CIVIL LAW IN THE EASTERN CHURCH

It seems that from the earliest times the Eastern Church especially, looked upon betrothal as approximating if not actually tantamount to marriage. The Council of Ancyra, for example, which was held in the year 314, declared that if a man abducted a woman betrothed to another she should be taken from the abductor, even though violence had been done to her, and restored to the man to whom she had been betrothed.[35] Similarly, a most strict view of the obligations incumbent in consequence of a betrothal was pre-

---

[32] Cf. *infra,* p. 31.

[33] Cf. *infra,* pp. 34-35.

[34] Wernz-Vidal, *Ius Canonicum* (7 vols. in 8, Tom. V, *Ius Matrimoniale,* 3. ed., Romae: Universitas Gregoriana, 1946), n. 363 (hereafter cited *Ius Matrimoniale*).

[35] "Desponsatas puellas, et postea ab aliis raptas, placuit erui et his reddi, quibus fuerant ante desponsatae, etiamsi à raptoribus florem pudoris sui amisisse constiterit."—Mansi, II, 531; Bruns, II, 9; cf. c. 46, C. XXVII, q. 2.

sented by the Council in Trullo (692). In canon 98 of that Council it was decreed that if a man married a woman who was betrothed to another he was to be punished as an adulterer.[36]

As Patriarch John VIII Xiphilinos (1064-1075) pointed out at a Council of Constantinople (1066), it seemed from this decree of the Council in Trullo that betrothal already constituted marriage.[37] The *Ecloga* of Emperor Leo III (717-741) and of his son Constantine V Copronymus (741-775) appeared to give the sanction of civil law to this decree of the Council by imposing the grave penalty of facial mutilation on any man who seduced the betrothed of another.[38]

Emperor Leo the Wise (Leo VI, 886-912) in the seventy-fourth Novel dealt with the question of the divergent views of the civil and canon law regarding the binding force of betrothal. He stated that the particular point around which the difficulty arose was that persons under the legal age for marriage received the blessing of the Church on their espousals.[39]

It seems that the blessing here referred to was the marriage benediction, for if there was question of a blessing proper to betrothals the difficulty would have been the same whether the parties were below the marriageable age or had already attained it. On the other hand, if there was question of the marriage blessing, a peculiar difficulty would have arisen inasmuch as the blessing of the Church sealed the legal marriage for those of marriageable age,

---

[36] Lauchert, *Die Kanones der wichtigsten altkirchlichen Concilien nebst den aposotolischen Kanones* (Leipzig, 1896), p. 137; Bruns, I, 63; cf. Esmein, I, 149.

[37] Mansi, XIX, 1043.

[38] XVII, 32; the reference is taken from *A Manual of Roman Law,* the *Ecloga,* translated by Edwin Hanson Freshfield, Cambridge: The University Press, 1926; cf. Marbach, *Marriage Legislation for the Catholics of the Oriental Rites in the United States and Canada,* The Catholic University of America Canon Law Studies, n. 243 (Washington, D. C.: The Catholic University of America Press, 1946), p. 5; Joyce, p. 99.

[39] Migne, *Patrologiae Cursus Completus, Series Graeca* (161 vols., Parisiis, 1857-1866), CVII, 582 (hereafter cited *MPG*); *Ius Graeco-romanum. Novellae et Aureae Bullae Imperatorum post Iustinianum,* ex editione C. E. Zachariae-A. Lingenthal (Athenis: in Aedibus Georgii Fexis et Filii, 1931). Vol. I, *Collatio II, Imp. Leonis Novellae Constitutiones inter 886-910 editae,* Novel LXXIV, p. 114 (hereafter cited Lingenthal, I).

whereas for those below the marriageable age it was devoid of any legal consequences.[40] The Emperor met the difficulty by decreeing that the blessing was not to be given until the legal age for marriage was reached, namely fourteen years for boys and twelve for girls.[41]

However, a new situation was created in the year 1066 when Patriarch John VIII Xiphilinos, in appealing for support to the Council in Trullo, issued a synodal decree which set forth that betrothal no less than actual marriage gave rise to the impediment of affinity. The Patriarch declared that this was true not only of betrothals which had received the blessing of the Church, but extended also to all betrothals recognized as such by the civil law.[42]

In 1080 Emperor Nicephorus III Botaniates (1078-1081) issued legislation which gave civil sanction to these decrees of Patriarch John VIII. The Emperor pointed out as his reason that the civil laws should be in conformity with the canons of the Church.[43]

It seems that some difficulties were engendered by this measure, for Emperor Alexius I Comnenus (1081-1118) introduced a change in the law. He issued two enactments, one in 1084[44] and another in 1092,[45] in which he decreed that the practice of having a special benediction for betrothal as distinct from that for marriage should be compulsory from that time onward. He further enacted that the decree of Patriarch John should be understood as referring only to betrothals that had received the blessing of the Church, and that the latter were to be considered as indissoluble as marriage itself. The blessing however was not to be given until the parties had reached the legal age for marriage.[46]

---

[40] *Espanagoge,* XVI, 1; the *Espanagoge* was a projected code drawn up under Basil the Macedonian (867-886) in 884, and it put the benediction of the Church on an equality with the simple contract of marriage. The reference is taken from Joyce, p. 195; cf. *Ecloga* II, 8; Joyce, pp. 99 and 195.

[41] *MPG,* CVII, 585; Lingenthal, I, 114.

[42] *MPG,* CXIX, 756; Joyce, p. 99; Mansi, XIX, 1043.

[43] Mansi, XIX, 1046; *MPG,* CXXVII, 1484.

[44] *MPG, CIV,* 1180; Lingenthal, I, *Collatio IV, Novellae Constitutiones Annorum 1057-1204; Imp. Alexii Comneni Novella XXXI,* p. 305.

[45] *MPG,* CXIX, 1283-1286; Lingenthal, I, Novella, XXXI, p. 319.

[46] The Emperor Alexius, mistakenly it seems, referred to the seventy-fourth Novel of Leo VI as having prescribed a special blessing for betrothals. The blessing with which Leo was concerned was almost certainly the matrimonial blessing; cf. *supra,* p. 19; Hörmann, *Quasiaffinität,* II, 200-202; Joyce, p. 100.

Contracts with a view to marriage could be entered by all who had reached the age of seven years, but these were to be purely civil contracts. They did, however, give rise to an impediment to marriage under the same conditions as *sponsalia* did in Roman law.[47] In his enactments Emperor Alexius acknowledged explicitly the doctrine of the Church that, when blessed, the bond is ratified by God, and so such a union should be as indissoluble as marriage itself. It was further prescribed that all questions relating to the civil contract should be judged according to the civil law, and not according to the canons. Furthermore, these civil law contracts regarding marriage could be rendered more secure by means of a stipulation that a fine would have to be paid if the contract was defaulted. It was strictly forbidden to make such a stipulation regarding a betrothal that received the blessing of the Church. Such a stipulation would have implied that the betrothal could be dissolved, but in fact such a betrothal was considered as indissoluble as marriage itself.[48]

The Ecloga ad Procheiron Mutata, which the unnamed scribe says was written in 1166, set forth that the betrothal of Christians was brought about through the actual payment of earnest money, or through the guarantee of such payment in the grant of a bond, or through a written document specifying the terms of the contract. The contract of betrothal could be made by children of seven years of age and upward by mutual consent and with the consent of their parents or guardians. If after the betrothal took place, and before either party was thirteen years old, anyone presumed to bring about the marriage through the blessing of the Church, or through the ceremony of crowning, the preceding betrothal as well as the would-be union was dissolved.[49] It is of interest to note how the

---

[47] Cf. *supra,* pp. 3-5; also Constitution CIX of Emperor Leo the Wise—*MPG,* CVII, 639.

[48] *MPG,* CXIX, 1283-1286; Joyce, p. 101.

[49] Chap. I, Sec. I, n. 1 and 10. *The Ecloga ad Procheiron Mutata* was based on the *Ecloga,* and like the *Ecloga* applied to Greek-speaking peoples in Southern Italy and Sicily. It combined elements of Byzantine-Roman and Norman laws and was in effect under the Norman Kings of Sicily in the twelfth century. *The Ecloga ad Procheiron Mutata* was mainly based on a manuscript in the *Bibliotheque Nationale* at Paris, and is identified as *Paris Gr. 1380.* The translation is by Edwin Hanson Freshfield (Cambridge: The University Press, 1927).

provisions of the *Ecloga ad Procheiron Mutata* carried out a pattern already in evidence in the legislation of Emperor Alexius I.

ARTICLE 3. EVIDENCE FROM CHURCH COUNCILS AND FROM EARLY CHRISTIAN WRITERS IN THE WEST

Perhaps it is not to be expected that Church councils in the West would deal with the subject of betrothals, much less with the impediment of public propriety. If, as seems likely, the betrothal and marriage contracts were identified, there was hardly any reason why betrothal should become a subject of conciliar legislation. At any rate, reference to betrothal in Church councils in the West is very meager. Reference to the impediment of public propriety seems to be entirely lacking, at least during the first eleven centuries. The Council of Elvira in Spain (300/306) mentioned betrothal to emphasize the obligation it imposed on parents. The Council decreed that parents who broke off the betrothal of a son or of a daughter were to be compelled to forfeit communion with the faithful for a period of three years.[50]

The Council of Rome which was held in the year 721 under Pope Gregory II (715-731) seemed to imply that a man had a right to marital relations with his betrothed, for while others were to be subjected to anathema for marrying an abducted virgin if they were not betrothed to her, the same penalty seemed not to be in effect under like circumstancs if a betrothal did exist between the two.[51] The so-called protocol canon (c. 31) of the Council of Tribur (895), on which Gratian based c. 31, C. XXVII, q. 2, contained a similar teaching.[52]

---

[50] Ivo *Decretum,* Lib. VIII, c. 46—*MPL,* CIXL, 594; Mansi, II, 14, note 5; Council of Elvira, Can. 54: "Si qui parentes fidem fregerint sponsaliorum, triennii tempore abstineantur; si tamen idem sponsus et sponsa in gravi crimine fuerint deprehensi, excusati erunt parentes; si in iisdem fuerit vitium et polluerint se, superior sententia servetur."—Hardouin, I, 256; Bruns, II, 9.

[51] C. II—"Si quis virginem quam sibi *non desponsaverit* rapuerit vel furatus fuerit in uxorem, vel consentiens ei, anathema sit."—Mansi, XII, 264; Jaffé, n. 1655; cf. c. 12, C. XXVII, q. 2; the gloss to this canon states that under the term "betrothed" there is to be understood a wife—"In secunda parte dicitur, quod nomine sponsae intelligitur uxor."

[52] "Quidam desponsavit uxorem et dotavit eam, et cum ea coire non potuit: quam clanculo frater eius corrupit et gravidam reddidit. Decretum est ut

Evidence of the development which combined betrothal and marriage into one act and identified betrothal with non-consummated marriage began to appear in early Christian writings. The early Christian Fathers often treated of the matter in their writings, when they commented on the marriage of the Blessed Virgin Mary and Saint Joseph. They employed the words, *desponsatio, desponsare, pactio coniugalis,* for the actual marriage ceremony, and applied the term *sponsa* to the married bride if the union was still unconsummated, but the term *nupta* when the union had become consummated. This terminology, while it was not always uniform, nevertheless reflects the fact that these meanings were recognized.[53]

Tertullian (c. 206) explained how the Blessed Virgin Mary, though she was a betrothed virgin—*"desponsata,"* could yet be said to be a married woman—*"nupta."* He pointed to the fact that one who is betrothed is already in a certain sense married.[54]

Saint Cyprian (+ 258) also spoke of a betrothed woman--

---

quamvis nupta esse non potuit legitimo viro, desponsatam tamen fratri, frater habere non possit."—*MPL,* CXL, 930. This canon (found in Burchard, *Decretum,* lib. XVII, c. 49; and in Ivo, *Decretum,* lib. IX, c. 100) according to Joyce, is not one of the canons actually issued by the Council of Tribur. It is found among certain *Judicia Concilii Triburensis* as contained in a manuscript preserved at Chalôns-sur-Marne. It is referred to by some authors as the *protocol canon,* since they accept it as the original draft of a canon for which canon 41 of the official series was substituted. Seckel (1864-1924), however, maintained that all the canons of the Chalôns manuscript are genuine canons of the Council of Tribur. Cf. Joyce, p. 601, n. 1; Seckel, "Zu den Acten der Triburer Synode (895)," *Neues Archiv des Gesellschaft fur ältere Geschichtskunde,* XVIII (1893), 365-409; Hörmann, *Quasiaffinität;* II, 309; Freisen, p. 498.

[53] Joyce, p. 600; Hörmann, *Quasiaffinität,* II, 24, 33, 80-96 and 218.

[54] *De Virginibus Velandis,* c. 6: "Sed et ad haec duo ingeniose quidam respondere sibi visus est: quoniam quidem desponsata est Maria, idcirco et ab angelo et ab Apostolo 'mulierem' pronunciatam: desponata enim quodammodo *nupta.* . . . Ceterum, si hic desponsatae adaequatur, ut ideo 'mulier' dicta sit Maria, non qua femina sed qua maritata, iam ergo Christus non ex virgine natus est, quia ex desponsata, quae virgo esse desierit ex hoc nomine. Quod si ex virgine natus est, licet ex sponsa tamen integra, agnosco 'mulierem' etiam virginem, etiam integram, dici."—*MPL,* II, 897.

sponsa—as already belonging to the man to whom she was betrothed.[55]

Saint Ambrose (+ 397) spoke of a betrothed woman as having the right to conjugal relations.[56]

Saint Jerome (+ 420), when treating of the perpetual virginity of Mary, explained that Christ was born of a betrothed virgin—*desponsata*—or, as the Scriptures stated it, a married virgin, rather than of a virgin without a spouse, lest she be stoned to death as an adulteress in accordance with the Mosaic law.[57]

Saint Augustine (+ 430), in speaking of the marriage of the Blessed Virgin Mary and Saint Joseph, stated that Mary, though she remained always a virgin, could be referred to as a wife—*coniux*—from the time she pledged her faith in betrothal.[58]

St. Isidore (+ 636) stated that persons were said to be married—*conjuges*—from the time that they pledged faith to each other in their betrothal, even though a carnal union had not intervened.[59]

Ivo of Chartres (1040-1116) in one of his letters stated that betrothal—*desponsatio*—which he said was effected through a union of the two wills, in a certain sense already constituted marriage even though a carnal union had not intervened, and that it gave rise to an impediment for marriage, so that a brother was

---

[55] *Ep. LXII* (ad Pomponium): "Si superveniens maritus *sponsam* suam jacentem cum altero videat, nonne indignatur, et fremit et per zeli dolorem fortassis et gladium in manu sumit? Quid Christus Dominus et iudex noster cum virginem suam sibi dicatam . . . iacere cum altero cernit."—*MPL,* IV, 368.

[56] *Exposition in Lucam,* Lit. II, n. 2: "Testis pudoris maritus adhibitus. . . . Videretur enim culpam obumbrare voluisse innupta praegnans? Causam autem mentiendi indesponsata habuit, *desponsata* non habuit, cum coniugii praemium et gratia nuptiarum partus sit feminarum."—*MPL,* XV, 1554.

[57] *De Perpetua Virginitate Beatae Virginis Mariae* (adversus Helvidium): "Si cui autem scrupulus commovetur quare desponsata et non potius sine sponso, sive ut Scriptura appellat, marito virgo conceperit: sciat triplicem fuisse rationem . . . secundo, ne juxta legem Moysi lapidaretur ut adultera."—*MPL,* XXIII, 187.

[58] *De Nuptiis et Concupiscentia,* lib. I, cap. XI, n. 12: "Conjux vocatur ex prima fide desponsationis quam concubitu nec cognoverat nec fuerat cogniturus."—*MPL,* XLIV, 420.

[59] *Etymologiae,* Lib. IX, C. 7: "Conjuges verius appellantur *a prima desponsationis fide,* quamvis adhuc ignoretur inter eos conjugalis concubitus."—*MPL,* LXXXII, 365; cf. c. 6, C. XXII, q. 2.

barred from marrying the wife of his deceased brother, and a sister from marrying the husband of her deceased sister.[60]

ARTICLE 4. TESTIMONY OF THE POPES

The earliest papal pronouncements that dealt with betrothals and the impediment that derived from them tended to emphasize the inviolable character of betrothals, thus indicating that they created a bond similar to marriage itself. The letters of the popes revealed a similar tendency. These letters, though generally addressed to individuals, often to bishops, not only constituted a legal norm for the persons to whom they were directed, but they were considered, to some extent at least, to have the force of law.[61]

Notwithstanding the fact that the papal decretals were addressed over a period of many centuries to persons in various parts of the Christian world, a remarkable uniformity is to be observed in their teaching regarding the existence of a marriage impediment between a betrothed person and the blood relatives of the other party in the betrothal. It is necessary to bear in mind, however, that there is question of a matter entirely within the competence of ecclesiastical law, and so it is not unlikely that some of the papal decisions, as found in the decretals, may contain concessions in the form of exceptions from the regulations existing at any particular time. That indeed seems a fact in the case of a decision rendered by Pope Alexander III (1159-1181).[62]

The first papal pronouncement on betrothal is attributed to Pope Siricius (c. 388). Siricius forbade in a general way that a man take as wife the betrothed of another, and at the same time stated that such action would partake of the nature of a sacrilege inasmuch

---

[60] Epistola XLIX: "His igitur auctoritatibus manifestum est, quia postquam *per desponsationis foedus* inter duas personas ex majore parte fuerit conjugium ex utrorumque voluntate compactum, non potest alterius frater uxorem fratris ducere, nec soror sororis marito nubere."—*MPL,* CIXII, 119.

[61] Van Hove, *Prolegomena,* pp. 139-141; cf. also Hörmann, *Quasiaffinität,* II, 293.

[62] C. 5, X, *de sponsalibus impuberum,* IV, 2; cf. Wernz, lib. IV, tit. XIX, n. 448, note 13; Freisen, p. 502.

as the betrothal contract was entered with the blessing of the Church.[63]

It is difficult to say with any certainty what exact meaning is to be attached to the word *nupturae* in the Pope's letter. It is true that the term *nupta* was usually applied to a married woman after conjugal life had already begun. However, according to Tertullian (ca. 160-ca. 240), it could also apply to a married woman before conjugal life began, and so could appropriately be applied to the Blessed Virgin Mary.[64] The word *nupturae*, then, in the present context may refer to a woman who only in the future was to give the matrimonial consent that would actually constitute marriage, or it may mean that the woman had given the consent at that time and was to enter the marital relation only at a later time. The prohibition is so strong that it seems rather to imply the latter meaning, in which case there then existed the impediment of *ligamen*.

There is a much discussed letter of doubtful authenticity that deserves mention here. The letter is attributed by some authors to Pope Benedict I (575-579).[65] Mansi (1692-1767), while he admitted that nearly all authorities considered the letter apocryphal, doubted if their rejection of it was justified. He himself attributed the letter to Benedict I and explained that, even though it were admitted that the inscription of the letter were spurious, it would not necessarily follow that the letter itself must be rejected. Mansi argued that the inscription, *"Benedictus Servus Servorum dei Grandensi Patriarchae Salutem. . . ,"* while it could not have been used in the time of Benedict I, inasmuch as Grado was not a patriarchate until a later date, may have been a later addition of a copyist. In a similar manner he explained the use of the expression *"Servus Servorum Dei,"* which also was used only at a later date by Gregory the Great (590-604).[66]

---

[63] *Epistola I*: "Hoc ne fiat, modis omnibus jubemus: quia illa benedictio, quam *nupturae* sacerdos imponit apud fideles, cujusdam sacrilegii instar est, si ulla transgressione violetur."—*MPL*, XIII, 1136; cf. Devoti, *Institutiones Canonicae* II, 213, note 2. Jaffé, n. 255.

[64] Cf. *supra*, p. 23.

[65] Smith, *Papal Enforcement of Some Medieval Marriage Laws* (Louisiana State University Press, 1940), p. 45 (hereafter cited Smith).

[66] Cf. Mansi, IX, 863-864.

Jaffé (1819-1870) indeed inserted the letter under the decretals of Benedict I (n. 1045), but designated it as spurious. However, he inserted the letter also among the decretal letters of Benedict VI (973-974) with the observation that, while it had not been determined to which of the two Benedicts the letter belonged, it was nevertheless to be considered genuine. Yet he also stated that because of the inscription the letter could not be assigned to Benedict I.[67]

The letter denied that an impediment to marriage arose between a woman and the brother of the man to whom she had been betrothed but who had died. It stated that such an impediment did not arise unless carnal intercourse had taken place. This letter constitutes the basis on which rests c. 18, C. XXVII, q. 2, which canon also denies that betrothal gave rise to the impediment of public propriety.[68] Gratian did not say to which Benedict the letter was to be attributed.

A letter attributed to Pope Gregory the Great (590-604), which contained a decision opposed to that ascribed to Benedict, is considered spurious.[69] The letter is not to be found among the various collections of Gregory's decretals.

In a letter of Pope Nicholas I (858-867), written to the Bulgarians in response to certain questions which they proposed, the amalgamation of betrothal and actual marriage in the act of espousal—*desponsatio*—may be clearly seen. However, even after such amalgamation some kind of preliminary agreement between the parties or their guardians regarding the espousal was still necessary. It is very likely that this preliminary agreement, which may have had no particular form other than that of a verbal understanding, constituted the first among the four states which the pope designated as effective elements of marriage.

This first stage was referred to by Nicholas as a promise of future marriage—*"sponsalia quae futurarum sunt nuptuarum*

---

[67] "Benedicto I merito abjudicatur haec epistola propter titulum: 'Benedictus servus servorum Dei Grandensi Patriarchae'; cui vero Benedictorum attribuenda sit, me ignorare confiteor. De fide ejus non dubito."—Jaffé, n. 3773; *MPL,* LXXII, 683.

[68] Cf. *infra,* pp. 36-37.

[69] Jaffé, n. 1856a; Smith in his work on p. 46, n. 47, erroneously stated that Jaffé accepted the letter as genuine.

promissa foedera."[70] The second stage was the rite of espousal (*desponsatio*), which meant the giving and the accepting of actual marriage consent, symbolized by the handing over of the earnest gifts (*arrhae*), the placing of the ring on the finger of the bride, and the delivering over to her of the deed of settlement. Thirdly came the Mass at which the pair received the blessing of the Church while a veil was held over their heads. Fourthly came the crowning as the parties left the Church to enter on conjugal life.

Since the first of these four stages is specified as a promise of future marriage, it can hardly be doubted that the ceremony of espousal (*desponsatio*), which constituted the second stage, was regarded as the actual marriage contract. The nuptial Mass could be celebrated immediately (*mox*), though when the parties were under the age prescribed by law this celebration was delayed until the time had come for conjugal life to begin (*tempore apto*).[71]

It is only by supposing that betrothal was considered the matrimonial union of wills that an adequate reason can be given for the letter of Pope John VIII (872-882) to Rostagnus, Archbishop of Arles, in which he directed that a man who abducted the betrothed of another as also the betrothed herself were to be excommunicated unless she returned to the man to whom she had been betrothed.[72]

---

[70] Cf. Joyce, p. 47.

[71] "Nostrates siquidem tam mares, quam feminae, non ligaturam auream vel argenteam, aut ex quolibet metallo compositam, quando nuptialia foedera contrahunt, in capitibus deferunt: sed post *sponsalia, quae futurarum sunt nuptiarum promissa foedera,* quaeque consensu eorum qui haec contrahunt, et eorum in quorum potestate sunt, celebrantur; et postquam arrhis sponsam sibi sponsus per digitum fidei a se annulo insignitum *desponderit,* dotemque utrique placitam sponsus ei cum scripto pactum hoc continente coram invitatis ab utraque parte tradiderit, *aut mox aut apto tempore,* ne videlicet ante tempus lege difinitum tale quid fieri praesumatur, ambo ad nuptialia foedera perducuntur."—*Monumenta Germaniae Historica, Epistolae Karolini Aevi,* Tom. IV (ed. Societas Aperiendis Fontibus Rerum Germanicarum Medii Aevi, Berolini: apud Weidmannos, 1925), 570; Jaffé, n. 2812; Hardouin, II, 354; Joyce, p. 599; cf. also Joyce, p. 47; *ASS,* XII (1879), 158.

[72] Jaffé, n. 2968; cf. c. 47, C. XXVII, q. 2; "Atho praesentium lator, dum in nostro servitio fideliter excubaret, quemdam virum foeminam sibi *desponsatam* queritur rapuisse. Et ideo fraternitas tua, auctoritate nostra suffulta, suffraganeos suos episcopos praesentialiter convocet: sicque unanimi sententia, si sponsam huic raptor non reddiderit, tam idem, quam rapta, si ad sponsum pristinum remeare noluerit, omni communione priventur."—Mansi, XVIIa, 241.

Alexander II (1061-1073), in a decision concerning a woman who when betrothed under oath to one man had married another, termed the marriage adulterous and ordered that the woman should be returned to her betrothed.[73]

There can hardly be any doubt that a letter of Pope Gregory VII (1075), in which he spoke of a cleric who had contracted marriage, considered betrothal as already constituting marriage.[74] On another occasion Gregory was quite explicit in stating that a union of this kind begot an impediment to marriage. The letter concerned the case of a certain Duke Boniface who wished to marry the betrothed of his deceased brother Anselm.[75] The pope stated that such a marriage would be alien to the laws of the Christian religion and contrary to the statutes of the Fathers of the Church. Promises of such a marriage, even if given under oath, were to be considered as not existing, and if by persisting in his intentions the duke contracted the marriage, he was to be excommunicated.

The evidence, gleaned from the writings of the Fathers, from the councils of the Church, and from the decretal letters of the popes, as presented above in support of the view that betrothal became identified with non-consummated marriage in one act of espousal—*desponsatio* or *pactio coniugalis*—seems to place the matter beyond reasonable doubt. It is difficult to say with any degree of accuracy at what time the identification took place, but the evidence tends to indicate an early date, at least in Roman law territories.[76] It is noteworthy also that the development in

---

[73] ". . . adulterio quidem, quoniam alterius sponsam vivente proximo concupivit et seduxit."—Mansi, XIX, 961; Jaffé, n. 4617.

[74] ". . . qua de re commotus, episcopus cum ei non solum hanc denegaret ecclesiam sed totum officium per summam interdiceret obedientiam, respondit se non debere sibi obedientiae reverentiam, quoniam archidiaconatus consecrationes ecclesiarum et ipsas ecclesias vendendo symoniaca heresi se commaculasset cum muliere quadam in publica fornicatione jaceret, de qua filium genuisset, quamque rumor esset *sacramento et desponsatione laicorum more sibi copulasse,* et praeterea quod nunnulli eum ad episcopatum pacione premii pervenisse discerent."—*MGH, Epistolae Gregorii* VII, *Registrum,* Lib. I-IV, Tom. II (ed. Societas Aperiendis Fontibus Rerum Germanicarum Medii Aevi, Berolini: apud Weidmannos, 1920), p. 141; Jaffé, n. 4883; *MPL,* CXLVIII, 370; cf. Hörmann, *Quasiaffinität,* II, 219.

[75] Mansi, XX, 294; Jaffé, n. 4145.

[76] Cf. Joyce, p. 46.

Church legislation approximated the development that had taken place in Germanic law, under which the complete marriage relation was brought about by two distinct legal acts, namely, by the betrothal and the *traditio puellae in domum.*[77]

In view of that development it is not surprising that the papal decretals, with practical unanimity, forbade marriage between one of the betrothed and the blood relations of the other, even after the death of one of the parties. In reality the impediment of affinity which in the early centuries of the Church arose from valid marriage whether consummated or not, as in Roman law, existed in such cases.[78]

Contrary to what some authors seem to indicate, the unanimity of the popes in denying marriage in such cases is quite manifest.[79] The only exception to this unanimity seems to be the very dubious and much disputed letter variously attributed to Benedict I and Benedict VI.[80] It is on this same letter that Gratian based the only canon that apparently denies the existence of an impediment as arising from betrothal, namely, c. 18. C. XXVII, q. 2.

But, with this development of the amalgamation of betrothal and actual marriage, another development had taken place with regard to the impediment of affinity. The theory that the impediment of affinity arose only from carnal intercourse, whether licit or illicit, instead of from marriage consent, which theory had its inception in the Frankish Church about the seventh or eighth centuries, was accorded general recognition about the eleventh or twelfth centuries.[81] This development cancelled out the possibility of the emergence of affinity as an impediment deriving from betrothal already identified with non-consummated marriage in the *desponsatio* or *pactio coniugalis.* In the absence of carnal intercourse the impediment of affinity could not arise. Hence it is not surprising that Hincmar of Rheims (+ 882) denied that any impediment to marriage arose from a union in which carnal inter-

---

[77] Cf. *supra,* p. 7.
[78] Cf. *supra,* pp. 17-18.
[79] Cf. Smith, pp. 45 and 46.
[80] Cf. *supra,* pp. 26-27.
[81] Cf. *supra,* pp. 15-18.

course had not intervened.[82] Yet this same basis on which the impediment of affinity had previously rested still existed, and in accordance with the traditional practice of the Church and the demands of Christian decency it postulated a marriage impediment between the parties involved in the betrothal, which came to be identified with non-consummated marriage,[83] and the respective blood relatives of the other party. The necessity was met in that the impediment of public propriety or quasi-affinity was presented in Gratian's *Decretum.*

---

[82] *Hincmari Rhemensis Archiepiscopi Epistola XXII*: "Dicat etiam, si post mortem Stephani virgo permaneat et se continere non potuerit, et nubere magis quam continere elegerit, utrum fratri ejusdem Stephani copulare valebit. Quibus cum contradicere non valebit, aut in quaestione sua deficiat, aut ei nostra solutio satisfaciat."—*MPL,* CXXVI, 144.

[83] Cf. *supra,* pp. 13-14.

CHAPTER III

Gratian's Presentation of the Impediment of Public Propriety

Article 1. The Source of the Canons in Gratian

The canons, namely canons 11, 12, 14 and 15, C. XXVII, q. 2, in which the impediment of public propriety was presented by Gratian are, to say the least, of uncertain origin.[1] In fact, many authors do not hesitate to state that these canons of Gratian are apocryphal.[2] The difficulty which Gratian had in finding a basis for the impediment of public propriety may be seen from his recourse to a text in Deuteronomy (22, 25) as a source of c. 11, C. XXVII, q. 2. One looks in vain for support of the impediment of public propriety in this text.[3]

The original authentic source of c. 11, C. XXVII, q. 2, if there is such a source, is still to be determined. Friedberg (1837-1910) in his edition of the *Decretum* of Gratian stated that canon 11 is a summary of canon 41 of the Council of Tribur, but no essential connection can be seen to exist between these canons.[4] C. 12 as well as c. 14, C. XXVII, q. 2, is attributed by Gratian to Gregory the Great, but neither canon is to be found in Gregory.[5] C. 15, C. XXVII, q. 2, is assigned to Pope Julius I (337-352) as its original source. It must however be regarded as apocryphal, since it is not to be found among the writings of Julius.[6]

Hörmann, in discussing the ultimate source of these canons as

[1] Wernz, lib. IV, tit. XIX, n. 448. Cappello, *De Matrimonio,* n. 555; De Smet, n. 635; Coronata, *Institutiones Iuris Canonici* (2. ed., 5 vols., Taurini, Romae: Marietti, 1939-1947), III, 551; Hörmann, *Quasiaffinität,* II, 306-318; Joyce, pp. 92-93.

[2] Freisen, p. 499; Scherer, II, 347; Gasparri, *De Matrimonio* (1904), n. 801; Petrovits, *The New Church Law on Matrimony* (2. ed., Philadelphia: John Joseph McVey, 1926), p. 292 (hereafter cited Petrovits).

[3] Cf. Hörmann, *Quasiaffinität,* II, 303.

[4] Scherer, II, 346; Freisen, p. 499.

[5] Scherer, II, 346; Freisen, p. 499.

[6] Joyce, note, pp. 92-93; Freisen, p. 499.

given in Gratian, considered two possible sources in pre-Gratian material. The first is canon 41 of the Council of Tribur (895). The text of this canon, according to Hörmann, may have been changed, either intentionally or because of a misunderstanding of the canon, in the construction of the Gratian canons. However, Hörmann considered that this possibility was to be ruled out inasmuch as canon 41 of the Council of Tribur stressed the delict of the brother, while the canons of Gratian stress the impediment to marriage with the betrothed of a relative.[7]

Hörmann further observed that the source of the Gratian canons is not to be found in the so-called protocol canon (c. 31) of the Council of Tribur.[8] There, according to Hörmann, the reason for the prohibition to marriage was the seduction of the woman by the brother.[9] A further possibility regarding the source of the Gratian canons, especially of c. 14, C. XXVII, q. 2, and one considered more probable by Hörmann, is to be found in a statute of Emperor Henry II.[10]

According to Hörmann, the regulation contained in this statute was received into the Lombardic law books and obtained the general force of law in the northern Italian ecclesiastical territories. Because of the similarity of this norm with canon 41 of the Council of Tribur it may have been influenced by the latter and, like so many canons concerning marriage between relatives, it may have been inscribed with the name of Pope Gregory.[11]

ARTICLE 2. GRATIAN'S *Matrimonium Initiatum* AND *Matrimonium Ratum*

Apart from the uncertain origin, not to say apocryphal character, of the canons in which Gratian presented the impediment of

[7] Council of Tribur (895), c. 41: "Si quis legitimam duxerit uxorem, et, impediente quacumque domestica infirmitate, uxorium opus non valens implere cum illa; frater vero ejus, suadente diabolo, adamatus ab ipsa, clanculum eam humiliaverit et violatam reddiderit: omnimodo separenter et a neutro ulterius eadem mulier contingatur. Igitur conjugium, quod erat legitimum, fraterna commaculatione est pollutum: et quod erat licitum, illicitum est factum."—Mansi, XVIII, 152; cf. Hörmann, *Quasiaffinität,* II, 301 and 304.

[8] Cf. *supra,* p. 22, note 52.

[9] Hörmann, *Quasiaffinität,* II, 311; Freisen, p. 498.

[10] Cf. *supra,* p. 7.

[11] Hörmann, *Quasiaffinität,* II, 313.

public propriety, the presentation itself is by no means free from ambiguity. This fact indicated that Gratian himself did not have very clear ideas on the whole development regarding marriage in general and the impediment of public propriety in particular.[12]

At the time of Gratian the question of the relative value of consent and of carnal intercourse in effecting marriage and in furnishing a basis for affinity was much discussed among canonists. Gratian, so it seems, tried to resolve this question by introducing the distinction of initiated marriage and consummated marriage—the so called *matrimonium initiatum* and *matrimonium ratum.* Marriage according to Gratian was initiated with the exchange of the parties' consent, but it was perfected through their carnal union.[13] It is when one keeps this distinction in mind that one can better understand why from cc. 5-10, C. XXVII, q. 2, of the *Decretum* it appears that betrothed persons are already married, while on the other hand in cc. 16, 17 and 39, C. XXVII, q. 2, a carnal union also seems necessary for a full marital status.[14]

Gratian's initiated marriage—*matrimonium initiatum*—was identical with espousal—*desponsatio* or *pactio coniugalis*—and so included in itself both the concept of betrothal and also that of non-consummated marriage. The later clarifying distinction of Peter Lombard (ca. 1100-1160) between consent of the future and consent of the present—*consensus de futuro et consensus de presenti*—had not yet been formulated.

Peter Lombard when in his *Book of the Sentences* (1147-1150) he cited the passages of Gratian, used those passages, not in order to prove from them the existence of the impediment of public propriety, but in order to explain through them the distinction be-

---

[12] Cf. Hörmann, *Quasiaffinität,* II, 218; Scherer, II, 347, n. 8; Freisen, p. 500.

[13] "Sciendum est quod coniugium desponsatione initiatur, commixtione perficitur. Unde inter sponsum et sponsam coniugium est, sed *initiatum;* inter copulatos est coniugium *ratum."—Dictum* ad c. 34, C. XXVII, q. 2; cf. Joyce, p. 34.

[14] "Coniuges verius appellantur a prima desponsationis fide, quominus adhuc *inter eos ignoretur coniugalis concubitus."*—c. 6, C. XXVII, q. 2. On the other hand, canon 16 states: "Non dubium est illam mulierem non pertinere ad matrimonium, cum qua docetur non fuisse conmixtio sexus."—c. 16, C. XXVII, q. 2; cf. also *Dictum* ad c. 5, C. XXVII, q. 2.

tween *sponsalia de presenti* and *sponsalia de futuro.*[15] This distinction, which was first used in clear terms by Lombard, was quickly seized and generally received by canonists, especially after its adoption by Pope Alexander III (1159-1181).[16] Lombard did not at all refer to the impediment of public propriety, nor did he list it in his catalogue of impediments.[17]

Bernard of Pavia (+1213), when commenting on the decretals of Alexander III, was quite explicit in stating that the initiated marriage of Gratian—*matrimonium initiatum*—was the same as the espousal—*desponsatio* or *pactio coniugalis.* He treated the matter at length in his commentary on various canons of Gratian.[18] Bernard further stated that a marriage thus initiated by *desponsatio* (*de praesenti*) could not be dissolved by means of a subsequent marriage.[19]

There is not in the *Decretum* any canon wherein it is expressly stated that the impediment of public propriety derives both from *sponsalia de presenti* and from *sponsalia de futuro.* However, it was precisely this comprehensive interpretation that was given to the canons of Gratian by the Glossators.[20] C. 11, C. XXVII, q. 2, then,

---

[15] "Efficiens autem causa matrimonii est consensus, non quilibet, sed per verba expressus, nec de futuro, sed de presenti. Si enim consentiunt in futurum dicentes: Accipiam te in virum et: ego te in uxorem, non est iste consensus efficax matrimonii."—*Libri IV Sententiarum,* Lib. IV, d. XXVII (Ed. ad Claras Aquas prope Florentiam: 2. ed., 2 vols., Ex Typographia Collegii S. Bonaventurae, 1916); *MPL,* CXCII, 910.

[16] Cf. Joyce, p. 61.

[17] Freisen, p. 500.

[18] "Nec illam vulgatam distinctionem credo silentio transeundam, scil. quod matrimonium dicitur initiatum in desponsatione, consummatum in carnis commictione, ratum efficitur in personam legitimatione vel separandi impossibilitate . . . de his habes C. XXVII, qu. 2 s. Apparet (dict. Gratiani ad c. 34)."—Bernardus Papiensis, *Summa Decretalium* (ed. Ern Ad. Theod. Laspeyres: Rathisbonae, 1860), Lib. IV, tit. 1, n. 22.

[19] "Illud autem matrimonium dicitur initiatum, quod initium per desponsationem accepit. . . . Cum igitur quis aliquam desponsavit et non cognovit, aliam vero postea desponsavit et cognovit, separendus est a secunda et reddendus priori, quia sequens matrimonium consummatum non praeiudicat initiato, ut C. XXVII, qu. 2, De coniugali (c. 50) et infra eodem in omnibus capitulis"—*ibid.,* tit. 4, n. 2.

[20] "Si quis desponsaverit sibi aliquam, et praeveniente mortis articulo eam cognoscere non potuerit; frater eius non potest eam ducere in uxorem."—c. 11, C. XXVII, q. 2; "Hoc canon intelligitur de sponsa de presenti; aliter

as the Glossator stated, was better understood solely of the *sponsalia de presenti,* but it could also be understood as inclusive of the *sponsalia de futuro.* The same may be said regarding c. 31, C. XXVII, q. 2.[21] The gloss on the word *licita* and on the word *moechus* indicated that the canon referred to both *sponsalia de praesenti* and *sponsalia de futuro.*[22]

Even though it appears that Gratian's initiated marriage (*matrimonium initiatum*) was identical with espousal (*desponsatio* or *pactio coniugalis*), a further difficulty is presented in the apparent contradiction existing between c. 18, C. XXVII, q. 2, and the canons by which Gratian established the impediment, in particular cc. 11, 12, 14 and 15, C. XXVII, q. 2. In canon 18 marriage is allowed between a man and the sister of the woman who upon his betrothal to her had died. The reason given was that no impediment arose when no carnal intercourse had intervened.[23]

As has been seen previously, the letter on which this canon is based has been variously attributed either to Benedict I or to

---

non faceret ad propositum, quia sponsa de futuro non est uxor; quod tamen sequitur quod non possit duci a fratre, obtinet etiam in sponsa de futuro; dum tamen post VII annos facta sit desponsatio."—Gloss to c. 11, C. XXVII, q. 2; cf. Scherer, II, 374; Freisen, p. 504; Joyce, pp. 92-93.

[21] "Quidam desponsavit uxorem, et dotavit, et cum ea coire non potuit; quam clanculo frater eius corrupit et gravidam reddidit. Decretum est, ut, quamvis nupta non potuerit esse legitimo viro, desponsatam temen fratri frater habere non possit; sed *moechus,* et moecha fornicationis quidem vindictam sustineant; *licita* vero coniugia eis non negentur."—c. 31, C. XXVII, q. 2.

[22] "Post mortem sponsi, si erat sponsa de presenti."—Gloss ad *licita;* cf. Wernz, Lib. IV, tit. XIX, n. 449, note 22.

[23] "Affatus est autem nos suis litteris eiusdem cathedrae sessorem, et percunctatus est quidam vestras nomine Iohannes, pro connubio filiae suae superstitis, cuius soror defuncta cuidam iuveni, Stephano nomine, *simplicibus verbis fuerat desponsata,* et ante, quam ad nuptias perveniret, morte preventa; utrum scilicet cum eodem iuvene possit matrimonium celebrari superstitis filiae, nec ne. . . . Qui ergo nequaquam mixtus est extraneae mulieri foedere nuptiali, quo pacto per nuda sponsionis verba possunt una caro fieri, nullatenus valemus intueri. Propinquitas enim sanguinis verbis dicitur, non verbis efficitur. Sed neque osculum parit propinquitatem, quod nullam facit sanguinis conmixtionem. Quoniam vero ita prorsus sese habet res Iohannis istius, ut velit secundam filiam illi nuptiis copulare, *cui primam iam decreverat desponsare,* censura apostolici magistratus mandamus, hoc absque ullius criminis vitio posse fieri, si utriusque partis sederit voluntati. . . ."—c. 18, C. XXVII, q. 2.

Benedict VI, and is generally considered doubtful.[24] Furthermore, the canon in itself is by no means clear. The ambiguity caused by the words *simplicibus verbis fuerat desponsata,* toward the beginning, taken with the words, *cui primam decreverat desponsare,* toward the end, led the Glossator to state of the canon that, although it was contrary to the other canons cited by Gratian, the father only promised the daughter but did not betroth her to Stephen, but that she was indeed said to be betrothed simply inasmuch as she had been promised by mere words, but not for the reason that she had given her consent.[25]

Bernard of Pavia (+ 1213) and Richardus Anglicus (+ 1237), in discussing the implications of the canon in question, stated that the expression *simplicibus verbis,* when considered in conjunction with *decreverat desponsare,* could be taken to mean a mere promise of the parents to betroth the daughter.[26] When it is borne in mind that under the Germanic system the father or guardian gave the woman in betrothal, even though at a later period it was necessary that the woman give her consent, the explanation as given assumes considerable probability.[27]

---

[24] Cf. *supra,* pp. 26-27.

[25] "Palea, quae hic solet esse, est contraria his quae diximus supra eadem. '*Si quis desponsaverit*' (c. 11). Sed loquitur cum pater promiserat filiam illi: sed ille non desponsaverat eam: sed quod dicitur desponsata, id est, promissa simplicibus verbis patris, illa non consentiente. Et hoc colligitur ex eo quod dicitur circa finem, *decreverat desponsare.*"—Gloss to c. 18, C. XXVII, q. 2.

[26] *Bernardi et Ricardi Casus Decretalium,* casus ad c. 1, X, de *desponsatione impuberum,* IV, 2.

[27] Huebner, p. 599; Joyce, p. 47.

CHAPTER IV

The Impediment of Public Propriety in the Decretal Collections of Gregory IX and of Boniface VIII

In the authentic collection of the Decretals of Gregory IX (1227-1241) the impediment of public propriety was more clearly set forth, although in the canons attributed to Pope Alexander III there seems to be some contradiction. In c. 5, X, *de sponsalibus et matrimoniis,* IV, 1, Alexander because of discord in the family tolerated—"*dissimulare et aequanimiter tollerare . . .*"—a marriage that a man had contracted in good faith with the mother of his betrothed. Furthermore, in a previous decision to a bishop in England, Alexander stated that a man and a woman were not one flesh until they were united in carnal union, and so, if such a union had not intervened, a man was free to marry the sister of the deceased woman to whom he had been betrothed.[1]

This decision of Alexander was not received into the decretal collection of Gregory IX.[2] In later decisions, however, setting aside his former views, Alexander declared that marriages contravening the impediment of public propriety were null.[3]

Freisen (1853-1932) tried to reconcile these varying decisions of Alexander by saying that in Gratian and in the Decretals of Gregory IX only the woman was forbidden to marry the relatives of her betrothed, whereas the man was not forbidden to marry the relatives of his betrothed.[4] The point he made is not substantiated. It is further weakened by the fact that c. 3, X, *de sponsalibus et matrimoniis,* IV, 1, which Freisen alleged in support of his argu-

[1] "Non sunt una caro vir et mulier, nisi cohaeserint copula maritali. Idcirco, defuncta sponsa intacta, eius soror a sponso hoc non impediente libere ducitur in uxorem."—c. 2, *de sponsalibus et matrimoniis,* IV, 1, in Compil. I.

[2] Cf. Wernz, lib. IV, tit. III, n. 448.

[3] Cf. cc. 4 and 6, X, *de desponsatione impuberum,* IV, 2; also c. 8, X, *de sponsalibus et matrimoniis,* IV, 1.

[4] *Geschichte des canonischen Eherechts,* p. 503.

ment, was erroneously attributed to Alexander III, whereas it rightly belonged to Pope Eugene III (1145-1153).[5]

In its 50th canon the IV General Council of the Lateran, held in the year 1215 under Pope Innocent III (1198-1216), abolished the impediment of public propriety which obtained between the offspring of a woman's second marriage and the relatives of her former spouse. This impediment—*publica proprietas ex secundis nuptiis*—was attributed to Pope Hyginus (136-140) in the *palea* contained under c. 4, C. XXXV, q. 10.[6] Although the impediment of public propriety was not given any other mention by the Council, it was considered that, because of its similarity to the impediments of affinity and consanguinity, the extent of which was reduced to the fourth degree, public propriety in its extent was also reduced to the fourth degree.[7] It was to the extent of the fourth degree that the impediment was received as law into the Collection of Gregory IX.[8]

In the Decretal Collection of Gregory IX a decretal letter of Pope Alexander III set forth that the impediment of public propriety did not arise from *sponsalia* contracted when one or both parties were under seven years of age, but that it did arise if they gave consent to such a contract after they had reached the age of seven.[9] *Sponsalia de futuro,* if invalid because of a lack of the proper consent, did not beget the impediment of public propriety. But once the *sponsalia* were validly contracted, the impediment retained its effect even though the *sponsalia* ceased to exist for any reason whatsoever. This provision of law was contained in a decretal letter of Alexander III to the Archbishop of York.[10]

---

[5] Cf. Jaffé, n. 6685; Wernz, lib. IV, tit. XIX, n. 488, note 13; Joyce, p. 92.

[6] Schroeder, *Disciplinary Decrees of the General Councils,* Original Text with English Translation (St. Louis: Herder, 1941), p. 578 (hereafter cited Schroeder); Mansi, XXII, 1038. Cf. Bernardus Papiensis, *Summa Decretalium,* lib. IV, tit. XIV, n. 1.

[7] Cf. c. 8, X, *de consanguinitate et affinitate,* IV, 14; Schroeder, p. 578; Freisen, p. 506; Scherer, II, 347; Wahl, p. 19.

[8] Bernardus Papiensis, *Summa Decretalium,* lib. IV, tit. I, n. 18.

[9] Cc. 4, 6, X, *de desponsatione impuberum,* IV, 2; cf. also Bernard's *casus* ad c. 4, *ibid.;* Jaffé, nn. 9009 and 9069.

[10] C. 5, X, *de desponsatione impuberum,* IV, 2; Jaffé, n. 8952; cf. Esmein, I, 149.

By a letter of Pope Clement III (1187-1191), *sponsalia* contracted with a minor below the age of seven years were declared to be invalid, but they became valid through mutual cohabitation after the age of seven, and thus gave rise to the impediment of public propriety.[11] In accordance with the provision of a letter of Innocent III (1198-1216), if someone below the age of puberty contracted marriage while he had not yet reached the physical development that implied a precocious fitness for marriage, it was not marriage that was contracted, but the *sponsalia,* and accordingly the betrothal gave rise to the impediment of public propriety.[12]

The impediment of public propriety arose also in the case wherein one of the parties in a valid betrothal had carnal intercourse with a blood relation of the other party. By such action the betrothal itself was dissolved, but the impediment of affinity—*affinitas superveniens*—arose between the parties, and a new impediment of public propriety arose between the guilty betrothed party and a relative of the other party in the first degree of the collateral line.[13]

At the II General Council of Lyons (1274) it was considered, by some of the Fathers of the Council, that the extension of the impediment of public propriety to the fourth degree was still too inclusive, so that they weighed the question of further restricting the extension of the impediment. However, no legislative measures on the question were adopted.[14]

The *Liber Sextus Decretalium* of Boniface VIII (1298) did much to dispel the many doubts that existed about the impediment of

---

[11] C. 12, X, *de desponsatione impuberum,* IV, 2; Jaffé, n. 10246.

[12] C. 15, X, *de desponsatione impuberum,* IV, 2; Potthast, *Regesta Pontificum Romanorum inde ab anno post Christum Natum MCXCVIII ad annum MCCCIV* (2 vols., Berolini, 1874-1875), n. 2775 (hereafter cited Potthast).

[13] Cf. cc. 1, 2, 4, 6, X, *de eo, qui cognovit consanguineam uxoris suae vel sponsae,* IV, 13; Reiffenstuel, *Ius Canonicum Universum* (ed. noviss., 5 vols. in 6, Romae, 1831-1834), Lib. IV, tit. XIV, n. 62 (hereafter cited Reiffenstuel); Schmalzgrueber, *Ius Ecclesiasticum Universum* (5 vols. in 12, Romae, 1843-1845), Lib. IV, tit. XIII, n. 10 (hereafter cited Schmalzgrueber); Wahl, p. 78.

[14] Ioannes Andreae, *In Quartum Decretalium Librum Novella Commentaria* (Venetiis, 1581), Lib. IV, tit. XIV; cf. Fagnanus, *Commentaria in Libras Decretalium* (5 vols., Romae, 1661), Lib. IV, tit. XIV, n. 26 (hereafter cited Fagnanus).

public propriety, both by establishing new legislation, and also by restating some statutes already in existence. The *Liber Sextus* enacted that the fact of the *sponsalia* had to be definitely certain before it gave rise to the impediment of public propriety.[15] Accordingly, *sponsalia* doubtfully contracted did not give rise to the impediment; nor did *sponsalia* which were contracted subject to a condition, until the condition had been fulfilled. The impediment of public propriety arose also from *sponsalia* entered into by parents for their children, when the latter were above the age of puberty, provided that the children consented to the contract antecedently or ratified it subsequently.[16]

There is not to be found in the decretal law of Gregory IX any clear text stating that the impediment of public propriety arose from *sponsalia de presenti* as well as from *sponsalia de futuro*. However, with an argument made *a fortiori*, it was deduced that *sponsalia de presenti* gave rise to the impediment of public propriety for the reason that an even stronger and more intimate bond was thus created than through the *sponsalia de futuro*.[17]

The earliest commentators on the decretals understood them to mean that the impediment of public propriety arose both from *sponsalia de futuro* and from *sponsalia de presenti*. Bernard of Pavia (c. 1198) was very clear in stating that public propriety arose from *sponsalia de presenti*.[18] On the basis of c. 4, C. XXXV, q. 10, Bernard made the further points that the impediment of public propriety arose between the children of a second marriage

[15] "Ex sponsalibus puris et certis, etiamsi consanguinitatis, affinitatis, frigiditatis, religionis aut alia quavis ratione sint nulla, dummodo non sint nulla ex defectu consensus, oritur efficax ad impediendum et dirimendum sequentia sponsalia vel matrimonia, non tamen ad praecedentia dissolvendum, impedimentum iustitiae publicae honestatis."—c. un., *de sponsalibus et matrimoniis*, IV, 1, in VI°; cf. Esmein, I, 150.

[16] C. un., *de desponsatione impuberum*, IV, 2, in VI°.

[17] Sanchez, *De Sancto Matrimonii Sacramento Disputationum Tomi Tres* (Lugduni, 1669), Lib. VII, disp. LXX, n. 1 (hereafter cited Sanchez); Schmalzgrueber, Lib. IV, tit. I, n. 98. Scherer, II, 347.

[18] *Summa de Matrimonio*, n. 12: "Nam ecce si quis aliquam desponsaverit de presenti et mortuus est ea non cognita, nullus de eius consanguinitate ipsam poterit accipere uxorem, similiter ac, si sponsa praemortua fuerit, sponsus non poterit aliquam accipere de eius consanguinitate." Cf. Laspeyres edition of Bernard's *Summa Decretalium*, Appendix I, p. 303.

and the relatives of the former spouse, and that the impediment did not extend beyond the fourth degree.

Bernard did not with equal explicitness state that the impediment of public propriety arose also from *sponsalia de futuro*. However, in commenting on a decision of Alexander III to the Bishop of Hereford, England, as contained in c. 4, X, *de desponsatione impuberum,* IV, 2, he clearly implied it. The case, as presented by Bernard, concerned a man of legal age who betrothed a girl below the age of seven. Later this man had carnal intercourse with the mother of the girl and married the mother. The question was, could the marriage stand? Bernard's solution was that, if the man married the mother before the girl reached the age of seven, the marriage held, since the *sponsalia* were invalid because of the girl's lack of age and so did not give rise to the impediment of public propriety. On the other hand, if the daughter had ratified the *sponsalia* after she reached the age of seven, and the marriage with the mother took place after this act of ratification, then the marriage was null because of the impediment of public propriety, and the parties were to be separated.[19]

Tancred (+ 1235) mentioned two cases as giving rise to the impediment of public propriety. He stated that the impediment arose between the children of a woman's second marriage and the blood relatives of her first husband, and also from the contract of *sponsalia*. But with reference to the word *sponsalia* he did not elaborate any closer specification of meaning.[20]

In stating that *sponsalia* gave rise to the impediment of public propriety Hostiensis (+ 1271) did not seem to make any distinction with reference to the effect as following from *sponsalia de presenti* or from *sponsalia de futuro*. The implication, however, was that public propriety as an impediment arose from both kinds of *sponsalia*. Hostiensis also stated that public propriety as a matrimonial impediment between the children of a second marriage

[19] *Bernardi et Ricardi Casus Decretalium,* ad c. 4, X, *de desponsatione impuberum,* IV, 2.

[20] "Una contrahitur ex desponsatione, puta, si aliquis desponsavit puellam septem annorum et licet eam non cognoscat, tamen nullus de consanguinitate eius poterit eam habere in uxorem, nec ipse aliquam eius consanguineam." Tancredus, *Summa de Matrimonio,* tit. XXVIII, n. 52; quoted from Freisen, pp. 501-502; cf. Scherer, II, 348.

and the blood relatives of the former spouse did not obtain at his time. As already seen, the IV General Council of the Lateran had abolished it.[21] He further stated that public propriety in its character of a matrimonial impediment arose even from invalid *sponsalia,* except in cases wherein the invalidity was due to a lack of proper consent, and that the impediment extended to the fourth degree.[22]

The teaching of Saint Thomas Aquinas (1225-1274) regarding the impediment of public propriety seems to imply a deviation from the common trend. St. Thomas stated that this impediment arose from *sponsalia de futuro,* and that *sponsalia de presenti* and carnal intercourse gave rise to the impediment of affinity.[23]

For this opinion he seemed not to win any adherents.[24] Nevertheless, the inherent merit of the doctrine propounded by St. Thomas, at a time when ideas on the subject were rather confused and not very clearly expressed, may be better judged from the closer relationship in which it stood both to the Roman law and to the present law of the Church as set forth in the Code of Canon Law. In Roman law as also in the present law of the Code that consent which was sufficient to constitute marriage—the *consensus de praesenti* of St. Thomas—was made to give rise to the impediment of affinity. Furthermore, in Roman law the consent that

---

[21] Cf. *supra,* p. 39.

[22] "Sponsalia ergo quae nulla sunt consensu deficiente vel aetate impediente nullam iustitiam publicae honestatis generant; secus, quando nulla sunt impediente consanguinitate, ut notatur supra *de sponsalibus* § *quis sit effectus.* Effectus etiam is est, nam si puella cum fratre tuo consanguineo sed non uterino sponsalia contraxit, quamvis sponsalia nulla sint ex eo quod fratri tuo attinet in quarto gradu ex parte matris ipsius fratris tui, te tamen qui de alia matre es, impediente publicae honestatis iustitia habere non potest in maritum." *Summa Aurea* (Venetiis: apud Juntas, 1568), Lib. IV, tit. 2, n. 8.

[23] "Matrimonium affinitatem causat non solum ratione carnalis copulae, sed etiam ratione societatis coniugalis. . . . Unde et affinitas contrahitur ex ipso contractu matrimonii *per verba de presenti* ante carnalem copulam: et similiter ex sponsalibus, in quibus fit quaedam pactio coniugalis societatis, contrahitur aliquod affinitati simile, scilicet publicae honestatis iustitia."—*Summa Theologica* (De novo edita cura et studio Collegii Provinciae Tolosanae Ordinis Praedicatorum, 6 vols., Parisiis; Andreas Blat, 1935), *Supplementum,* Q. 55, art. 4, ad 2.

[24] Cf. Freisen, p. 505; Esmein, I, 148.

denoted merely the promise of a future marriage—the *consensus de futuro* of St. Thomas—was made to give rise to the marriage impediment of quasi-affinity or public propriety.[25]

Panormitanus (1386-1453) in his commentary on the decretals was also explicit in stating that the impediment of public propriety arose *a fortiori* from *sponsalia de praesenti.*[26] Panormitanus was likewise quite emphatic in stating that the impediment of public propriety did not extend further than the fourth degree.[27]

---

[25] *Supra,* pp. 3 and 4.

[26] "Quaero primo pro intellectu litterae; utrum hoc procedat in sponsis de futuro, an *autem* de presenti? Dic secundum doctores quod utroque casu procedit desponsatio. Nam si non licet ducere sponsam consanguinei de futuro, multo fortius si est de presenti, nam maior est honestas, ut non ducatur sponsa de presenti cum qua matrimoniale vinculum est iunctum quam sponsa de futuro cui solum facta est promissio futurarum nuptiarum."—*Commentaria,* Lib. IV, tit. 1, n. 1.

[27] *Commentaria,* Lib. IV, tit. 1, n. 4.

CHAPTER V

The Impediment of Public Propriety From the Council of Trent to the Code of Canon law

ARTICLE 1. CHANGES IN THE DECRETAL LAW ON PUBLIC PROPRIETY AS INTRODUCED BY THE COUNCIL OF TRENT

After the Council of Trent (1545-1563) the law regarding the impediment of public propriety underwent further development more by way of doctrinal interpretation and canonical jurisprudence than through legislative enactments. With the exception of the Decree *Ne Temere* of the Sacred Congregation of the Council as promulgated on August 2, 1907, which prescribed a determinate form for the validity of betrothals, there was no universal legislation affecting the impediment of public propriety until the appearance of the Code of Canon Law.

As a result it may be said that legal development was manifested not so much in the emergence of a clear system of law as in the clarifying of ambiguities inherent in the decretal law. Much of the jurisprudence was concerned with the attempt to resolve or at least to bring into sharper focus the numerous doubts that had arisen. Notwithstanding certain authentic decrees issued by the Sacred Congregations as well as decisions in particular cases, the manifold and grave controversies continued for the most part in full vigor as long as the impediment arising from betrothal and non-consummated marriage was extant, that is to say, up to the time of the promulgation of the Code of Canon Law.

To explore the merits of the arguments that were marshalled in support of the various opinions that were held regarding the particular points of controversy would practically entail a commentary on the whole decretal law concerning the impediment of public propriety. That law today has little more than a historic interest, for the corresponding law contained in the present Code has changed the whole basis of the impediment. Accordingly, no more extensive treatment will be attempted here than an outline of the general scope of the impediment along with a brief statement of the outstanding controversies that centered around it.

The Council of Trent decreed a twofold change in the pre-existing law regarding the impediment of public propriety. The Council declared that betrothals (*sponsalia*), if invalid for any reason whatsoever, did not give rise to the impediment, and that the impediment of public propriety arising from a valid betrothal did not extend beyond the first degree whether in the direct or in the collateral line of blood relationship. This action was taken by the Council because, as was stated, the former wider extension of the impediment had by that time outlived the advantages it formerly had.[1]

One of the first questions to arise after the issuance of the new decree regarding the impediment of public propriety by the Council of Trent was whether the decree which limited the extension of the impediment to the first degree of blood relationship was applicable also to public propriety in the nature of an impediment as arising from an unconsummated marriage. The reason for the doubt was that the decree spoke of *sponsalia,* and the expression *sponsalia de praesenti,* meaning non-consummated marriage, as well as the expression *sponsalia de futuro,* meaning betrothal or the promise of future marriage, was in common use.[2] The question was settled in the year 1568 by Pope St. Pius V (1566-1572) in the Constitution *Ad Romanum,* in which it was authentically declared that the decree of the Council of Trent, which limited the impediment of public propriety to the first degree, referred only to public propriety as arising from betrothals. The impediment as

---

[1] Conc. Trident., sess. XXIV, *de ref. matrim.,* c. 3; "Justitiae publicae honestatis impedimentum, ubi sponsalia quacunque ratione valida non .erunt, sancta synodus prorsus tollit. Ubi autem valida fuerint, primum gradum non excedant, quoniam in ulterioribus gradibus iam non potest huiusmodi prohibitio absque dispendio observari." Cf. Wernz, Lib. IV, tit. XIX, n. 448; Feije, n. 387. Sanchez, Lib. VII, disp. LXVIII, n. 8; *Acta et Decreta Sacrorum Conciliorum Recentiorum, Collectio Lacensis* (7 vols., Friburgi Brisgoviae, 1870-1892), VII, 842.

[2] Feije, n. 387.

arising from a non-consummated marriage still continued to extend to the fourth degree inclusive.[3]

The impediment of public propriety was contracted only with the blood relatives of the other party in the betrothal or with the partner of the non-consummated marriage. It was, however, contracted with all blood relatives both legitimate and illegitimate, but not with those who were related to the other party simply by affinity.[4]

The impediment of public propriety arising from non-consummated marriage connotated a firmer bond than that which was occasioned in consequence of a simple betrothal. Accordingly its extension after the Council of Trent was more comprehensive, for, as was explicitly stated in the Constitution *Ad Romanum,* the Council restricted solely the extension of the impediment of public propriety as arising from betrothals. It was also more difficult, and a more weighty reason was required, to obtain a dispensation from the impediment of public propriety when it existed in consequence of a non-consummated marriage.[5]

---

[3] "Motu proprio et auctoritate apostolica, tenore praesentium declaramus et definimus decretum Concilii huiusmodi omnino intelligendum esse et procedere in sponsalibus de futuro dumtaxat, non autem in matrimonio sic, ut praefertur, contracto, sed in eo durare adhuc impedimentum in omnibus illis casibus et gradibus quibus de iure veteri ante praedictum Concilii decretum introductum erat, et ita ab omnibus iudicari debere mandamus, atque statuimus."—*Bullarum Diplomatum et Privilegiorum Sanctorum Romanorum Pontificum Taurinensis Editio* (24 vols. et Appendix, Augustae Taurinorum, 1857-1872), VII, 578 (hereafter cited *Bull. Rom.*) ; cf. S.C.C., *Caesenaten.,* 18 iun. 1611, as reproduced by Monacelli in his *Formularium Legale Practicum Fori Ecclesiastici* (nova ed., 4 vols. in 3, Romae, 1844), II, tit. 16, n. 32 ; cf. also *supra,* p. 39.

[4] Giovine, *De Dispensationibus Matrimonialibus Consultationes Canonicae* (2 vols. in 5 parts, Neapoli, 1863-1866), Vol. I, Pars II (1865), p. 534 (hereafter cited Giovine) ; Benedictus XIV, *De Synodo Dioecesana* (2 vols., Romae, 1806), II, lib. IX, c. 13, n. 4; Lombardi, *Iuris Canonici Privati Institutiones* (2 ed., 3 vols., Romae, 1901), II, 276 (hereafter cited Lombardi) ; Gasparri, *De Matrimonio* (1904), n. 707; Sanchez, Lib. VII, disp. LXVIII, n. 3.

[5] Conc. Trident., sess. XXIV, *de ref. matrim.,* c. 3; Pius V. Const. *Ad Romanum,* I iul. 1568—*Bull Rom.,* VII, 578; *Ojetti, Synopsis Rerum Moralium et Iuris Pontifici Alphabetico Ordine Digesta* (3. ed., 4 vols., Romae, 1909-1914), II, 2202 (hereafter cited *Synopsis*) ; Feije, n. 386.

Once the impediment of public propriety had arisen it continued in existence perpetually in the absence of any dispensation to remove it. Hence the impediment continued to bind even after the betrothal became legitimately dissolved, or after the non-consummated marriage had come to an end through the death of one of the parties.[6]

ARTICLE 2. THE IMPEDIMENT OF PUBLIC PROPRIETY ARISING FROM BETROTHALS

The law in its enactment that a betrothal—(*sponsalia*)—had to be *valid* and *absolute* to give rise to the impediment of public propriety seemed in itself to be quite clear.[7] Yet a divergence of opinion arose on these points. From the text of the decree of the Council of Trent it seemed that all validly contracted betrothals, even though they were private or occult in the sense that they were known only perhaps to the parties themselves, gave rise to the impediment. Nevertheless, from the underlying reason for the impediment rooted as it was in public decency, some authors by laying special emphasis on the concept connected with the word *public* maintained that the betrothal had to be public to give rise to the impediment.[8] This doctrine was opposed by the more commonly held opinion that the impediment arose also in the case of occult betrothals.[9] The question of whether occult betrothals gave

---

[6] Barbosa, *Collectanea doctorum, tam veterum quam recentiorum, in ius pontificium universum* (6 vols. in 5, Venetiis, 1716-1719), II, lib. IV, tit. II, n. 1 and 2; Faganus, Lib. IV, tit. XIV, n. 29; Scavini, *Theologia Moralis Universa ad Mentem S. Alphonsi M. de Ligorio* (9. ed., 4 vols., Mediolani, 1869), III, 640.

[7] Cf. c. un., *de sponsalibus et matrimoniis,* IV, 1, in VI°; Conc. Trident., XXIV, *de ref. matrim.,* c. 3; cf. *supra,* p. 46.

[8] Pitonius, *Disceptationes Ecclesiasticae, Pars II* (Romae, 1704), p. 102, n. 98 (hereafter cited Pitonius); cf. Scherer, II, 347, note 13, and also Gonzalez-Tellez, *Commentaria Perpetua in Singulos Textus Quinque Librorum Decretalium Gregorii* IX (5 vols., Venetiis, 1699), Lib. IV, tit. I, n. 6 (hereafter cited Gonzalez-Tellez).

[9] Benedictus XIV, *De Synodo Dioecesana,* II, Lib. VIII, c. 12; Rosset, III, n. 1991; Schmalzgrueber, Lib. IV, tit. 1, n. 99; Feije, n. 263; cf. S.C.S. Off., 11 aug. 1852—*Collectanea S. Congregationis de Propaganda Fide* (2 vols., Romae: Typographia Polyglotta S. C. de Propaganda Fide, 1907), n.

rise to the impediment of public propriety was definitely decided for Spain and Latin America after 1880 and 1900 respectively, when a prescribed form was made necessary for the validity of betrothals.[10]

Another question, closely allied to the foregoing one, also gave rise to much discussion and difference of opinion. The question was: if the betrothals were entered publicly, and were apparently valid, though in reality they were invalid because of some occult cause, did they give rise to the impediment of public propriety? Some authors, again basing their argument on the underlying reason for the impediment, namely the demand inherent in the public sense of decency, but in apparent contradiction to the decree of the Council of Trent, which stated that betrothals which were not valid for any reason—*quacunque ratione valida non erunt*—did not give rise to the impediment, maintained that the impediment did arise.[11] Other authors, however, relying on the more literal interpretation of the words of the Council, held that the impediment did not arise in the case under consideration.[12]

Similarly, controversies arose concerning the other requirement of the law, namely, that betrothals must be *absolute* to give rise to the impediment. It was, however, generally agreed that a betrothal subject to a suspensive condition did give rise to the impediment once the suspensive condition was either fulfilled or revoked.[13]

A very notable exception to this general agreement presented

1078 (hereafter cited *Collectanea*); Alberti, *Theologia Pastoralis* (4 partes, Romae: pars I, 3. ed., 1901; pars II, 3. ed., and pars IV, 1904; pars III, 1903), IV, n. 96 (hereafter Pars IV will be cited *De Sacramento Matrimonii*).

[10] Cf. *infra*, pp. 53-54.

[11] Sanchez, Lib. VII, disp. LXVIII, n. 14; Gonzalez-Tellez, Lib. IV, tit. 1, n. 6; Pitonius, pars II, p. 103, n. 99.

[12] Alphonsus Maria de Ligorio, *Theologia Moralis* (ed. nova, cura et studio L. Gaude, 4 vols., Romae: Typis Polyglottis Vaticanis, 1905-1912), Lib. VI, n. 1062; Giovine, Vol. I, pars II, p. 532: Scherer, II, 374; Gasparri, *De Matrimonii* (1904), n. 713; Feije, n. 391. Wernz (Lib. IV, tit. XIX, n. 450, note 29) stated that the opposite opinion lacked probability.

[13] Cf. c. un. *de sponsalibus et matrimoniis,* IV, 1, in VI°; Sanchez, Lib. VII, disp. LXVXIX, n. 2; Schmalzgrueber, Lib. IV, tit. 1, n. 108; Gasparri, *De Matrimonio* (1904), n. 717.

itself in the case wherein betrothal was entered subject to the condition that the pope would grant a dispensation from the diriment impediment which barred marriage between the parties. Some authors denied the validity of betrothals subject to such a condition, and consequently, in accordance with the decree of the Council of Trent, denied that the impediment of public propriety arose in such a case. Their reasoning was based on the consideration that such a condition was illicit inasmuch as it was opposed to the public good to make part of a contract a condition that depended on the will of the supreme legislator. Furthermore, these authors claimed that certain decisions of the Sacred Congregation of the Council supported their view.[14]

Others distinguished by contending that the betrothals were invalid if the impediment in question was of such a nature that a dispensation could not be granted, or customarily was not given, or if there was no just cause for a dispensation. The betrothals were valid, they maintained, if there was question of an impediment from which Rome usually dispensed and in regard to which a reason existed for the granting of the dispensation. The impediment arose only when the dispensation was granted, but before that time there was the obligation of petitioning the dispensation and of awaiting the reply.[15]

It was generally agreed that betrothals which were contracted subject to a condition attended with a vitiating effect gave rise to the impediment of public propriety.[16]

---

[14] Bangen, *Instructio Practica de Sponsalibus et Matrimonio* (IV fasc., I [1858]; II, III & IV [1860], Monasterii), I, 3; Scavini, III, 641; Gury. *Compendium Theologiae Moralis* (ed. in Germania 4., Ratisbonae, 1868), n. 471; Giovine, Vol. I, pars II, pp. 305 and 531; cf. S.C.C., *Brugnaten. Sponsalium,* 26 ian. 1709—*Thesaurus Resolutionum Sacrae Congregationis Concilii* (167 vols., Romae, 1718-1908), VI, 176-178 (hereafter cited *Thesaurus*).

[15] Reiffenstuel, Lib. IV, tit. 1, n. 19; S. Alphonsus de Ligorio, *Theologia Moralis,* Lib. VI, n. 1061; De Angelis, *Praelectiones Iuris Canonici ad Methodum Decretalium Gregorii IX Exactae* (5 vols. in 9, Romae-Parisiis, 1877-1891), Lib. IV, tit. V, n. 4 (hereafter cited De Angelis); Giovine, Vol. I, pars II, p. 531; Rosset, II, n. 898.

[16] Sanchez, Lib. VII, disp. LXVII, n. 3; Gasparri, *De Matrimonio* (1904), n. 718; Wernz, Lib. IV, tit. XIX, n. 450; Scavini, III, 640.

Scherer (*Handbuch des Kerchenrechtes,* II, 348, n. 12), arguing from the

Almost from the first appearance of the impediment of public propriety in Church legislation through the *Decretum* of Gratian the tendency throughout had been the limitation of the scope of the impediment. A limitation was imposed by the IV General Council of the Lateran (1215). A further limitation was proposed but not enacted into law at the II General Council of Lyons (1274). Finally, at the Council of Trent (1545-1563) another limitation was put in effect by the law.[17]

A similar trend was in evidence at the Vatican Council (1869-1870). A number of French bishops were in favor of placing further restrictions on the impediment of public propriety which arose from non-consummated marriage. Together with some Italian, Belgian and Canadian bishops, they were in favor of the complete abolition of the impediment which arose from betrothals.[18] The Council, however, took no legislative action in this regard.

The tendency toward restriction was entirely in keeping with the manner of development of the impediment of public propriety in Church legislation. As has been maintained above, for many centuries non-consummated marriage and betrothal had been identified, and in the character of the "initiated marriage" (*matrimonium initiatum*) of Gratian gave rise to the impediment of public propriety. Later, when in the clarifying distinction of Peter Lombard the two concepts were clearly set apart into *sponsalia de praesenti* and *sponsalia de futuro,* each separately was considered to give rise to the impediment, and so it was quite natural to expect a tendency that sought to reduce the scope of the impediment, especially in the event that it arose from *sponsalia de futuro*—betrothal—since the latter connoted a less firm bond of union.[19]

Indirectly also numerous attempts sought to reduce the scope of

---

words *"puris et certis"* of c. un., *de sponsalibus et matrimoniis,* IV, 1, in VI°, held that betrothals subject to a condition which was attended with a vitiating effect were not valid, and hence after the change introduced by the Council of Trent did not give rise to the impediment of public propriety.

[17] Cf. *supra,* pp. 39, 40, 46.

[18] Granderath, *Histoire du Concile du Vatican* (Edité par C. Kirch, Bruxelles, 1914), *Appendices et Documenta,* pp. 150-151; Martin, *Omnium Concilli Vaticani Documentorum Collectio* (Paderbornae, 1873), pp. 162, 183, 187; cf. *Collectio Lacensis,* VII, 842.

[19] Cf. *supra,* pp. 34-35.

the impediment of public propriety which arose from betrothals by requiring a determinate form for their validity. These efforts were finally rewarded when on August 2, 1907, the decree *"Ne temere"* of Pope Pius X (1903-1914), prescribing a definite form for the validity of betrothals, became the universal law of the Church.[20]

As early as the thirteenth century attempts had been made in local Church councils with a view to remedying some of the many evils, not the least of which were family enmities, which arose from clandestine betrothals.[21] Again at the Council of Trent the question of making a definite form necessary for the validity of betrothals entered into some of the preliminary discussions on the decree dealing with clandestinity, but mention of this particular question is not to be found in the subsequent discussions.[22]

From time to time the question was brought to the attention of the Sacred Congregation of the Council, but the reply on each occasion was to the effect that no change was to be made—*nihil est innovandum*. Such was the import of the reply to the Archbishop of Braga on January 26, 1715.[23] Such also was the reply given by the Holy Office to the Archbishop of Quebec on August 11, 1852. In view of the evils arising from clandestine betrothals the Archbishop had petitioned that a definite form be made necessary for the validity of betrothals. The reply set forth that no change was to be introduced, but that care should be taken for the instruction of the faithful on the seriousness of the betrothal contract and regarding the impediment of public propriety to which it gave rise.[24]

When local ordinaries imposed on their dioceses legislation which

---

[20] S.C.C., decr. *Ne temere,* 2 Aug. 1907—*ASS,* XL (1907), 525.

[21] Provincial Council of Trier (1227), c. 5—Mansi, XXIII, 29; Synod of Langeais (1278), c. 3—Mansi, XXIV, 212; Synod of Lambeth (1330), c. 5—Mansi, XXV, 894; cf. Feije, n. 558; Wernz, Lib. IV, tit. XIX, n. 89.

[22] Pallavicino, *Istoria del Concilio di Trento* (6 vols., Faenza, 1792-1797), Vol. V (1796), Lib. XXII, cap. IV, nn. 1-2; cap. VIII, nn. 9-15; Feije, n. 558, note 6.

[23] *ASS,* I (1865), 529-530; cf. S.C.C., *Ugentina Sponsalium,* 23 mart. 1878—*Thesaurus,* CXXXVII, 152; S.C.C., *Anconitana et Aliarum* 14 maii 1898—*Analecta Ecclesiastica,* VI (1898), 189-190.

[24] *Analecta Ecclesiastica,* VI (1898), 190; cf. De Angelis, Lib. IV, tit. III, n. 9; Feije, n. 558.

required a determinate form for the validity of betrothals, such legislation was not sustained by Rome. The Sacred Congregation of the Council, on July 27, 1863, declared that local ordinaries lacked authority to impose such legislation. The Sacred Congregation referred back to similar decisions issued by it on December 19, 1596, and on January 26, 1715.[25]

Benedict XIV (1740-1758) related that in the Archdiocese of Valencia in Spain the Archbishop was petitioned to issue synodal legislation which would require for the validity of betrothals the presence of the pastor and of two witnesses. The Archbishop refused to do so, since he felt that he did not possess the needed authority. The question was then brought to the attention of the Sacred Congregation of the Council. The Congregation commended the Archbishop for the position he had taken and stated that, since the Council of Trent had not introduced any new legislation on this matter, the pre-Tridentine law should prevail.[26]

Soon, however, a change was to take place in the attitude of the Apostolic See towards clandestine betrothals. On April 28, 1804, a pragmatic sanction of the Spanish King Charles IV (1788-1808) decreed that validity would be acknowledged for only those betrothals which were contracted by means of a public written document. Although this decree was in itself invalid inasmuch as it was issued by incompetent authority, in practice it was observed and so attained the force of Church law also by reason of at least a tacit approval on the side of the competent ecclesiastical authority. In reply to a query the Sacred Congregation of the Council, on January 31, 1880, gave it official recognition by stating that betrothals were invalid if they were not contracted according to the prescribed form.[27]

At a later time the civil law which had required that, for validity, betrothals were to be contracted by means of a public written document became abolished. The question was then asked of the Sacred Congregation of the Council if the former legislation still retained

---

[25] *ASS,* I (1865), 529-530.

[26] Benedictus XIV, *De Synodo Dioecesana,* Lib. XII, c. 5, n. 1; Benedictus XIV, *Institutiones Ecclesiasticae* (Prati, 1844), Instit. 46, n. 12.

[27] S.C.C., *Placentina,* 31 ian. 1880—*ASS,* XIII (1880), 185-188; cf. Wernz, Lib. IV, tit. II, n. 89, note 40; De Angelis, Lib. IV, tit. III, n. 10.

its validity as Church law. The reply of the Congregation on April 11, 1891, was in the affirmative.[28]

The Fathers of the Plenary Council of Latin America, held in Rome in 1899, requested Pope Leo XIII (1878-1903) to extend to Latin America the provisions of the declaration which the Sacred Congregation of the Council on January 31, 1880, had made in favor of Spain. The Pope through the Sacred Congregation for Extraordinary Ecclesiastical Affairs granted the extension *in perpetuum* on January 1, 1900.[29]

No doubt these special provisions of law in favor of Spain and Latin America paved the way for the decree *Ne temere* enacted by Pope Pius X through the Sacred Congregation of the Council. This decree became the law of the universal Latin Church on April 19, 1908, and prescribed that for their validity betrothals had to be in writing and signed by the parties and by the pastor or local ordinary, or by two witnesses.[30]

With slight variation the provisions of the decree *Ne temere* have been received into the Code of Canon Law in canon 1017. In the law of the Code, however, betrothals no longer give rise to the impediment of public propriety.

ARTICLE 3. THE IMPEDIMENT OF PUBLIC PROPRIETY ARISING FROM NON-CONSUMMATED MARRIAGE

The other source of the impediment of public propriety under the Decretal and Tridentine laws was non-consummated marriage —*sponsalia de praesenti.* Non-consummated marriage gave rise to the impediment even though the marital union was invalid, except in two cases. The two exceptions obtained, first, when the invalidity was due to a lack of the proper consent, and, secondly, when the invalidity was due to a suspensive condition which in

---

[28] S.C.C., *Compostella,* 11 apr. 1891—*ASS,* XXIV (1891-1892), 34-39.

[29] S. C. pro Negotiis Eccles. Extraord.—*ASS,* XXXII (1899-1900), 698-701, and 553-556; *Analecta Ecclesiastica,* VII (1900), 167-168; cf. Wernz, Lib. IV, tit. II, n. 89, note 40.

[30] S.C.C., decr. *Ne temere,* 2 aug. 1907—*Codicis Iuris Canonici Fontes,* cura Emi Petri card. Gasparri editi (9 vols., Romae [postea Civitate Vaticana]: Typis Polyglottis Vaticanis, 1923-1939 [Vols. VII-IX, ed. cura et studio Emi Iustiniani Card. Seredi]), n. 4340 (hereafter cited *Fontes*).

reality was tantamount to a temporary lack of consent. The impediment of public propriety which arose from a non-consummated marriage extended to the fourth degree even after the Council of Trent.[31]

Much controversy centered around the nature of the consent necessary in the case of a non-consummated marriage if it was to give rise to the impediment of public propriety. What if a consent sufficient according to the demand of the natural law but insufficient according to the requirements enacted in canon law was present in the case? Did the impediment of public propriety arise in such a case? Did the impediment of public propriety on the consummation of the marriage give way to affinity, or did it continue in existence side by side with the impediment of affinity? How about those who when they were still under the age of puberty attempted to contract marriage? For these the marriage was invalid, but before the change introduced by the Council of Trent, which eliminated invalid betrothals as a basis of public propriety, the attempted marriage was considered to be resolved into at least an invalid betrothal, and hence was considered to give rise to the impediment of public propriety, provided that the parties did not exclude betrothal by means of a positive act of their wills.[32] What was to be said of the clandestine marriages of those who had reached the age of puberty? Did such marriages give rise to the impediment of public propriety? These questions taxed the minds of canonists and occasioned much controversy.

The question whether a clandestine marriage gave rise to the impediment of public propriety was only partially solved in the decree of the Sacred Congregation of the Council, dated March 13, 1879, and confirmed by Pope Leo XIII on March 17, 1879. This decree set forth that in places where the Tridentine decree *Tametsi* held sway the so-called civil marriage had no resemblance

---

[31] C. 3, X, *de sponsalibus et matrimoniis,* IV, 1; c. un., *de sponsalibus et matrimoniis,* IV, 1, in VI°; Conc. Trident., sess. XXIV, *de ref. matrim.,* c. 3; Pius V, Const. *Ad Romanum,* 1 iul. 1568—*Bull. Rom.,* VII, 578; cf. *supra,* pp. 46-47; Sanchez, Lib. VII, Disp. LXVIII, n. 2; Schmalzgrueber, Lib. IV, tit. XIII, nn. 98-99; Gasparri, *De Matrimonio* (1904), n. 719; Gonzalez-Tellez, Lib. IV, tit. I, n. 5; Scherer, II, 349, note 17.

[32] C. 15, X, *de desponsatione impuberum,* IV, 2; cf. *supra,* p. 40.

to a real marriage, and in consequence did not give rise to the impediment of public propriety. This was true whether the parties in performing the act intended only to contract a civil ceremony or intended also to enter betrothals, or whether in ignorance or in contempt of the law of the Church they intended to contract a real marriage.[33]

But the scope of this decree became itself a subject of controversy. Canonists were not at all agreed as to the exact force of the decree. Some canonists considered it merely declarative in character, while others looked upon it as effecting a restrictive interpretation of the law and thus becoming tantamount to a new law.[34]

Moreover a grave controversy continued regarding the emergence of the impediment of public propriety from clandestine marriages. The emphasis was, however, shifted to the more particular question, namely, whether in places subject to the decree *Tametsi* an invalidly contracted clandestine marriage, otherwise than a purely civil marriage, gave rise to the impediment of public propriety. The canonists who engaged in the controversy were rather evenly matched in authority and in weight of numbers in the defense of their mutually controverted doctrine.

The juridic basis of the affirmative side of the controversy, which held that the impediment of public propriety did arise in the case, was the fact that before the Council of Trent clandestine marriage had given rise to the impediment, and also the fact that, as Pius V had stated in the Constitution *Ad Romanum,* the impediment of public propriety which derived from non-consummated marriage

---

[33] "Praememoratum actum, qui vulgo dicitur matrimonium civile, in locis ubi promulgatum est decretum Conc. Trid., sess. 24, c. 1, *de reform. matr.*, sive fideles actum ipsum explentes intendant, uti par est (matrimonio ecclesiastico iam rite celebrato, vel cum animo illud quantocius celebrandi), meram caeremoniam civilem peragere, sive intendant sponsalia de futuro inire, sive tandem ex ignorantia, aut in spretum ecclesiasticarum legum intendant matrimonium de praesenti contrahere, impedimentum iustitiae publicae honestatis non producere."—*ASS,* XII (1879), 147-175; *Thesaurus,* CXXXVIII, 182; cf. De Angelis, Lib. IV, tit. I, n. 13; *ibid.,* tit. IV, n. 9; Feije, nn. 781 and 783.

[34] Cf. De Angelis, Lib. IV, tit. IV, n. 10; Rosset, III, n. 2015; Wernz, Lib. IV, tit. XIX, n. 456, note 52; Benedictus XIV, *Institutiones Ecclesiasticae, Instit.* 46, n. 23.

continued in all cases and to the same degree as before the Tridentine law.[35] Furthermore, in support of their view these authors alleged a decision of the Sacred Congregation of the Council, which stated that public propriety did arise from a not civilly contracted clandestine marriage in places where the decree *Tametsi* prevailed as law.[36]

The negative side of the controversy, which maintained that a clandestine marriage, whether or not it was contracted as a civil marriage, did not give rise to the impediment of public propriety in places subject to the law of the decree *Tametsi,* contended that it was misleading to speak of clandestine marriage before the Council of Trent, for prior to the Council of Trent there did not exist any prescribed form for the validity of the marriage, and consequently there was no such thing as clandestine marriage. Further, they claimed that after the enactment of the decree *Tametsi* a clandestine marriage was invalid through lack of consent for the very reason that the consent was not given in the prescribed form, and thus the marriage which was invalid for the lack of a properly given consent did not give rise to the impediment of public propriety. Indeed, such an attempt at marriage could not even be called a *matrimonium ratum.*[37]

---

[35] Cf. *supra,* p. 46; Faganus, Lib. IV, tit. XIV, n. 11; Schmalzgrueber, Lib. IV, tit. XIII, n. 102; De Angelis, Lib. IV, tit. III, n. 8; Santi, *Praelectiones Juris Canonici* (4 ed., cura M. Leitner, 5 vols. in 3, Ratisbonae-Romae; Pustet, 1903-1905), Lib. IV, tit. IV, n. 33; Mansella, *De Impedimentis Matrimonium Dirimentibus ac de Processu Judiciali in Causis Matrimonialibus* (Romae, 1881), p. 60; Scherer, II, 350; Rosset, III, n. 2005; Feije, n. 407.

[36] "Praesupposita declaratione per Constitutionem S. D. N. Pii V super hoc decreto: Censuit Congregatio oriri impedimentum justitiae publicae honestatis ex sponsalibus per verba de praesenti etiam nulliter contractis, omissa forma decreti Conc. Trid., cap. I, hujus Sessionis (24)."—This decision is found in Gallemart (+ 1625), *Sacrosanctum Oecumenicum Concilium Tridentinum, additis declarationibus Cardinalium Concilii Interpretum* . . . (Tridenti, 1737), in sess. XXIV, c. 1, and is cited from Gallemart by the Sacred Penitentiary in a rescript of March 13, 1820; cf. Wernz, Lib. IV, tit. XIX, n. 456; Feije, n. 401; cf. also *ASS,* XII (1879), 154.

[37] Sanchez, Lib. VII, disp. LXX, n. 13; Barbosa, *Pastoralis sollicitudinis sive de officio et potestate episcopi tripartita descriptio* (Lugduni, 1716), Pars III, alleg. LI, n. 181; *Pirhing,* Lib. IV, tit. V, n. 62; Pitonius, Pars II, 102, n. 98.

The outstanding exception contraposed by Boniface VIII to the general rule that an invalid marriage did give rise to the impediment of public propriety was the case in which the invalidity of the marriage was due to a lack of consent.[38] All canonists were agreed that the impediment did not arise when the invalidity of the marriage was due to an absence of the consent requisite according to the demand of the natural law itself. There was no such unanimity, however, when the consent as required by the natural law was present, but when at the same time the giving of the consent as required by the positive law of the Church was absent. The merits of the opinion which denied that the impediment arose in this latter case were based on the general character of the words used by Boniface, *"dummodo non sunt nulla ex defectu consensus."* This latter opinion came in the course of time to be acknowledged as the more common opinion.[39]

Another question which gave rise to no small amount of controversy after the Tridentine law came into effect was the following: Did invalid marriages contracted by persons of whom one or even both were below the age of puberty give rise to the impediment of public propriety? Before the Council of Trent such invalid marriages were by the positive law considered to have the same effect as betrothals, and so they accordingly gave rise to the impediment of public propriety.[40] Did this disposition of the positive law still hold after the Council of Trent, or was it abrogated by the Tridentine legislation, which stated that betrothals for whatever reason invalid did not give rise to the impediment of public propriety?[41] The more common opinion was that the Decretal law still prevailed, and that the impediment did arise from such invalid

[38] C. un, X, *de sponsalibus et matrimoniis,* IV, 1. in VI°.

[39] Cf. cc. 14, 15, X, *de sponsalibus et matrimoniis,* IV, 1; Wernz, Lib. IV, tit. XIX, n. 453, note 45; Feije, n. 598; Giovine, I, pars II, p. 535; Sanchez, Lib. II, disp. LXX, n. 22; Gasparri, *De Matrimonio* (1904), n. 727. De Smet held that, if the marriage was invalid solely for the reason that it was contracted in the face of a purely ecclesiastical impediment which neutralized the efficacy and validity of the given consent, then there nevertheless emerged the impediment of public propriety.—*De Sponsalibus et Matrimonio,* n. 64, footnote 1.

[40] Cc. 1, 15, X, *de desponsatione impuberum,* IV, 2; cf. *supra,* p. 40.

[41] Consc. Trident., sess. XXIV, *de ref. matrim.,* c. 3.

marriages, but extended only to the first degree of relationship as in the case of betrothals.[42]

The impediment of public propriety arose from non-consummated marriages as well as from betrothals. When the marriage became consummated the impediment of affinity arose. Did the emergence of this impediment cancel out the previously extant impediment of public propriety, or did both impediments continue to exist simultaneously? This was a mooted question. It was never definitely decided.

Those canonists who maintained that both impediments existed after the consummation of the marriage argued from the premise that the basis of each impediment still continued to exist, so that both impediments continued also to exist. They likewise claimed on their behalf certain decisions of the Sacred Congregation of the Council.[43] The opponents in the controversy held that, since consummation was the natural culmination of the marriage, the resultant affinity absorbed the pre-existing impediment of public propriety.[44]

---

[42] Sanchez, Lib. VII, disp. LXX, n. 8; Wernz, Lib. IV, tit. XIX, n. 452, note 41, n. 455; Benedictus XIV, *Institutiones Ecclesiasticae,* Instit. 46, n. 23; Feije, n. 389. Scherer (*Handbuch des Kirchenrechtes,* II, p. 349, note 13) and De Smet (*De Sponsalibus et Matrimonio,* n. 634) denied that the impediment of public propriety arose from the marriages which were contracted invalidly in consequence of the fact that one or both of the contracting parties were below the age of puberty; cf. Alberti, *De Sacramento Matrimonii,* n. 96.

[43] Rosset, III, n. 2000; Vlaming, *Praelectiones de Iure Matrimonii* 3. ed., 2 vols., Bussum in Hollandia, 1919-1921), I, 367 (hereafter cited as Vlaming); De Smet, n. 633; Wernz, Lib. IV, tit. XIX, n. 395; cf. S.C.C., *Brixien. Matr.,* 3 de. 1667—cited by S.C.C., *Dubium Matr.,* 21 nov. 1722— *Thesaurus,* II, 239-242; S.C.C., *Valentina Dispen.* 15 apr. 1752—*Thesaurus,* XVI, 44-45.

[44] D'Annibale, *Summula Theologiae Moralis* (4 ed., 3 vols., Romae, 1894-1897), III, n. 434, note 25; Gasparri, *De Matrimonio* (1904), nn. 698 and 721.

PART II

Canonical Commentary

INTRODUCTION

The present discipline of the Church regarding the impediment of public propriety is contained in canon 1078:

> *Impedimentum publicae honestatis oritur ex matrimonio invalido, sive consummato sive non, et ex publico vel notorio concubinatu; et nuptias dirimit in primo et secundo gradu lineae rectae inter virum et consanguineas mulieris, ac vice versa.*

It is apparent from this canon that the impediment of public propriety springs from a twofold source: invalid marriage, whether consummated or not, and public or notorious concubinage. Considered in its origin in an invalid marriage, the impediment of public propriety in the law of the Code agrees to a limited extent with both the impediment of affinity and that of public propriety in the pre-Code legislation. Inasmuch as it arises from an invalid consummated marriage, the impediment of public propriety agrees with the pre-Code impediment of affinity, and inasmuch as it arises from an invalid non-consummated marriage, the impediment of public propriety in the present law agrees with the pre-Code impediment of public propriety. The impediment of public propriety bears also a certain resemblance to the diriment impediment of affinity in the present law. Like the impediment of affinity, that of public propriety arises from a marriage, but unlike that of affinity, which derives only from a valid marriage,[1] the impediment of public propriety has its origin in an invalid marriage.

Furthermore, the reason for the existence of the two impediments in Church legislation is similar. It is to be found, not in a blood relationship as is the impediment of consanguinity, but in the impropriety of marriage between the parties of a valid marriage and the blood relations of the other party in the case of affinity, and between the parties of an invalid marriage or of a public or a notorious concubinage and the blood relatives of the other party in the case of public propriety. The prohibition of marriage in those instances contributes to the protection of good morals.

[1] Canon 97, § 1.

It is to be noted that, as its second source, the impediment of public propriety springs from two species of concubinage, namely, from public concubinage and from notorious concubinage. These two species of concubinage are specified disjunctively in canon 1078 as sources of the impediment. Considered in its source in concubinage, public propriety bears a resemblance to the impediment of affinity as based on illicit carnal copulation in the pre-Code legislation. However, it will be seen that the Code has inaugurated an entirely new legislation regarding the impediment of public propriety. This fact is emphasized by the absence in the Code of even a single footnote reference to any part of the former legislation.

Under the present discipline the impediment of public propriety may be defined as "a certain propinquity of persons or quasi-affinity, arising from an invalid marriage and from a public or a notorious concubinage, which, on account of public decency, invalidates the marriage of a baptized person with the blood relations, even illegitimate, of the other party, within the degrees established by law."[2] The two sources of the impediment, namely, an invalid marriage whether consummated or not, and a public or a notorious concubinage, will be considered separately and in the order in which they are stated in canon 1078. Hence, in the first place, the impediment of public propriety as arising from an invalid marriage will be treated.

Like the pre-Code law on the impediment of public propriety the present law of the Code is shrouded in the mists of controversy. The wording of the law appears clear enough in itself, but the exact scope of the impediment has given rise to much doubt. From the first this ambiguous nature of the law was recognized.[3] The result is that, even today, any work in the nature of a comprehensive treatment of the impediment of public propriety must, for the most part and of necessity, consist in an attempt to resolve a series of doubts as reflected in the commentators' explanation of this law of the Church.

---

[2] Wernz-Vidal, *Ius Matrimoniale,* n. 373.

[3] Cf. Gearin, "The Matrimonial Law According to the New Code," *The Ecclesiastical Review* (from 1889-1905, and from 1943 onward, *The American Ecclesiastical Review,* Philadelphia, 1889-1943; Baltimore, 1944-), LVIII (1918), 486 (hereafter cited *ER* and *AER* respectively).

CHAPTER VI

PUBLIC PROPRIETY ARISING FROM AN INVALID MARRIAGE

ARTICLE 1. MEANING OF THE EXPRESSION INVALID MARRIAGE IN CANON 1078

In the sequence of canon 1078 the first source of the impediment of public propriety to be considered is invalid marriage. Canon 1081, § 1 states that the consent of the parties, when legitimately manifested by persons capable before the law, makes the marriage.[1] Consequently, whenever any one of these three essential elements, namely, the consent of the parties, their capacity according to the law, which means the absence of a diriment impediment, or the legitimate manifestation of the consent, is lacking, there is an invalid marriage.[2]

---

[1] "Matrimonium facit partium consensus inter personas iure habiles legitime manifestatus."

[2] In the strict etymology of the words a distinction may be made between the terms *null* and *void* (*nullum et irritum*). The term null is more properly applied to a marriage that is invalid on account of the non-observance of the necessary juridical form, with the result that the union between the parties does not have even the semblance or the figure of a marriage. The term void, on the other hand, is more fittingly applied to a marriage which is invalid on account of a diriment impediment (cf. canon 1036, § 2) or on account of vitiated consent (cf. canon 1081, § 1), but which simultaneously retains the appearance of a marriage in that it was contracted according to the proper form.

Generally, however, no distinction of this kind is made in common usage, and the law itself does not strictly hold to this distinction. The Code uses the terms *null, void, invalid* (*nullum, irritum, invalidum*) to designate a marriage that lacks validity. Cf. canons 1070, § 1; 1076, § 1; 1072; De Smet, n. 158; Payen, *De Matrimonio in Missionibus ac Potissimum in Sinis Tractatus Practicus et Casus* (2. ed., 3 vols., Zi-ka-wei: In Typographia T'ou-ae-we, 1935-1936), I, n. 139 (hereafter cited *De Matrimonio*).

Civil law terminology, in most States, is somewhat different. The term *invalid* is given a twofold meaning. It may signify either void or voidable. A marriage that is void is juridically null or non-existent. Thus, for example, a marriage of persons not yet seven years of age is void in Common law.

Not every invalid marriage, however, gives rise to the impediment of public propriety. For example, the Pontificial Commission for the Interpretation of the Code has given a reply to the effect that a so-called civil marriage contracted by persons who are bound to observe the canonical form of marriage does not beget public propriety.[3] Authors seem to be agreed that in order to give rise to the impediment of public propriety an invalid marriage must have the semblance or figure of a marriage.[4] It will be necessary, therefore, to determine what is meant by the semblance of marriage, and to consider the various kinds of invalid marriages in order to ascertain whether or not they reflect an appearance of marriage.

The semblance of marriage may be said to consist in the expression of marital consent according to the necessary external substantial form.[5] Accordingly, if the form required for the validity of a particular marriage is not externally observed, the union lacks the semblance or the appearance of marriage. In fact it may be said that the form and the appearance of a marriage are one and

---

The term voidable is used in different senses, but in general it is true to say that a voidable marriage, while according to the civil law it is rescissible, can be validated by the voluntary cohabitation of the parties when the impediment or other cause of nullity has ceased. Cf. Alford, *Ius Matrimoniale Comparatum* (Romae: Anonima Libraria Cattolica Italiana; New York: P. J. Kenedy & Sons, 1938), pp. 48-49, n. 74; Goldsmith, *The Competence of Church and State over Marriage-Disputed Points,* The Catholic University of America Canon Law Studies, n. 197 (Washington, D. C.: The Catholic University of America Press, 1944), p. 71; Bishop, *New Commentaries on Marriage, Divorce and Separation* (6. ed., Vol. I, Chicago, 1891), I, n. 571.

[3] Cf. *infra,* p. 91.

[4] Coronata, *Tractatus Canonicus de Sacramentis* (3 vols., Romae: Marietti, 1943-1946), III, n. 412 (hereafter cited *De Sacramentis*); Gasparri, *Tractatus Canonicus de Matrimonio* (ed. nova ad mentem Codicis I. C., 2 vols., Typis Polyglottis Vaticanis, 1932), I, n. 731 (hereafter cited *Tractatus de Matrimonio*); Bouscaren-Ellis, *Canon Law, A Text and Commentary* (Milwaukee: Bruce, 1946), p. 491 (hereafter cited Bouscaren-Ellis); Doheny, *Canonical Procedure in Matrimonial Cases* (2 vols., Milwaukee: Bruce Publishing Co., 1938-1944. Vol. I, *Formal Procedure,* 1938; Vol. II, *Informal Procedure,* 1944), I, 473 (hereafter cited *Formal Procedure* and *Informal Procedure* respectively); Payen, *De Matrimonio,* I, n. 1538; Capello, *De Matrimonio,* n. 543.

[5] Cf. Gasparri, *Tractatus de Matrimonio,* I, n. 47; *De Smet,* n. 158; Payen, *De Matrimonio,* I, n. 137; Vlaming, I, n. 56; Feije, n. 406.

the same if under the expression *form of marriage* there is included the seemingly proper, but yet invalid, form which is attended with some essential defect.

Thus the form of marriage for all persons baptized in the Catholic Church, for those who have been converted to the Church from heresy or schism, and for Catholics of the Oriental rite if they contract marriage with Latins,[6] as given in canon 1094, postulates the presence of the pastor of the parish where the marriage takes place, or of the ordinary of the place, or of a priest delegated by either of these, and in addition the presence of at least two witnesses. A marriage contracted in accordance with this prescribed form, even though it is invalid by reason of a lack of proper delegation in the assisting priest, for example, has yet the appearance of marriage. Even a marriage contracted when the invalidity of the form is more manifest, as long as the form had not been entirely neglected, as for instance when only one witness was present in place of two required witnesses, could be held to have the appearance of a marriage.[7] So also a marriage contracted in accordance with the exceptional form mentioned in canon 1098, namely without the presence of the pastor, the ordinary, or a priest delegate, even though it be invalidly contracted, has yet the appearance of a marriage in that it was contracted according to the form required by law under the circumstances.

In considering the question of the presence or the absence of the appearance of marriage in the marriages of persons not bound by the canonical juridical form, one must make a threefold distinction. It is necessary to consider separately the marriages of unbaptized persons among themselves, the marriages of baptized persons not bound to the observance of the canonical form of marriage among

[6] Canon 1099, § 1, 1° and 2°. It is apropos to note here that the exception to the canonical form of marriage, as granted by canon 1099, § 2, in favor of persons baptized in the Catholic Church, but born of non-Catholic parents (*ab acatholicis nati*) and reared from infancy in heresy, in schism, in infidelity, or without any religion, when they contracted marriage with non-Catholics, has been revoked through a *Motu proprio* of His Holiness Pius XII, dated August 1, 1948, which became legally effective on January 1, 1949 —*AAS*, XL (1948), 305-306.

[7] Wernz, IV, n. 29, note 11; Vlaming, *loc. cit.*; Cappello, *De Matrimonio*, n. 893; Coronata, *loc. cit.*

themselves, and the marriages of baptized persons not bound by the canoncial form when they contract marriage with unbaptized persons.

Inasmuch as the Church does not legislate for the non-baptized, infidels are not bound by the canonical form of marriage.[8] However, although the question is not entirely outside the pale of controversy, the more common opinion holds that the unbaptized are bound by the civil laws in regard to marriage, and therefore also regarding the form of marriage.[9] Hence, as indicated by an Instruction of the Sacred Congregation of the Holy Office to the Bishop of Quebec on September 16, 1824,[10] the marriage of non-baptized persons has the appearance of marriage when contracted according to the laws or customs of the place, even though the marriage may be invalid on account of a diriment impediment set up by the state.[11] Accordingly, common law marriage,[12] where it is

---

[8] Cf. canons 12 and 1099, § 2.

[9] Cf. S. C. de Prop. Fide, 5 dec. 1631—*Collectanea,* n. 71; Ottaviani, *Institutiones Iuris Publici Ecclesiastici* (2. ed., 2 vols., Civitate Vaticana: Typis Polyglottis Vaticanis, 1935-1936), II, n. 340; Cavagnis, *Institutiones Iuris Publici Ecclesiastici* (4. ed., 3 vols., Romae, 1906), III, nn. 184-191; Vromant, *Ius Missionariorum,* Tom. V, *De Matrimonio* (Louvain: Museum Lessianum, 1931), nn. 13-16; Wernz-Vidal, *Ius Matrimoniale,* n. 73.

[10] *Collectanea,* n. 784.

[11] Cf. Gasparri, *op. cit.,* n. 415; (Gasparri, *ibid.,* note 1, incorrectly assigned March 3, 1825, as the date of this Instruction); Vlaming, I, n. 364; Payen, *De Matrimonio,* I, n. 137.

[12] Common law marriage, since it owes its existence *de facto* to the sufferance of the state, may be considered a civil law marriage in this connection. A common law marriage is a marriage contracted without the formalities of the statutory solemnities prescribed for civil marriage. "All that is required for a valid common law marriage is that marriageable parties take each other as husband and wife, their intent or consent being declared by words, or even by letter. But only words in the present tense have this effect. A present intention to be husband and wife at some future time is ineffective, however expressed. The consent can only be *per verba de presenti.* The rule that consent given *per verba de futuro cum copula* constitutes marriage does not affect the principle, for it is a rule of evidence by which parties are presumed to have converted their future promises into actual marriage."—Dept. of Commerce and Labor, *Special Reports*: *Marriage and Divorce* (2 vols., Washington: U. S. Government Printing Office, 1909), I, 184; cf. Koegel, *Common Law and Its Development in the United States* (Washington: John Byrne & Co., 1922), pp. 138-140.

recognized by the state, is a valid form of marriage for the unbaptized. It thus possesses the figure and appearance of marriage.[13]

In and of themselves all baptized persons are bound by all the laws of the Church.[14] Yet, foreseeing the difficulties that might arise if it enforced obedience on all, even on heretics and schismatics, the Church has wisely limited the binding force of certain of its laws to Catholics. Thus canon 1099, § 2, declares that non-Catholics, whether baptized or not, are not bound to observe the Catholic form of marriage when they contract marriage among themselves.

According to a declaration of the Sacred Congregation of the Council on March 28, 1908,[15] in explanation of the term non-Catholic as used in the decree *Ne temere,*[16] which also stated non-Catholics were not obliged to the canonical form of marriage, there were to be included under the term non-Catholic the schismatics and the heretics of the Oriental rites. Hence on the one hand whenever baptized Protestants, or schismatics or heretics of the Oriental rites contracted marriage among themselves they were not bound to the observance of the Catholic form of marriage. On the other hand, the civil law was then, as now, incompetent to legislate for the marriage of baptized persons.[17]

Accordingly the only requirements for the celebration of marriage for such persons was the freedom of the parties to marry and the expression of true marital consent according to the requirements of the natural law. The informal marriage of such persons, in the absence of a diriment impediment, was valid.[18] Furthermore, even though the marriage had been invalid, it yet could have the appearance of marriage.[19] All this, as it was applicable then, is

---

[13] Cf. Gasparri, *op. cit.,* I, n. 47; Vermeersch-Creusen, *Epitome Iuris Canonici* (3 vols., Mechliniae-Romae: H. Dessain, Vol. I, 6. ed., 1937; Vol. II, 5. ed., 1934; Vol. III, 5. ed., 1936), II, n. 277 (hereafter cited *Epitome*).

[14] Canon 87.

[15] *Fontes,* n. 4340.

[16] S.C.C., decr. *Ne temere,* 2 aug. 1907, Art. XI, § 3—*Fontes,* n. 4340.

[17] Canon 1016.

[18] Cf. *Jus Pontificium* (Romae, 1921-1940), IX (1929), 171; Wernz-Vidal, *Ius Matrimoniale,* n. 22, note 14; Payen, *loc. cit.*

[19] S.C.C. Off., 16 sept. 1824—*Collectanea,* n. 784; Payen, *De Matrimonio,* I, n. 137.

applicable also now, for the same meaning still attaches to the term non-Catholic.

This same position is held, and it seems rightly so, by many authors[20] in regard to the marriage of baptized persons, both Catholic and non-Catholic, with unbaptized persons. According to this view, because of the indivisible nature of the marriage contract, the non-baptized party is indirectly brought under the jurisdiction of the Church by reason of the baptized party who is directly under its jurisdiction. Therefore, as in the case of two baptized persons who are exempt from the Catholic form of marriage, the informal or clandestine marriage of a baptized person exempt from the canonical form with an unbaptized person may be valid. Hence, such a marriage, since it may be a valid marriage, may also have the figure and appearance of a marriage, even though it be invalid because of a diriment impediment.

Under the pre-Code law some authors[21] admitted an exception to the doctrine that the prescribed external form had to be observed in order that an invalid marriage be considered to have the appearance of marriage.

This exception concerned marriages contracted between heretics and Catholics. It was held that the invalid marriage of a Catholic with a heretic if both of them were bound to the Tridentine form of marriage had the appearance of marriage, even though the form prescribed by the Council of Trent had been entirely ignored, provided that the marriage was contracted according to the customs of the region. The reason for the exception was based on a response of the Sacred Congregation of the Holy Office to the Bishop of Quebec on September 16, 1824, in answer to certain questions.[22]

---

[20] Wernz, IV, n. 60; Wernz-Vidal, *Ius Matrimoniale,* n. 52; De Smet, n. 438 bis; Vromant, *De Matrimonio,* V, 5-9; Grandclaude, *Ius Canonicum* (3 vols., Parisiis, 1883), III, 33; Dillon, *Common Law Marriage,* The Catholic University of America Canon Law Studies, n. 153 (Washington, D. C.: The Catholic University of America Press, 1942), pp. 79-83; Grandclaude, "Competence de l'etat touchant le mariage des infideles," *Le Canoniste Contemporain* (Paris, 1878-1922; ab anno 1924-1926, *Le Canoniste*), X (1887), 241-257.

[21] Wernz, IV, n. 29, note 11; Gasparri, *De Matrimonio* (1904), n. 52.

[22] "6. In facultatibus extraordinariis, quas Summus Pontifex concedere solet missionariis vel Episcopis in longinqua agentibus, dicitur: *Dispensandi quoad matrimonia praeterita etiam in secondo solo (gradu affinitatis et con-*

The response seems to speak of the marriages of baptized persons with infidels, of Catholics with heretics and of heretics among themselves or with infidels as having the appearance of marriage if contracted according to the customs followed by infidels or heretics of the region. Although the response does not so state, it was understood by those authors to refer also to the marriages of Catholics and heretics bound by the Tridentine decree *Tametsi.*

Feije (1820-1894), on the other hand, denied that the clandestine marriages of persons bound to observe the Tridentine form of marriage had the semblance or the figure of marriage.[23] This author, in treating of the above mentioned response of the Holy Office, limited its application to the determining of conditions under which bishops and missionaries could use the faculties granted to them by the Holy See to dispense in different types of marriages.[24]

Such, in fact, was the purpose of the response. It seems clear from the document itself that the Holy Office was not giving ex-

---

sanguinitatis), *dummodo nullo modo attingat primum gradum, cum iis qui ab haeresi vel infidelitate convertantur ad fidem catholicam.* De quo quaeritur an per matrimonium praeteritum (Form. 1, n. 6) intellegenda sit coniunctio quae obtinuisset inter virum catholicum et mulierem haereticam, vel inter virum fidelem et mulierum infidelem, vel viceversa, ita ut praedicta facultate uti liceat quando alterutra tantum pars contrahens ab haeresi vel infidelitate redit ad fidem catholicam.

Ad 6. Manifestum est per matrimonia praeterita in quibus uti possunt Episcopi vel missionarii facultate sibi ab Apostolica Sede delegata dispensandi ut in dubio, intelligi non coniunctiones quascumque etiam fornicarias, sed eas tantummodo, quae, iuxta mores regionum vel infidelium vel haereticorum formam habent et figuram matrimonii, habenturque pro legitimis matrimoniis, quae tamen irrita sunt ob ecclesiasticum impedimentum secundi gradus affinitatis et consanguinitatis.

Intelliguntur itaque matrimonia hoc obstante impedimento nulliter contracta ab iis qui legibus subduntur Ecclesiae. Huiusmodi sunt: 1. fidelium cum infidelibus inita absque Apostolica dispensatione super cultus disparitate: 2. Catholicorum cum haereticis: 3. denique haereticorum pariter cum infidelibus, vel etiam inter se, quippe et ipsi ecclesiae legibus tenentur. Non autem intelligenda veniunt matrimonia inter utramque partem infidelem."—*Collectanea,* n. 784.

[23] "E contra vero extrinsica haec species deest matrimoniis clandestine etiamsi matrimoniali aliqua forma; ex. gr. juxta mores regionis celebratis in loco ubi ex hac causa notorie sunt invalida."—*De Impedimentis et Dispensationibus Matrimonialibus,* n. 768.

[24] *Op. cit.,* n. 625.

amples of marriages which had the appearance of marriage when contracted according to the customs of the place. Otherwise it would not have excluded, as it did, the marriages of unbaptized persons. Such marriages of the unbaptized, since they certainly could be valid when contracted according to the laws and customs of the region, could also have the appearance of marriage even though invalidly contracted. The response merely cited examples of marital unions with reference to which the bishops and the missionaries could grant a dispensation through their use of the faculties that had been granted to them, and so it excluded the marriages of the unbaptized, since they were not subject to ecclesiastical laws. It did not state categorically that the marriages of Catholics with heretics when contracted according to the custom of the heretics of the region had the appearance of marriage.

The opinion, as based on this response to the Bishop of Quebec, namely that the marriage of a Catholic with a heretic, when it was contracted according to the customs of the region, had the appearance of marriage even in territories where the Tridentine Decree Tametsi was in effect as law, was exposed to still more serious difficulties. In the first place, the diocese of Quebec was among those places concerning which there was grave doubt whether at any time it was brought under the decree *Tametsi,* which prescribed a form for the validity of marriage. It is doubtful whether the decree *Tametsi* was ever published in the diocese of Quebec.[25] In the event that the decree had not been published in the diocese of Quebec the clandestine marriages of Catholics with heretics in the absence of a diriment impediment would have been valid, as would also the marriages of Catholics with heretics when contracted according to the customs of the region. Since such marriages would thus have been valid, they would also necessarily have had the appearance of marriage. Hence the Holy Office could well refer to them as having the appearance of marriage.

Furthermore, even if, for the sake of the discussion, it were admitted that the decree *Tametsi* was extended to the diocese of Quebec, the marriages of heretics with Catholics when contracted

---

[25] Ojetti, *In Ius Antepianum et Pianum ex Decreto Ne temere de forma celebrationis sponsalium et matrimonii commentarii* (Romae, 1908), p. 53; Zitelli, *Apparatus Iuris Ecclesiastici* (Romae, 1888), p. 436.

according to the customs of the region would still have had the appearance of marriage at the time when the response of the Holy Office was directed to the Bishop of Quebec. The reason is that the Benedictine Declaration, which Pope Benedict XIV had published on November 4, 1741,[26] for the Federated States of Holland and Beligum, was extended to Canada in the year 1764, when that colony was taken over by the English.[27]

The Benedictine Declaration stated that the marriages of heretics among themselves, if they were bound by the decree *Tametsi* on the form of marriage, whether already contracted or yet to be contracted, were to be considered as valid, even though they were not contracted according to the form prescribed by the Decree. This same concession was granted to heretics when they contracted marriage with Catholics, even if the latter were bound by this Tridentine decree.[28]

Hence in 1824, when the response in question was issued, the marriage of a Catholic with a heretic in Canada did not for its validity depend on the observance of the Tridentine form. A Catholic and a heretic could contract a valid marriage either clandestinely or according to the customs of the region. Since in the absence of

---

[26] Fontes, n. 3527.

[27] Zitelli, *op. cit.*, p. 436; Ojetti, *op. cit.*, p. 56, note 1. Gasparri (*De Matrimonio* [1904], II, Alleg. VI) explicitly stated that the Benedictine Declaration was extended to Canada in the year 1764, but in an earlier part of his work (n. 52) he held the view, as based on the response of the Holy Office to the Bishop of Quebec, that the marriage of a Catholic with a heretic, if both of them were bound by the decree *Tametsi* on the form for the contracting of marriage, and if it was contracted according to the customs of the region, had the appearance of marriage.

It is difficult to see how these two positions can be reconciled. In the subsequent edition (1932) of his work Gasparri admitted no exception to the rule that, in order to have the appearance of marriage, a marriage must have been entered according to the prescribed external form. Likewise he did not refer, in this connection, to the response of the Holy Office on September 16, 1824, to the Bishop of Quebec. (Cf. Gasparri, *Tractatus de Matrimonio* [1932], n. 47). The decree *Tametsi,* which prescribed a determinate form for the validity of marriage, was never published in England. (Cf. Ojetti, *op. cit.*, p. 50; Zitelli, *op. cit.*, p. 431). Hence, there was no question of the extension of the Benedictine Declaration to that country.

[28] Cronin, *The New Matrimonial Legislation* (London, 1909), pp. 256-258; Wernz, IV, n. 167; Feije, n. 307; Scherer, p. 216, note 238.

any diriment impediment the marriages contracted by such persons according to the customs of the region were valid, they also had, of necessity, the appearance of marriage. Accordingly the Holy Office was referring to marriages not subject to the Tridentine form of marriage for their validity and so quite properly referred to them as having the appearance of marriage when contracted according to the customs of the region. Hence it is difficult to see how the view which regarded the invalid marriages of Catholics with heretics, when contracted according to the customs of the region in places where both parties were bound by the Tridentine form, as having the appearance of marriage could claim as its basis this response of the Holy Office.

Of the authors who wrote after the Code, Vlaming (+ 1935)[29] alone seemed to state apodictically that the response of the Holy Office to the Bishop of Quebec contained an exception to the commonly accepted doctrine, which held that a marriage had to be contracted according to the prescribed external form if it was to have the appearance of marriage, and that this exception still obtained under the Code Law. This author, however, did not put forward any reasons in substantiation of his view. Other post-Code authors who refer to the response in question hesitate to state that, if under the earlier law it did contain an exception, that exception still holds under the law of the Code.

Vidal (1868-1939)[30] gave a resume of the response, but he did not, as Wernz (1842-1914)[31] had done, deduce from it that the marriage between a Catholic and a heretic, if contracted otherwise than according to the canonical form, could still possess the appearance of marriage. Nor did Vidal state that this response retains any efficacy under the present law of the Code. De Smet (1868-1927)[32] indeed quoted the opposite doctrine but he did so without giving it his approval. Payen (1941)[33] stated that the exception, which he assumed as having effect under the earlier law, still holds under the same conditions in the present law. Yet he thereupon im-

---

[29] *Praelectiones Iuris Matrimonii,* I, n. 76.

[30] *Ius Matrimoniale,* n. 22, note 44.

[31] *Loc. cit.*

[32] *De Sponsalibus et Matrimonio,* p. 135, n. 158, note 1.

[33] *De Matrimonio,* I, n. 137.

mediately declared that the marriage between a Catholic, who as such is subject to the canonical form of marriage, and a non-Catholic, whether baptized or unbaptized, reflects the appearance of a marriage in only a wide sense.[34]

Payen further stated that the ordinary, or the pastor after consulting the ordinary, can declare such a marriage invalid, since the form that should have been observed was entirely neglected. He likewise stated, in the same paragraph, that the appearance, the figure, and the form of marriage point to the same or approximately the same notion.[35]

In the very next paragraph, however, this author stated that any union which has the appearance of a marriage can be declared invalid only by means of a judicial process, but he again makes an exception for what is termed a union which has the appearance of a marriage in only a wide sense. Apparently, then, he left room for the exception admitted by the authors already mentioned, but in doing so he insisted that a union contracted by a Catholic with a non-Catholic when the canonical form is totally neglected has the appearance of a marriage in only a wide sense, and then denied to it the canonical consequences that are attendant on an invalid marriage which has the appearance of a marriage, so that correspondingly there was no need of a judicial process for the declaration of its invalidity.[36] All of this seems tantamount to not admitting, if not actually denying, that the marriage of a Catholic with a heretic when the canonical form is entirely neglected can nevertheless have the appearance of a marriage.

Most of the authors, including Cappello, Coronata, Chelodi (+ 1922), Vermeersch (+ 1936)-Creusen, Doheny, Bouscaren-Ellis, Woywod (+ 1941), Ayrinhac (+ 1930), Prümmer (+ 1931), Noldin (+ 1922)-Schmitt (+ 1948) who have written since the law of the Code came into effect do not so much as mention any exception to the generally accepted doctrine that a union lacks the appearance of a marriage if under total neglect of the

---

[34] "Haec tamen matrimonia *latiori tantum sensu* figuram matrimonii retinent."—Payen, *loc. cit.*

[35] ". . . nam haec tria, species, figura, forma idem aut fere idem sonant." Payen, *loc. cit.*

[36] Cf. *infra*, pp. 76-77.

canonical form it has been contracted by a heretic or a non-baptized person with a Catholic who is bound to the observance of the prescribed form. Nor do any of these authors refer in this connection to the response of the Holy Office to the Bishop of Quebec on September 16, 1824.

In view of certain responses of the Pontifical Commission for the Interpretation of the Code, it seems difficult to see how it can be maintained with any degree of probability that the marital union of a person bound to the observance of the canonical form for the contracting of marriage can have the appearance of a marriage when that canonical form is entirely ignored. On October 16, 1919, the Commission declared that neither a judicial process nor the intervention of the defender of the bond is required for declaring invalid the marriage of a Catholic who in disregard of the laws of the Church married a non-Catholic in a Protestant church in a place formerly subject to the decree *Tametsi* of the Council of Trent, if at the same time the Benedictine Declaration was never extended to that territory, or of a Catholic who under similar circumstances contracted such a union after the decree *Ne temere*.[37]

Since a union which has the appearance of a marriage postulates a judicial process if it is to be declared invalid,[38] it seems clear that the Commission did not regard the marriage of a Catholic with a Protestant, when the canonical form of marriage was ignored in a place where either the decree *Tametsi* or the decree *Ne temere*

---

[37] "Utrum Ordinarius, praetermissis iuris solemnitatibus in Constitutione *Apostolica Dei miseratione* requisitis, matrimonium possit declarare nullum cum interventu tamen defensoris vinculi matrimonialis, quin opus sit secunda sententia, hisce in casibus, nempe:

. . . 2) Aut sic catholica pars, quae cum acatholica, spretis Ecclesiae legibus, in templo sectae protestanticae (in loco certe antehac obnoxio cap. *Tametsi* Conc. Tridentini, et ubi Benedictina declaratio extensa non est, vel post Decretum *Ne temere*) matrimonium contraxit, obtento civili divortio, in facie Ecclesiae novum matrimonium cum catholico consorte inire vult.

Resp.: Casus supra memoratus nullum iudicialem processum requirit aut interventum defensoris vinculi, sed resolvendus est ab Ordinario ipso, vel a parocho, consulto Ordinario, in praevia investigatione ad matrimonii celebrationem, de qua in can. 1019 et seqq."—*AAS*, XI (1919), 479; S. C. de Sacramentis, instr. *Provida Mater*, 15 aug. 1936, Art. 231—*AAS*, XXVIII (1936), 358.

[38] Cf. canon 1014; *infra*, p. 80.

were in effect, as having the appearance of a marriage. Still another reply of the same Commission on March 12, 1929, stated that the civil marriage of persons bound to the observance of the canonical form of marriage does not give rise to the impediment of public propriety.[39] Therefore the civil marriage of a Catholic with a heretic, as long as the Catholic is bound to the observance of the canonical form, even though the union was contracted according to the customs of the region, cannot be said to have the appearance of a marriage, for a union that reflects the appearance of a marriage definitely gives rise to the impediment of public propriety.[40] Ayrinhac, in reference to this reply, appositely stated that the marriage of a Catholic who does not observe the canonical form cannot be called an invalid *marriage,* since it lacks the very appearance of a marriage.[41]

Furthermore, marriages contracted according to the customs of the region, as referred to in the response of the Holy Office to the Bishop of Quebec, almost certainly included civil marriages. But it has been the consistent teaching of the Church that civil marriages of persons bound to the observance of the canonical form of marriage lack all real appearance of a marriage.[42] Therefore, in the absence of any conclusive evidence it cannot be admitted that the Church wished to make an exception to its general doctrine in the specific instance here considered.

There are two types of invalid marriage, namely putative marriage and attempted marriage which inasmuch as they may or may not possess the appearance of marriage, call for special consideration here. An invalid marriage is said to be putative if it is contracted in good faith by at least one of the parties, and it remains a putative marriage until such time that both of the parties become

---

[39] Cf. *infra,* p. 91.

[40] Cf. *supra,* p. 67.

[41] "Catholics who attempt marriage without observing the canonical form (can. 1094, 1099) do not contract validly, but the union is not properly called *matrimonium invalidum,* since it lacks the semblance of marriage."—*Marriage Legislation in the New Code of Canon Law,* revised and enlarged by P. J. Lydon (New York: Benziger Brothers, 1932), p. 10; cf. also O'Neill, "The Impediment of Public Propriety," *The Irish Ecclesiastical Record* (Dublin, 1864-), 5. series, XXXIII (1929), 424-425.

[42] Cf. *infra,* pp. 86-87.

certain of its invalidity.[43] In the pre-Code law, if an invalid marriage was to be considered as also a putative marriage, it was postulated that persons who were bound to the observance of the canonical form as prescribed by the Tridentine decree *Tametsi,* or after April 19, 1908, by the decree *Ne temere,* had contracted their union according to the prescribed form (*in facie Ecclesiae*). That is to say, before a union could exist as a putative marriage, it had at the same time to possess the appearance of a marriage.[44]

The only requirement which canon 1015, § 4 demands for a putative marriage is good faith in one of the parties. It does not require the observance of the prescribed form. Hence, under the law of the Code there is a solidly probable opinion, held by many notable authors[45] that an invalid marriage to be a putative marriage need not necessarily have the appearance of a marriage. On the other hand, a putative marriage may have and in fact generally will have the appearance of a marriage, since it will rarely happen that even one of the parties will be in good faith if the substantial form has not been observed.

In general parlance an act is said to be attempted when it is knowingly undertaken against the prescript of an invalidating or incapacitating law.[46] A marriage may be said to be attempted when it is contracted by parties if at least one of them knows that he is incapable of validly entering marriage. If one of the parties is in bad faith and the other is in good faith, then an attempted marriage may at one and the same time be both an attempted and a putative marriage.[47] An attempted marriage, like a putative marriage, may or may not possess the appearance of a marriage depending on whether or not the parties observed the prescribed form when they contracted their union.[48]

---

[43] Canon 1014, § 4.

[44] Cf. c. 2, X, *de clandestina desponsatione,* IV, 17; Esmein, II, pp. 33-37; De Becker, *De Sponsalibus et Matrimonio Praelectiones Scholastico-Dogmaticae* (2. ed., Lovanii, 1903), pp. 371-372; Freisen, p. 859; Wernz, IV, n. 29, note 11; Wernz-Vidal, *Ius Matrimoniale,* n. 610.

[45] Wernz-Vidal, *op. cit.,* n. 22, note 14; Chelodi, *Ius Matrimoniale,* n. 9; De Smet, n. 158, note 3; Payen, *De Matrimonio,* I, n. 135.

[46] Cf. canons 1069, § 1; 1072; 1073, 1075, 1°.

[47] Payen, *loc. cit.;* Cappello, *De Matrimonio,* n. 48; Wernz-Vidal, *op. cit.,* n. 22; Vermeersch-Creusen, *Epitome,* II, n. 277.

[48] Vlaming, I, n. 360; De Smet, n. 626; Wernz-Vidal, *op. cit.,* n. 376.

From what has been said so far, it is clear that a marriage may fail in an essential quality and yet have the appearance of a marriage. The contrary, however, is not true. If a union fails in possessing the appearance of a marriage it must fail in an essential quality, namely, the legitimate expression of consent. In the final analysis, the question whether a particular union possesses or lacks the appearance of a marriage depends not so much on whether the union has the essential qualities inseparable from marriage as on whether it is recognized by the legislator as furnishing at least a semblance of marriage.[49]

It cannot be maintained that no distinction is to be made between invalid marriages that possess or lack the appearance of a marriage, for the reason that any substantial distinction between them is simply inconceivable. While it is true that both types of invalid marriage are equally devoid of the true marriage bond, there is no reason why the legislator may not attach certain canonical effects to an invalid marriage which possesses at least the semblance of a marriage, while at the same time he denies any juridical effect for an invalid marriage that lacks even the semblance of a marriage. The difference between the action of persons who enter a union that is no marriage, and the action of those who enter a union that is an invalid marriage, was stated clearly by the Secretary of the Sacred Congregation of the Council on March 13, 1879. Canonically, the persons who attempt a union that is no marriage effect entirely nothing, whereas persons who enter a union that is an invalid marriage contract a marriage which indeed because of some defect is invalid, but which at least through its semblance gives rise to canonical consequences.[50]

Thus, in the case of an invalid union which has at least the appearance of a marriage, the principle "*. . . in dubio standum est pro valore matrimonii . . . ,*" as stated in canon 1014, is fully applicable.

---

[49] Cf. Feije, n. 768; Gasparri, *Tractatus de Matrimonio,* n. 47; Vermeersch-Creusen, *loc. cit.;* Coronata, *De Sacramentis,* III, n. 412.

[50] ". . . ecquis non videt diversitatem inter has locutiones: nullum contrahi matrimonium et contrahi matrimonium nullum? Prima indicat contrahentes nihil prorsus agere; altera inire quidem matrimonium quod tamen ex aliquo defectu est nullum."—*ASS* (1879), 172-173; cf. *De Angelis,* Lib. IV, tit. I, n. 13.

Wherefore, unlike an invalid marriage which has the appearance of a marriage and as a result can be declared invalid only by means of a judicial process,[51] there is not required any judicial process whatsoever, nor even the intervention of the defender of the bond, for declaring the invalidity of an invalid marriage which lacks even the semblance of a marriage.[52]

The distinction is important also because of its bearing on the impediment of public propriety. Every invalid union which has the appearance of a marriage and under certain conditions, even the union invalidly contracted by persons who at the time were unbaptized,[53] gives rise to the impediment of public propriety, while on the other hand, an invalid union which lacks even the semblance of marriage does not beget the impediment of public propriety.[54] It must be further borne in mind that if a null and void union fails to give rise to the impediment of public propriety on the score of lacking even the semblance of a marriage, as, for example, the civil union contracted by persons who are bound to the observance of the canonical form of marriage,[55] it may nevertheless give rise to the impediment of public propriety on the score of existing as a public or notorious concubinage. Thus Pope Benedict XIV referred to the civil marriage of persons bound by the law regarding the canonical form of marriage as iniquitous concubinage.[56] Hence the coming into being of a pseudo-marital union and the subsequent cohabitation of the parties must also be taken into account. This distinction is somewhat analogous to the distinction between the *matrimonium in fieri* and the *matrimonium in facto esse.*

---

[51] Cf. canons 1576, § 1, 1°, and 1990; S. C. de Sacramentis, instr. *Provida Mater,* 15 aug. 1936, Art. 13—*AAS,* XXVIII (1936), 315.

[52] *AAS,* XI (1919), 479; Bouscaren, *The Canon Law Digest* (2 vols., Milwaukee: Bruce, 1934, 1943), I, 810-811; Gasparri, *loc. cit.;* Vermeersch-Creusen, *loc. cit.*

[53] Cf. *infra,* p. 133.

[54] Doheny, *Informal Procedure,* p. 581; Payen, *op. cit.,* I, n. 1538; Woywod, *A Practical Commentary on the Code of Canon Law* (2 vols., tenth printing as edited by C. Smith, New York: J. Wagner, Inc., 1946), I, 1073 (hereafter cited *A Practical Commentary*); Chelodi, *Ius Matrimoniale,* n. 104.

[55] Cf. *infra,* pp. 91 and 115.

[56] Ep. *Redditae Nobis,* 5 dec. 1774—*Fontes,* n. 350.

The relationship which a so-called civil marriage on the part of persons who are bound by the law regarding the canonical form of marriage bears to the impediment of public propriety calls for a special discussion. This discussion appears in the following article.

ARTICLE 2. PUBLIC PROPRIETY IN ITS RELATION TO A SO-CALLED CIVIL MARRIAGE

So-called civil marriage, inasmuch as it is made obligatory in many civil jurisdictions on the baptized as well as on the unbaptized, must be considered from the point of view of its relation to the impediment of public propriety. In general a civil marriage may be said to be a matrimonial union which is entered according to the requirements of the civil law by persons who are considered by the same civil law to be capable of entering such a union. The civil authority recognizes the union as a marriage, and accords to it the civil effects of marriage.[57]

In certain countries, as for example in France, Germany, and Belgium, civil marriage is obligatory in the sense that, unless the parties present themselves before a representative of the civil power for the purpose of entering marriage, their marriage is considered to be non-existent and to lack all civil effects, including the right to the protection of the civil law. In other countries, such as the United States and England, civil marriage is optional. Given to the parties is the option of marrying either before a minister of religion or before a functionary authorized by the state, provided that these parties have obtained from the civil authority a license to marry.[58] In still other countries, as for example in Spain and

---

[57] Gasparri, *Tractatus de Matrimonio,* II, n. 1288; De Smet, n. 449; Wernz-Vidal, *Ius Matrimoniale,* n. 583; Coronata, *De Sacramentis,* III, n. 701.

[58] All States and extra-territorial possessions of the United States require that all persons, without exception, obtain a license from the civil authority before they contract marriage. Similarly, all States as well as all extra-territorial possessions have decreed penalties against any person, whether he be a civil functionary or a minister of religion, who officiates at the marriage of parties who have not previously obtained a license from the civil authority; cf. Alford, *Ius Matrimoniale Comparatum, passim.*

Moreover, certain jurisdictions (Hawaii, District of Columbia, Arkansas, Delaware, Kentucky, Maine, Massachusetts, Minnesota, Nevada, New Hampshire, Ohio, Oklahoma, Oregon, Rhode Island, Virginia, Wisconsin, and the

Portugal, a subsidiary civil marriage is recognized. It is a civil ceremony made obligatory by the State on those who cannot or who will not contract marriage before the Church, as for instance on people who do not recognize the jurisdiction of the Church.[59]

In the treatment of so-called civil marriage it must be taken into account that persons not bound by the law regarding the canonical form of marriage stand in a different relationship to civil marriage than do persons who are bound by this law. Again, a further distinction must be made between the non-baptized and the baptized persons who are exempted by the Church from subjection to the law regarding the canonical form of marriage.

According to the more common and, so it seems, also the better opinion, non-baptized persons are bound by the civil laws regulating marriage.[60] Hence, if the civil laws prescribe a determinate form for the validity of marriage, non-baptized persons must adhere to the prescribed form in order to contract marriage validly. If the non-baptized adhere to the civil form that is prescribed, their union will have the appearance of a marriage even though it is invalid because of some diriment impediment set up by the civil law. Such an invalid marriage of the unbaptized may be considered as giving rise to the impediment of public propriety if later one of these unbaptized parties proposes within the forbidden degrees to contract a marriage with the baptized relative of the other party.[61] If, on the other hand, non-baptized persons attempt, in opposition to the prescribed civil form to contract a marriage, their union cannot be considered to have the appearance of a marriage, and as a union that is null and void it cannot in any way be considered as giving rise to the impediment of public propriety. Yet, if this union connotes the existence of a concubinage, it may be considered as giving rise to the impediment of public propriety be-

---

cities of New York and Philadelphia) under the authority of the United States demand that a minister of religion be authorized by the civil authority before he can assist at a marriage; cf. Alford, *op. cit.*, p. 247, n. 346; Bouscaren-Ellis, p. 463, note 12.

[59] Gasparri, *loc. cit.;* Prümmer, *Manuale Theologiae Moralis* (8. ed. recognita a E. M. Münch, 3 vols., Friburgi Brisgoviae: Herder, 1935-1936), III, n. 885; Chelodi, *Ius Matrimoniale,* n. 147.

[60] Cf. *supra,* p. 68.

[61] Cf. *infra,* p. 132.

tween either one of these parties and the baptized relatives of the other party, if the relationship exists in the first or the second degree of the direct line.[62]

Baptized non-Catholics are exempted by canon 1099, § 2, from the law regarding the canonical form for the contracting of marriage. Yet, they are not in consequence of this bound to observe the form of marriage as prescribed by the civil law, for the civil authority is incompetent to legislate for the marriage of baptized persons.[63] Accordingly such persons are not bound to any particular form for the contracting of marriage when they marry among themselves. They may accommodate themselves to the form of marriage prescribed by the state.[64] They may, however, exchange a true and valid marriage consent privately and informally, provided that no diriment impediment stands between them. Baptized heretics, then, may contract a valid marriage civilly, and if they do so their marriage gives rise not to the impediment of public propriety, but to the diriment impediment of affinity.[65]

If the civil marriage of heretics is invalid, in consequence of the presence of some diriment impediment, it gives rise to the impediment of public propriety, provided that it has the appearance of a marriage. Moreover, the observance of the form of marriage as prescribed by the civil law establishes the legal presumption that their invalid marriage nevertheless still suffices to furnish the appearance of marriage.[66] However, since heretics and schismatics may contract marriage among themselves informally, a union informally but also invalidly contracted by them may present the appearance of a marriage, and thus may give rise to the impediment of public propriety.[67]

It is often difficult, however, to distinguish such an informal invalid marriage from a mere meretricious union. One must ex-

[62] Cf. *loc. cit.*

[63] Canon 1016.

[64] Noldin-Schmitt, *Summa Theologiae Moralis,* III, n. 675.

[65] Canons 87, 97 and 1077.

[66] Cf. S.C.C. Off., 16 sept. 1824—*Collectanea,* n. 784; Wernz-Vidal, *Ius Matrimoniale,* n. 22, note 14; Doheny, *Formal Procedure,* p. 434; Prümmer, *op. cit.,* III, n. 888.

[67] De Smet, n. 158.

amine each case on its merits if one is to determine whether or not the union reflects the appearance of a marriage.[68] So the answer to the question whether the invalid civil union of baptized heretics, of itself and apart from cohabitation, gives rise to the impediment of public propriety depends on whether such an invalid union has at least the semblance of a marriage. If, in its appearance it can be regarded as a marriage, then the impediment of public propriety arises. If not, on that score, the impediment does not arise in the case.

What has been said in the preceding paragraphs concerning the relationship of the civil marriages on the part of heretics and schismatics among themselves to the impediment of public propriety applies equally to the marriages of heretics or schismatics with unbaptized persons. According to the more common view,[69] the marriages of heretics with non-baptized persons are governed by the same authority as the marriages of heretics among themselves.

It remains to discuss in some detail the so-called civil marriage of persons, if one or both of them are bound to the adherence of the canonical form of marriage,[70] in its relationship to the impediment of public propriety. Even though such persons may wish to express a true matrimonial consent according to the form prescribed by the civil law, their consent is rendered ineffectual by the contrary invalidating prescript of the positive law of the Church.[71] The question then that calls for an answer is: does such an invalid civil marriage, independently of cohabitation, give rise to the impediment of public propriety? This is precisely the question which was asked of the Pontifical Commission for the Interpretation of the Code, and to which the Commission replied on March 12, 1929. A similar question had been submitted to the Sacred Congregation of the Council, and its reply in the negative, given by that Sacred Congregation on March 13, 1879, was approved and ordered to be made a decree by Pope Leo XIII on

---

[68] Prümmer, *loc. cit.;* Doheny, *loc. cit.;* cf. also Wernz-Vidal, *Ius Matrimoniale,* n. 590; Chelodi, *Ius Matrimoniale,* n. 147.

[69] Cf. *supra,* p. 70.

[70] Cf. canon 1099, § 1.

[71] Cf. canons 1094-1103.

March 17 of that year.[72] Although the question was thus authentically decided under the earlier law, it again became the subject of controversy under the law of the Code.

Some authors held that this decree of Leo XIII was abrogated by the law of the present Code, and that accordingly the impediment of public propriety arises from civil marriage in the law of the Code.[73] The radical change inaugurated by the present law concerning the impediment of public propriety, including as it did the introduction of an entirely new source of the impediment, namely public or notorious concubinage, was alleged in favor of this view. In addition, the arguments that had been employed in support of this same position under the former legislation were accommodated to the provisions of the law of the Code, and thus were again made to apply.[74]

It was held that the Code itself, by referring to civil unions as marriages, implied that a civil union had the appearance of a marriage, and accordingly could be considered as an invalid marriage that gave rise to the impediment of public propriety. For example, canon 2386, § 1, states that clerics in major orders, if they presume to contract marriage even civilly, incur *ipso facto* an excommunication simply reserved to the Holy See.[75]

The Code, in decreeing that certain juridical, and especially penal, effects attach to certain specified acts, treats of civil marriages

---

[72] "An actus qui vulgo audit matrimonium civile, pariat impedimentum iustitiae publicae honestatis?"

Resp. "Negative: et consulendum SSmo, ut id declarare ac statuere dignetur."—*ASS,* XII (1879), 176.

[73] Sebastiani, *Summarium Theologiae Moralis* (ed. octovo minor, Taurini: Marietti, 1925), n. 557; Cerato, *Matrimonium a Codice I. C. integre desumptum* (4. ed., Patavii, 1927), n. 73; Cance, *Le Code de Droit Canonique* (6. ed., 3 vols., Paris: J. Cabalda et Fils, 1930), II, n. 307; Genicot-Salsmans, *Institutiones Theologiae Moralis* (10. ed., 2 vols., Bruzellis, 1922), II, n. 506; Prümmer, *op. cit.,* III, n. 845; O'Neill, "The Impediment of Public Propriety," *The Irish Ecclesiastical Record* (5. series, XXXIII (1929), 524-424.

[74] Cf. Maroto, "De Impedimento publicae honestatis: animadversiones," *Apollinaris* (Romae, 1928-), II (1929), 245-251.

[75] "Clerici . . . matrimonium etiam civiliter tantum contrahere praesumentes, incurrunt in excommunicationem latae sententiae Sedi Apostolicae simpliciter reservatam."

as on a par with other invalid marriages with reference to the incurring of these effects. Canon 188, 5° decrees that an office becomes *ipso facto* vacant through a tacit renunciation of it if a cleric has contracted marriage, even a civil marriage, as it is called.[76] And canon 2356 states that bigamists, that is, those who despite an existing matrimonial bond have attempted another marriage, although only a civil marriage, as it is called, *ipso facto* fall a prey to legal infamy through their attempted second marriage.[77]

Moreover, canon 1139, § 1, declares that any marriage whatsoever, if entered with the naturally sufficient consent of the two parties, can be rectified in its essentially basic status.[78] Marriages contracted civilly are frequently thus rectified. Accordingly there must be inherent in a civil marriage the possibility of a true matrimonial consent, and, so it seems, a civil marriage is comprised in the expression *"quodlibet matrimonium"* as occurring in canon 1139, § 1. Therefore a civil marriage should be considered as furnishing the semblance of marriage and as giving rise to the impediment of public propriety.[79]

The majority of the authors,[80] however, held that the decree of Pope Leo XIII still retained its efficacy, and that under the law of the Code, as under the former legislation, the impediment of public propriety does not arise from a merely civil marriage. The arguments which had been used in favor of this doctrine in the pre-Code law retained their validity under the law of the Code, for although the law on the impediment of public propriety had been changed by the Code, the attitude of the Church towards the so-called civil marriage did not change.

The Church never treated a so-called civil marriage as a union that had the appearance of a marriage. In its official documents the

---

[76] ". . . matrimonium, etiam civile tantum, ut aiunt, contraxerit."

[77] "Bigami, idest qui, obstante coniugali vinculo, aliud matrimonium, etsi tantum civile, ut aiunt, attentaverint, sunt ipso facto infames." Cf. also canons 646, § 1, 3°; 985, 3°; 1075, 1°.

[78] "Quodlibet matrimonium initum cum utriusque partis consensu naturaliter sufficiente . . . potest in radice sanari."

[79] *Apollinaris, loc. cit.*

[80] Gasparri, *Tractatus de Matrimonio,* I, n. 735; Wernz-Vidal, *Ius Matrimoniale,* n. 377; Coronata, *De Sacramentis,* III, n. 412; Cappello, *De Matrimonio,* n. 544; Chelodi, *Ius Matrimoniale,* n. 104.

Church repeatedly declared that the so-called civil marriage was nothing more than a mere civil act devoid of any canonical effect. Pope Benedict XIV, when writing to the Carmelite missionaries in Belgium on September 17, 1746, declared that a union contracted before a civil magistrate or a heretical minister could be regarded neither as a sacrament, nor as a contract, nor as in any way valid. Catholics were warned that when they contracted such a civil marriage they performed merely a civil act by which they showed their submission to the laws and institutions of the state.[81]

Similarly, Pope Pius VI (1775-1799), in the letter *Perlatae sunt* to the Bishop of Luçon on May 28, 1793, stated that Catholics in appearing before a civil functionary did not contract marriage, but only performed a mere civil act.[82] In like manner Pope Pius IX (1846-1878) in an allocution of September 27, 1852, condemned as iniquitous concubinage, any marital union valid only in the civil forum.[83]

Moreover, it cannot be said that the Code in its use of the expression *civil marriage* implies that such a union has the appearance of marriage or is in any way regarded as a marriage. On the contrary, when the Code uses the expression *civil marriage* it regularly qualifies these words with the addition of the phrase *"ut aiunt,"* "as it is called." In this way it is indicated that for baptized persons the expression *civil marriage* is really a misnomer.[84] Even when the qualifying phrase *"ut aiunt"* is not employed

---

[81] Litt. Ap. *Exposuistis Nobis*: ". . . neque in ratione sacramenti, neque in ratione contractus sustineri aut ullo pacto validum reputari posse. . . . Sciant itaque catholici vestrae curae concrediti, cum civili magistratui, aut haeretico ministello matrimonii celebrandi causa se sistunt, actum mere civilem se exercere, quo suum erga leges et instituta Principum obsequium ostendunt; caeterum tunc quidem nullum a se contrahi matrimonium."—*Collectanea*, n. 359.

[82] ". . . nullum ab ipsis contrahi matrimonium, sed actum mere civilem exerceri. . . ."—*ASS*, XII (1879), 172.

[83] *Acerbissimum*, n. 3—*ASS*, XII (1879), 157; *Fontes*, n. 515.

[84] Can. 188, 5°: "matrimonium, etiam civile tantum, ut aiunt"; Can. 646, § 1, 3°: "matrimonium aut etiam vinculum, ut aiunt, civile"; can. 985, 3°: "qui matrimonium attentare aut civilem tantum actum ponere ausi sunt"; can. 1063, § 3: "ad actum civilem dumtaxat explendam"; can. 1075, 1°: "vel ipsum matrimonium, etiam per civilem tantum actum, attentarunt"; can. 2356: "aliud matrimonium, etsi tantum civile, ut aiunt, attentaverint"; can.

in the Code,[85] the distinction between a merely civil marriage and an invalid or attempted marriage is indicated with the use of the word *civil* itself. If the so-called civil marriage did not differ from an invalid marriage, there would not have been any necessity to set it apart in a category by itself, as is actually done each time it receives mention in the Code.[86]

Furthermore, as was pointed out by the Secretary of the Sacred Congregation of the Council, in the light of the basic principles of jurisprudence it can readily be seen that a merely civil marriage cannot beget the impediment of public propriety. The Church has constantly taught that the so-called civil marriage is merely a civil act. As such it is incapable of producing any ecclesiastical effect, including the effect of begetting the impediment of public propriety, unless the Church recognizes it as producing that effect.[87] When the Church attaches other effects, especially penal effects, to a civil marriage,[88] these effects depend solely on the will of the legislator, and do not indicate that of itself the civil act has any juridical significance, but indicate that it is a delict to be punished with ecclesiastical penalties.

This argument, based on the total incompetency of the civil ruler in the ecclesiastical forum, is confirmed by the response of the Pontifical Commission for the Interpretation of the Code on October 16, 1919, regarding canon 1990. The response stated that no juridical process, not even the intervention of the defender of the bond, was necessary to declare invalid the civil marriage of two Catholics subject to the decree *Ne temere,* or of apostates from the Catholic faith who in apostasy contracted civil marriage, but

---

2388, § 1: "matrimonium etiam civiliter tantum contrahere praesumentes." Cf. "Le ulteriori risposte della Commissione interprete del Codice su l'impedimento di publica onesta," *Studi, Il Monitore Ecclesiastico* (Maratea, 1876-1881; Conversano, 1882-1898; Roma, 1899-), XLI (1929), 181-182.

[85] Cf. cans. 985, 3°; 1063, § 3; 1075, 1°; 2388, § 1.

[86] O'Neill, "The Impediment of public propriety," *The Irish Ecclesiastical Record,* 5. series, XXXIII (1929), 525.

[87] ". . . Ex his tamen nihil inferri potest favore figurae matrimonialis in actu civili: nisi accederet enim recognitio ac dispensatio Ecclesiae, consensus maneret actus mere civilis ad effectum ecclesiasticum gignendum impar."—*ASS,* XII (1879), 137.

[88] Cf. canons 2356; 2388, § 1.

later, upon having obtained a divorce and having done penance, wished to marry in the Church.[89] This response can only be interpreted to mean that the so-called civil marriage has no juridical effect whatever in the Church.[90]

It cannot be argued that the Church's granting of a radical sanation for a so-called civil marriage militates against the doctrine that a civil union cannot in any way be considered even as an invalid marriage, such as would give rise to the impediment of public propriety. It is true that Pope Benedict XIV, in his Epistle *Redditae Nobis* of December 5, 1744, declared that a radical sanation was granted only for a putative marriage,[91] and that at that time a marriage was considered putative only if it had the appearance of a marriage.[92] Later, however, there seemed to be a relaxation on this point, for there is evidence which points to the fact that the Holy See granted a general sanation for civil marriages that had been contracted in France during the Revolution.[93]

[89] "Utrum Ordinarius, praetermissis iuris solemnitatibus in Constitutione Apostolica *Dei miseratione* requisitis, matrimonium possit declarare nullum cum inventu tamen defensoris vinculi matrimonialis, quin opus sit secunda sententia hisce in casibus, nempe: 1) si duo catholici, in loco certe antehac obnoxio cap. *Tametsi* Conc. Tridentini, vel post Decretum *Ne temere,* matrimonium civile tantum inierunt omisso ritu ecclesiastico, et, obtento civili divortio, novem in Ecclesia inire student matrimonium vel novum matrimonium, civiliter initum, in foro Ecclesiae invalidare. . . 3) Aut apostatae a fide catholica, qui in apostasis civiliter . . . se iunxerunt, obtento civili divortio, poenitentes ad Ecclesiam redire et cum parte catholica alteras nuptias in Ecclesia celebrare desiderant?

Resp: Casus supra memorati nullum iudicialem processum requirunt aut interventum defensoris vinculi, sed resolvendi sunt ab Ordinario ipso, vel a parocho, consulto Ordinario, in praevia investigatione ad matrimonii celebrationem, de qua in can. 1019 et seqq."—*AAS,* XI (1919), 479.

[90] Cf. Ayrinhac, *Marriage Legislation,* p. 10.

[91] 40: "Porro legitimatur proles incestuosa, ope dispensationis, quae dicitur *in radice matrimonii.* Ut autem obtineatur huiusmodi dispensatio . . . requiritur quod proles nata sit ex copula non manifeste fornicaria, sed putative matrimoniale. . . ."—*Fontes,* n. 350.

[92] Cf. *supra,* p. 78; Benedictus XIV, *De Synodo Dioecesana,* II, Lib. XIII, c. XXIV, n. 7; Sanchez, Lib. VIII, disp. VII, n. 4; Harrigan, *The Radical Sanation of Invalid Marriages,* The Catholic University of America Canon Law Studies, n. 116 (Washington, D. C.: The Catholic University of America, 1938), p. 40.

[93] Cf. Harrigan, *loc. cit.*

At any rate, exceptions were made so that, even long before the law of the present Code came into effect, all that was demanded for the grant of a radical sanation of marriage was the presence of a marital consent which of its nature sufficed for a matrimonial contract.[94] That is to say that the figure or the semblance of marriage was not a necessary pre-requisite for the granting of a radical sanation as it formerly had been.[95]

As the Secretary of the Sacred Congregation of the Council pointed out when he spoke of the so-called civil marriage in the Instruction already referred to above,[96] the natural element necessary for marriage, namely the mutual and deliberate consent of the will, could be present in particular cases even though there was lacking even the semblance of a marriage, and hence a rectification of the union in its basic status could be granted.[97]

The actual semblance of a marriage or its seeming validity in a pseudo-marital union is not made a necessary condition for the granting of a radical sanation of the marriage according to the law of the Code. The Code excludes from this prospective benefit only those marriages which are invalid by reason of an impediment of the divine or the natural law.[98] The effective granting of a radical sanation necessarily presupposes only that the parties have intended and expressed a true marriage consent, which still con-

---

[94] S.C.S. Off., 11 nov. 1868—*Fontes,* n. 1004; 22 aug. 1906—*Fontes,* n. 1278; 12 apr. 1899—*Fontes,* n. 1219; Aichner, *Compendium Iuris Ecclesiastici* (11. ed., Brixinae, 1911), p. 661; Ojetti, *Synopsis, s.v. Sanatio in Radice.*

[95] Cf. Feije, n. 768; Wernz, IV, n. 657.

[96] Cf. *supra,* p. 79.

[97] "Matrimonium civile patet extrinsecam formam *iusti matrimonii* nullatenus habere et copulam esse manifeste fornicariam, cum ab Ecclesia definitum fuerit exitialis concubinatus. In casibus tamen particularibus fieri posse ut contrahentes elementum naturale, mutuum nempe deliberatumque consensum ponant; quod elementum nullius est valoris ob legis Tridentinae obicem, et quia sub civili forma ab Ecclesia nullatenus recognoscitur. Ast, si ob graves causas, constito de perseverantia consensus, Ecclesia dispenset a lege Tridentini, tunc elementum naturale suas exerit vires, et ubi effectus huius dispensationis retrotrahitur ad initium habetur sanatio in radice."—*ASS,* XII (1879), 173; cf. Feije, n. 403; De Angelis, Lib. IV, tit. I, n. 131.

[98] "Matrimonium vero contractum cum impedimento iuris naturalis vel divini, etiamsi postea impedimentum cessaverit. Ecclesia non sanat in radice, ne a momento quidem cessationis impedimenti."—canon 1139, § 2.

tinues and with the removal of the impediment proves sufficient, in accord with the demand of the natural law, for the sealing of the contract of marriage.[99]

No contradiction is involved in the statement that a civil union lacks the appearance of a marriage the while it is also maintained that in a civilly contracted union the parties who are bound to the observance of the canonical form for the valid contracting of a marriage can nevertheless give expression to a naturally adequate consent for marriage. It is quite possible for such persons, within the form that is prescribed by the civil law, to exchange a true marriage consent, whether they proceed in good faith as the result of their ignorance of the Church's law, or whether they act in bad faith in their attempt to elude the law of the Church. The Code appositely states that the internal consent of the will is presumed to correspond to the words or the signs employed by the parties when they undertake to seal the contract of marriage.[100] Consequently one cannot lightly conclude that as a rule a true marital consent is lacking when parties who are bound to observe a special juridical form for expressing a *valid* matrimonial consent contract a purely civil union. Each case must be judged on its own merits if a definite answer is to be reached in this matter.

The doctrine that a so-called civil marriage of itself and apart from cohabitation does not beget the impediment of public propriety under the law of the Code was finally confirmed by the response of the Pontifical Commission for the Interpretation of the Code on March 12, 1929.[101]

ARTICLE 3. PUBLIC PROPRIETY IN ITS RELATION TO A MARRIAGE INVALID BECAUSE OF LACK OF CONSENT

Although canon 1078 makes the apodictic statement that the impediment of public propriety arises from an invalid marriage—

---

[99] Gasparri, *Tractatus de Matrimonio,* n. 1225; Cappello, *De Matrimonio,* n. 853; Payen, *De Matrimonio,* III, n. 2614.

[100] Canon 1086, § 1.

[101] "An vi can. 1078 ex solo actu, ut ainut, civili inter eos de quibus in can. 1099, § 1, independenter a cohabitatione, oriatur impedimentum publicae honestatis?"

Resp. "Negative."—*AAS,* XXI (1929), 171.

"oritur ex matrimonio invalido"—some authors[102] maintain that the impediment does not arise when the invalidity of the marriage is due to lack of consent. Other authors, while acknowledging it to be the better opinion that the impediment does arise in the case, nevertheless hold that a doubt of law is involved, and hence by reason of canon 15 the impediment does not arise.[103]

The authors who maintain that public propriety does not arise from a marriage invalid because of lack of consent argue that, since the impediment of public propriety did not originate in marriage invalid because of lack of consent under the earlier law,[104] the same condition should obtain under the present law. To justify their appeal to the earlier law and the application of the latter to the interpretation of canon 1078, these authors claim that public propriety in the Code agrees in part with the pre-Code law on public propriety. The point of agreement consists in this that in the Code, as in the pre-Code law, an invalid non-consummated marriage gives rise to the impediment.

Because of this similarity these authors say that canon 1078 must be interpreted according to the norm of canon 6, 3°. This section of canon 6 prescribes that canons of the Code which agree in part with the earlier law must be interpreted in accord with the earlier law within the limits of existing harmony. There is the greater reason to invoke this interpretation here, so they allege, since the natural foundation of the impediment consists in union of wills, and if there is no consent then there is no union of wills, and hence no foundation for the impediment. Moreover, this interpretation, which limits the scope of the impediment, is more in accord with the mind of the legislator, for the history of the impediment clearly demonstrates that the tendency in canonical legislation has been towards the restricting of the scope of this impediment.[105]

---

[102] Pighi, *De Sacramento Matrimonii* (2. ed., Veronae, 1921), n. 79;—Aertnys-Damen, *Theologia Moralis* (14. ed., 2 vols., Taurini-Romae: Marietti, 1939), II, n. 767.

[103] Wernz-Vidal, *Ius Matrimoniale,* n. 376; Cerato, *Matrimonium a Codice integre desumptum,* n. 73; Coronata, *De Sacramentis,* III, n. 412.

[104] Cf. *supra,* p. 58.

[105] Cf. canon 18; also *supra,* pp. 51-54.

The great majority of authors, however, relying on the clear statement of canon 1078, namely that the impediment arises from an invalid marriage—*"oritur ex matrimonio invalido"*—hold that the impediment arises from a marriage that is invalid for any cause whatsoever, even if the invalidity results from the total lack of matrimonial consent.[106] At least one author, Cappello,[107] considers the statement of the law so clear in itself that he holds this opinion to be incontestable.

Gasparri,[108] in adhering to this latter opinion, stated that it is confirmed from the preparatory acts of the Code. This author recalled that those canonists who prepared the canons, which were later to be examined and approved by the consultors, noted that public propriety under the law as it was then in effect arose from an invalid marriage provided that the invalidity did not arise from a lack of consent. Since the consultors, in the final draft of canon 1078, passed over in silence this limitation, the obvious conclusion seems to be that they wished to abolish it. The authors who hold that public propriety arises also from a marriage that is invalid because of a lack of consent maintain in effect, and it appears that they do so with excellent foundation in the law, that the prescript of canon 18 rather than the prescript of canon 6, 3° should be applied in the interpretation of canon 1078. That is to say that canon 1078 should be interpreted in accordance with the proper signification of the words considered in their text and context. The law clearly states that the impediment of public propriety arises from an invalid marriage—*"ex matrimonio invalido"*—and it does not distinguish marriages invalid through lack of consent from marriages invalid because of any other reason. *"Ubi lex non distinguit nec nos distinguere debemus."*[109]

In view of this clear statement in the law itself it seems unwarranted to invoke the prescript of canon 6, 3°, as the norm

---

[106] Vlaming, I, n. 360; De Smet, n. 627; Chelodi, *Ius Matrimoniale,* n. 104; Vermeersch-Creusen, *Epitome,* II, n. 337; Noldin-Schmitt, *Summa Theologiae Moralis,* II, n. 506; Payen, *De Matrimonio,* I, n. 1538; Knecht, *Handbuch des katholischen Eherechts* (Friburg im Breisgau: Herder, 1928), p. 523.

[107] *De Matrimonio,* n. 543.

[108] *Tractatus de Matrimonio,* I, n. 732.

[109] Payen, *De Matrimonio,* I, n. 1538.

of interpretation of canon 1078. In the first place, the whole nature of the law on the impediment of public propriety has undergone a radical change in the law of the Code.[110] Whereas before the Code the impediment was based on a non-consummated marriage and on betrothal, it is now based on an invalid marriage and on public or notorious concubinage.

That is to say, the nature of the impediment has been changed in its very basis, which formerly consisted in the mutual union of the wills of the two parties, but now has become rather closely identified with the notion of their carnal union, so that it actually evinces a greater similarity to the pre-Code impediment of affinity than to the pre-Code impediment of public propriety. This indicates a substantial change in the law. On the other hand, the only point of agreement between the two legal systems regarding the impediment of public propriety is that in the law of the Code, as in the pre-Code law, the impediment arises also from an invalid non-consummated marriage.[111] This sole point of similarity, which involves a condition that is but rarely apt to arise, seems to be less substantial than it is accidental.[112]

In the nature of things the substantial supersedes the accidental, so that the accidental similarity between the law of the Code and the pre-Code law regarding the impediment of public propriety must follow the substantial change in the law, with the result that canon 1078 should be interpreted according to the norm of canon 18, that is, according to the proper meaning of the words taken in their text and context, rather than according to the norm of canon 6, 3°.[113]

---

[110] Prümmer, *Manuale Theologiae Moralis,* III, n. 843; Cappello, *De Matrimonio,* n. 543; Cerato, *Matrimonium a Codice Iuris Canonici integre desumptum,* n. 73; Wernz-Vidal, *Ius Matrimoniale,* n. 375; Doheny, *Informal Procedure,* II, 472.

[111] Payen, *De Matrimonio,* I, n. 1537.

[112] Wernz-Vidal, *Ius Matrimoniale,* n. 379, note 33.

[113] "In a substantial change of anything the accidents vanish with the substantial form. Accidents of the new substance may be similar to those of the old substance, but their value emanates from the new and not the old, so too in law. When an enactment submits to a substantial change the accidents follow the substance. But this is not applicable *vice versa.* Accidents may change while the substance remains the same. This is the form of muta-

Furthermore, the earlier law stated explicitly that an invalid marriage gave rise to the impediment of public propriety except when the invalidity arose from a lack of consent—*"dummodo non sunt nulla ex defectu consensus."* Yet under the earlier law it was held by authors of repute[114] that, if the parties exchanged a consent that met the demand of the natural law, but the consent became nullified in its effect in consequence of the presence of an impediment of the ecclesiastical law, as for example through the impediment of abduction or error about the servile condition of the other party, then the impediment of public propriety arose. This doctrine seems to have run directly counter to the precise statement of the pre-Code law, which contained the exceptive clause, *"dummodo non sunt nulla ex defectu consensus."*[115]

In the law of the Code these words have been omitted. Hence, in entire abstraction from the consideration that the earlier law is abrogated, the position of the canonists who hold that under the law of the Code the impediment of public propriety arises from a marriage that is invalid because of a lack of consent, as well as from a marriage that is invalid for any other cause, is much stronger than was the similar position of the pre-Code authors, since the exception, *"dummodo non sunt nulla ex defectu consensus,"* was not carried over into the present law of the Code. This exceptive clause, however, must be considered as abrogated, for it has been entirely omitted from the law of the Code. The evidence rather favors the view that, far from being an oversight, the omission

---

tion found in the foregoing paragraph, i.e., canon 6, 3°. Where the substance of the law is rearranged how are the accidentals or the extension to be interpreted? The rules of canon 18 are employed."—Neuberger, *Canon 6 or the Relation of the Codex Iuris Canonici to Preceding Legislation,* The Catholic University of America Canon Law Studies, n. 44 (Washington, D. C.: The Catholic University of America, 1927), p. 80; cf. Pöschl, *Lehrbuch des katholischen Kirchenrechts* (Graz, 1921), p. 47.

[114] Cf. *supra,* p. 58; Sebastiani, *Summarium Theologicae Moralis,* n. 557; Chelodi, *Ius Matrimoniale,* n. 103; Wernz-Vidal, *Ius Matrimoniale,* n. 375, note 22; Slater, "The Impediment of Public Propriety," *The American Ecclesiastical Review* (Vols. I-XXXII, Philadelphia, 1889-1905; from 1905: *The Ecclesiastical Review,* Vols. XXXIII-CIX, Philadelphia, 1905-1943; from 1944: *The American Ecclesiastical Review,* Vol. CX, Washington, D. C., 1944-   ), LXV (1921), 492-498.

[115] C. un., *de sponsalibus et matrimoniis,* IV, 1, in VI°.

was the result of a deliberate act of the legislator.[116] In the supposition of the opposite view, namely that the provision of the earlier law has not been abrogated, it is difficult to explain why the legislator should have been willing to carry over into the law of the Code a controversy that had persisted throughout the preceding centuries.

Moreover, unlike the pre-Code legislation, the present law does not postulate marriage consent as a requisite element for giving rise to the impediment of public propriety. Together with an invalid marriage a second root of the impediment is public or notorious concubinage. Since the impediment arises from concubinage, in which marriage consent is not only not present but as a rule even positively excluded, it is difficult to see why it should not arise from an invalid marriage even though no true marriage consent is present. This argument evinces its force not only *a pari* but also *a fortiori*.[117]

The argument for the opposite view, drawn from a consideration of the foundation of the impediment, can hardly withstand close scrutiny. While it was held, and rightly so, before the present law came into effect that the basic reason on account of which the Church established the impediment of public propriety was the natural and juridic relationship between the parties brought about by a union of their wills,[118] no such claim can be made under the present legislation. No author, since the advent of the Code, has claimed that the impediment of public propriety is founded on a union or a consent of the wills of the parties. As Vidal[119] indicates,

---

[116] Vermeersch-Creusen see in the notion of discrepancy both a positive and a negative element. The discrepancy is negative when the prescript of the earlier law is not contained either explicitly or implicitly in the Code. Suppression by silence according to these authors is a negative discrepancy, and so the rule of canon 6, 6° applies. That is to say that the earlier law is abolished.—*Epitome,* I, n. 76; cf. Woywod, *A Practical Commentary,* I, n. 1073.

[117] Cappello, *De Matrimonio,* n. 543; Vermeersch-Creusen, *Epitome,* II, n. 361.

[118] Wernz, IV, n. 446; cf. *ASS,* XII (1879), 175.

[119] *Ius Matrimoniale,* n. 373; cf. also Gasparri, *Tractatus de Matrimonio,* I, n. 729; Cappello, *De Matrimonio,* n. 545; Chelodi, *Ius Matrimoniale,* n. 103; Payen, *De Matrimonio,* I, n. 1537, note 1.

the foundation of the impediment is to be found rather in an illegitimate carnal union.

It cannot be rightly alleged that the doctrine which holds that the impediment of public propriety arises from a marriage that is invalid through a lack of consent is out of harmony with the mind of the legislator, for admittedly the law has tended towards a restriction of the scope of the impediment.[120] In the first place, inasmuch as the nature of the impediment has been changed, the argument is of very doubtful validity. Even if the validity of the argument were admitted, which however is not the case, it can hardly be denied that the scope of the impediment has undergone a drastic curtailment in the law of the Code. The impediment of public propriety in the pre-Code law, inasfar as it arose from betrothals, extended to the first degree of the direct and collateral lines, and, inasfar as it derived from a non-consummated marriage it extended to the fourth degree inclusive of the direct and collateral lines.[121] Certainly, that was a much wider extension than the impediment reveals in the present legislation. In the present law the impediment of public propriety extends only to the second degree of the direct line.[122]

In view of the compelling nature of the evidence it can readily be seen why Cappello[123] regards as certain the doctrine that public propriety arises from a marriage that is invalid because of a lack of consent as well as from a marriage that is invalid for any other cause. On the other hand, the arguments which deny that the impediment of public propriety arises from a marriage that is invalid because of the absence of consent seem to lack a solid juridical basis.

However, the authority of the authors who support this view is too weighty to be overlooked. While not subscribing to the view expressed by Vidal,[124] namely that the existence of the impediment in the case is involved in doubt by the law itself, and therefore in accordance with canon 15 is without any binding force at least until such time that an authentic declaration resolves the doubt,

---

[120] Cf. *supra,* pp. 51-54.

[121] Cf. *supra,* pp. 46-47.

[122] Cf. canon 1078.

[123] *Op. cit.,* n. 343.

[124] *Op. cit.,* n. 376.

the present writer is inclined to favor the practical course of action advocated by Payen,[125] for it furnishes a safe guide. Payen counsels that in the circumstances a dispensation *ad cautelam* should be obtained.

Closely allied to this question is the further question, namely: does the impediment of public propriety arise if a marriage is invalid because of a lack of consent which is entirely occult, so that this lack of consent cannot be established by means of proof in the external forum? In adherence to the doctrine maintained above it must be held, in theory at least, that the impediment of public propriety arises. In practice, however, the solution of the question would follow along other lines. Since the marriage would be presumed in the external forum to be valid, and since in the hypothesis proof to the contrary could not be obtained, the diriment impediment of ligamen would have to be presumed to exist and even on the death of one of the parties the impediment of affinity would have to be presumed as present. Affinity in turn would bar the contracting of marriage between either of the parties and the blood relatives of the deceased party in all the degrees of the direct line and inclusive of the second degree of the collateral line.[126]

---

[125] *Op. cit.*, I, n. 1538.

[126] Cappello, *loc. cit.;* Payen, *op. cit.*, I, n. 1538, note 5.

CHAPTER VII

Public Propriety Arising From a Public or a Notorious Concubinage

ARTICLE 1. CONCUBINAGE IN ROMAN LAW

Concubinage was a recognized institution in Roman law. It was the cohabitation of a man with a woman for which the law had no approving provision, but against which the law did not level any disapproving prohibition.[1] Concubinage seemed to owe its legal recognition to the restrictive legislation of the early Empire for certain classes of persons, and particularly to the restrictions with reference to marriage as imposed on soldiers in the service and on provincial officials.[2] Concubinage connoted a permanent relationship that remained free from the stigma of *stuprum*.[3]

Although ordinarily it involved loss of caste in the woman,[4] concubinage obtained between persons of equal rank, and sometimes, though rarely, between women of higher rank and men of lower rank.[5] Between a freed woman (*libertina*) and her patron or his son concubinage was honorable, and the woman was still entitled to be called matron (*matrona*).[6]

---

[1] Cf. D. (25. 7) 3; Meyer, *Der römische Konkubinat* (Leipzig, 1895), p. 89; Cooper, *Institutes of Justinian* (3. ed., New York, 1842), p. 112, note 9.

[2] D. (24. 7) 5.

[3] *Stuprum* in Roman law may be defined as sexual relations, apart both from marriage and from recognized concubinage, with a free woman who was not engaged in prostitution or some other despised occupation, such as tavern service. *Stuprum* could be committed by a married or an unmarried man with an unmarried woman. In married women the offense was adultery. Both parties guilty of *stuprum* were liable to the penalties of the *Lex Iulia de Adulteriis* on conviction.—Cf. D. (48. 5) 35; D. (25. 7) 3; C. (9. 9) 22 and 28; Corbett, *The Roman Law of Marriage* (Oxford: The Clarendon Press, 1930), p. 141.

[4] D. (23. 2) (41. 1); D. (25. 7) (3. 1 and 5); D. (32. 49) 4.

[5] Cf. D. (25. 7) 3; Meyer, *Der römische Konkubinat,* pp. 47 and 65; Buckland, *A Text Book of Roman Law from Augustus to Justinian* (Cambridge: University Press, 1932), p. 128.

[6] D. (25. 7), 1; D. (48. 5) 14.

As in the case of marriage a freed woman could not end concubinage at will, at least not if the manumission had been voluntary.[7] In the event that the concubine was convicted of immoral relations with another man she was liable to the penalties of the *Lex Iulia de Adulteriis*.[8]

Concubinage could obtain with any woman capable of Roman marriage, and after the time of Severus (193-211) also with a woman of non-citizen status (*peregrina*). However, Constantine forbade concubinage on the part of persons of senatorial rank as well as on the part of some other high officials with freed women and certain other abject persons grouped with them, on pain of loss of citizenship.[9] A man could have as his concubine a woman convicted of adultery, though he could not marry such a woman.[10] Since only a married woman could be convicted of adultery under the *Lex Iulia de Adulteriis*,[11] it seems that a man could have as his concubine a woman who had been married.

Concubinage was subject to restrictions similar to those of marriage. Thus a man could not have a wife and a concubine or two concubines at the same time.[12] The parties in concubinage could not be so near akin that marriage was forbidden to them; for example, a man could not have his niece as his concubine.[13] Like marriage, concubinage could not exist between tutor and ward.[14] It was necessary, also, that the parties in the concubinage were of marriageable age, and that they gave their consent to the union. The consent thus given was not a marriage consent and it did not evince the *affectio maritalis;* it was simply a consent to concubinage, and accordingly manifested the *affectio concubinaria*.[15]

Thus it was not always easy to distinguish between concubinage and marriage. The absence of the *affectio maritalis,* which was es-

---

[7] *Loc. cit.;* cf. Meyer, *op. cit.,* p. 82.

[8] D. (48. 5) 14; cf. Corbett, *The Roman Law of Marriage,* p. 145.

[9] C. Th. (4. 6) 3; c. (5. 27) 1. This regulation was modified by Justinian—N. (87. 15).

[10] D. (25. 7) 2.

[11] C. (9. 9) 22 and 28; cf. Corbett, *op. cit.,* p. 141.

[12] C. (2. 20) 1; C. (5. 26) 1; cf. Nov. (18. 5); Buckland, *loc. cit.*

[13] D. (23. 2) 56; D. (7. 1) 3.

[14] D. (25. 7) 1; cf. Meyer, *Der römische Konkubinat,* p. 61.

[15] D. (24. 1) 3; D. (25. 7) 1 and 4.

sential to marriage, was the only real distinguishing feature.[16] Dowry (*dos*) was the best evidence of the distinction. There was no dowry in concubinage, and the legal presumption militated in favor of the status of marriage in the event the woman was a free woman.[17]

The Christian Empire was hostile to concubinage. Constantine (306-337), the first Christian Emperor, abolished the right to give or leave property to the concubine or her child, but this right was restored soon after.[18]

The legitimation of children could be effected in various ways. The usual way, however, obtained through the contracting of a subsequent marriage. Constantine enacted that for cases then existing, but not for future cases, marriage with the concubine would legitimate the children already born, provided that she herself had been born a free woman (*ingenua*), was not one of the abject classes, and provided also that the children consented and that the male party in the concubinage had no wife or legitimate child. Emperor Zeno (474-491) seems to have repeated this provision in the year 477.[19]

Anastasius I (491-518) in the year 517 extended this provision to future cases as well, and to all concubines capable of marriage, provided that the marriage was attested in writing and through the granting of a dowry.[20] Two years later this concession was repealed by Justinian I (527-565).[21] Through a series of enactments Justinian regulated the matter anew. He allowed legitimation by means of a subsequent marriage even when the concubine was a freed woman, provided that the marriage was attested through the *instrumentum dotis* or some other writing, that the woman was capable of marriage at the conception or birth of the child, and that the children consented. Justinian permitted legitimation under these circumstances even though there were legitimate children.[22]

---

[16] D. (2. 20).
[17] D. (25. 7) 3; Buckland, *A Text Book of Roman Law,* p. 128.
[18] D. (38. 4) 4; Inst. (3. 5) 4.
[19] C. (5. 27) 5; Buckland, *loc. cit.*
[20] C. (5. 24) 6.
[21] C. (5. 27) 7.
[22] C. (5. 27) 5, 8, 10 and 11; Inst. (3. 1) 2; Novs. (12. 4), (18. 11), (74. 4).

ARTICLE 2. CONCUBINAGE IN CANON LAW

Concubinage according to the concept of Roman law pointed to a marital union which in its legal character was of a status inferior to that of marriage. It was similar to a *morganatic marriage.*[23] The words with which Pope Leo XIII in the Encyclical Letter *Arcanum* of February 10, 1880, reproved civil legislators could have been applied with equal aptitude to the attitude of Roman law towards marriage. The Pope pointed out that the requirement of solemn rites when arbitrarily devised by the legislators results in the anomalous condition which haphazardly lets some women enjoy the decent name of wife while others become designated under the dishonorable name of concubine.[24]

Confronted with the institution of concubinage as recognized by Roman law, the Church had no alternative but to take cognizance of it. As was to be expected, the Church in its marriage regulations did not feel constrained to follow the prescripts of the Roman law, least of all in the measure in which they affected the marriage of persons of different social standing. By baptism men are made the children of God. Hence all men, despite their diverse social status, were considered equal before God and in the eyes of the Church.

Accordingly it is not altogether surprising to find that Pope St. Callistus I (217-222), formerly a slave himself, was reproached for having allowed women of high social standing to marry freedmen or slaves.[25] The reproach proves that the Pontiff regarded persons of diverse social status free to intermarry. St. Jerome (+ 420) called attention to the difference between the law of the

---

[23] ". . . *Quasi come matrimonio morganatico.*"—Ferrini, *Pandette* (3. ed., Romae, 1908), n. 711, note 1. A morganatic marriage is a validly contracted marriage in which neither the wife nor the children who are born of the marriage have a right to the social status of the husband; they have only such other rights as are specified in accordance with the contractual agreement made at the time of the marriage. The marriage itself is not affected by such a contract; only its civil effects become modified thereby. Cf. Gasparri, *Tractatus de Matrimonio,* n. 44.

[24] N. 5: "Solemnes ritus arbitrio legumlatorum inventi, efficiebant ut honestum uxoris, aut turpe concubinae nomen mulieres nanciscerentur."—*ASS,* XII (1879); Fontes, n. 580.

[25] Hippolytus, *Philosophumena,* lib. IX, c. 12—*MPG,* XVI, 3386.

Church and the Roman law when, in treating of the divorce of Fabiola (+ 399), he pointed out that the laws of the Caesars were very different from the laws of Christ, just as also the commands of Papinian (+ 212) were very different from the commands of St. Paul.[26]

The I Council of Toledo (400) emphasized the difference between the attitude of the Church and the civil law relative to the intermarriage of persons of different social standing. Canon 17 of that Council decreed that a man who did not have a wife, but who had a concubine in place of a wife, was not to be barred from the reception of Holy Communion. But he was to be content with one woman in his union, whether wife or concubine, in accordance with his own predilection in this matter.[27] The reference here was to the sacrament of Holy Communion rather than to the social and civil communication with the faithful.[28] Severinus Binius (1573-1641), in commenting on this canon of the Council, stated that by the word concubine in the text was to be understood a true wife but one who had married without the furnishing of a dowry and apart from the celebration of external solemnities. He mentioned Agar and Cetura in Genesis XXV, 6, as examples from the Old Testament of true wives who were called concubines. He further stated that Justinian in Novel 18, cap. 5, equated concubines with wives who contracted marriage without the solemnity of signing the dowry tablets.[29]

Gratian in his *Dictum* to c. 4, D. XXXIV, which reproduces canon 17 of the Council of Toledo, stated that by a concubine was to be understood a woman who, once the legal disabilities were removed, was admitted in view of her conjugal intent and will to a

---

[26] *MPL*, XXII, 698.

[27] "Caeterum, is qui non habet uxorem, et pro uxore concubinam habet, a communione non repellatur, tantum ut unius mulieris, aut uxoris aut concubinae (ut ei placuerit) sit conjunctione contentus."—Bruns, I, 206; Mansi, II, 109; cf. c. 4, D. XXXIV.

[28] Cf. Benedictus XIV, *De Synodo Dioecesana*, I, Lib. VII, c. IX, n. 8; Reiffenstuel, Lib. III, tit. II, 12; Dillon, *Common Law Marriage*, p. 18.

[29] "Per concubinam hic intelligitur vera uxor, sed sine dote et sine solemnitate in matrimonium ducta. Sicut Genes. 25 Agar et Cethura verae uxores Abrahae dicuntur concubinae."—*Notae Severini Binii ad Conc. Tol. I* c. 17; Mansi, *loc. cit.*

status equal to that of the husband. This conjugal intent and will, with which Gratian no doubt implied the *affectio maritalis* of the Roman law, gave to a woman the status of a wife although the law designated her as a concubine.[30] The *Correctores Romani* in their remarks on this canon accepted and illustrated the interpretation of Gratian.[31]

The gloss relative to this same canon stated that concubines were regarded as wives who were married in a less solemn manner.[32] Similarly a text attributed by Ivo of Chartres and by Gratian to St. Isidore (+ 636), though not to be found in the writings of Isidore, permitted a man to have a concubine.[33]

The legislation of the I Council of Toledo (400) regarding concubinage was repeated by Halitgar, Bishop of Cambrai (817-831),[34] and by the Council of Mainz in 852.[35] Though the canons which were issued in 960 under the rule of King Edgar (959-975) did not advert to what then existed as a general practice, they demanded of any man who lived in union with a wife together with a concubine to maintain his union with but the one or the other of these in token of his amendment of life. The option thus granted seems to indicate that in comparison with the wife the concubine could be selected with equal right.[36]

Concubinage, however, had another and less honorable meaning.

---

[30] "Concubina autem hic ea intelligitur, quae cessantibus legalibus instrumentis unita est, et coniugali affectu asciscitur; hanc coniugem facit affectus, concubinam vero lex nominat. De hac dicitur in Concilio Toletano I, c. 17."—*Dictum* ad c. 4, D. XXXIV.

[31] Cf. Benedictus XIV, *loc. cit.*

[32] ". . . habebanturque tamquam uxores minus solemniter ductae."—*glossa* ad c. 4, D. XXXIV.

[33] *Decretum Ivonis,* I, VIII, c. 66: "Christiano non dicam plurimas, sed nec duas simul habere licitum ėst, nisi unam tantum aut uxorem, aut certe loco uxoris (si coniux deest) concubinam."—*MPL,* CLXI, 598; c. 5, D. XXXIV; cf. Joyce, p. 592.

[34] *De Poenitentia,* I, IV, c. 12—*MPL,* CV, 683.

[35] C. 15—*MGH, Leges,* I, 415.

[36] Canones editi sub R. Edgaro, *De Poenitentia,* c. 19: "Si quis habet uxorem et concubinam, etiam nullus sacerdos ei ullum aliquod officium praestet cum christianis, nisi ad emendationem revertatur; unam sibi retineat, sive uxorem sive concubinam."—Wilkins, *concilia Magnae Brittaniae et Hiberniae* (4 vols., Londini, 1737), I, 232; cf. Joyce, p. 596.

It connoted the illicit pseudo-marital relations of a man with a woman for a temporary duration only, and it pointed to the still more shameful sexual cohabitation of a married man with a woman other than his wife. The first section of the aforementioned canon 17 of the I Council of Toledo spoke of concubinage in the bad sense when it decreed that a man who had a wife could not communicate if he kept a concubine also.[37]

Pope St. Leo I (440-461) declared that a concubine was not the same as a wife.[38] St. Nicephorus (750-829), Patriarch of Constantinople (806-815), declared that the Church should have nothing to do with a man who refused to marry his concubine with the sacramental rite.[39]

The words used by Gratian in c. 6, D. XXXIV, and attributed by him to St. Augustine, also refer to unlawful concubinage. In this canon it was stated that a man could have but one wife and that, even though he was without a wife, he nevertheless could not retain as a concubine any woman whom he proposed to espouse only later as his wife. But worthy of even greater condemnation was the action of a man who dismissed his wife and thereupon assumed a concubine.[40]

C. 5, C. XXXII, q. 2, likewise spoke of concubinage as an unlawful union. This canon stated that even the desire of begetting children did not constitute a just cause for concubinage with

---

[37] "Si quis habens uxorem fidelem, si concubinam habeat, non communicet. . . ."—Bruns, *loc. cit.;* Mansi, *loc. cit.*

[38] *Ep. 167* (ad Rusticum): "Aliud est nupta, aliud concubina. . . ."—*MPL*, LIV, 1205; Jaffe, n. 554.

[39] *Ex Constitutionibus ejusdem* (*Nicephori*) *et Sanctorum cum eo Patrum*, c. 90—Pitra, *Iuris Ecclesiastici Graecorum Historia et Monumenta* (2 vols., Romae, 1864-1868), II, 336. It is not generally admitted that these Constitutions attributed by Pitra to Nicephorus belong to him. Cf. *Lexikon für Theologie und Kirche,* s.v. *Nikephorus.*

[40] In a footnote to Gratian's excerpt from Augustine the critical edition of the *Corpus Iuris Canonici* prepared by Friedberg, offers the following explanation: "In hac praecipue parte non sunt relata propria verba B. Augustini; sed nonnulla omissa et mutata. Nam ipse ita scribit: 'Sufficiant vobis uxores, aut nec uxores, concubinas vobis habere non licet . . . non licet vobis habere concubinas, quas postea dimittatis ut ducatis uxores; quanto magis damnatio vobis erit, si habere volueritis, et concubinas et uxores dimittatis.' "

reference to the retaining of a concubine for a temporary duration only.[41] The gloss to this canon stated that the question turned about whether a woman became a wife when she entered a temporary union. The answer to this question was rendered in the negative.[42]

The latter and less honorable acceptation by which the word concubinage was accepted in the sense of a protracted illicit relationship between a man and a woman in a false imitation of the conjugal life, became the prevailing usage. St. Thomas Aquinas (1225-1274) spoke of a concubine as a woman who lived in a sexual union with a man outside of the marital state. He showed how concubinage implied an opposition to the natural law, and hence could never be regarded as lawful, but was always to be branded as a mortal sin.[43]

The Council of Trent, while deploring the rising licentiousness of the age, at the same time decreed severe penalties against persons guilty of concubinage.[44] The Council solemnly declared it to be a grave sin for unmarried men to have concubines, but a most grave sin, and one committed in singular contempt of the great sacrament of marriage, when married men lived in the damnable

---

[41] "Concubinae ad tempus adhibitae, nec etiamsi causa filiorum concumbant, iustum faciunt concubinatum suum."

[42] "In qua quaeritur an fit uxor quae dicitur ad tempus. . . . Et dicitur quod non."—glossa ad c. 5, C. XXXII, q. 2.

[43] *Summa Theologica,* Supplementum, 3. pars., Q. 65, Art. 3, 4 and 5.

[44] "Grave peccatum est homines solutos concubinas habere; gravissimum vero, et in hujus magni sacramenti singularem contemptum admissum, uxoratos quoque in hoc damnationis statu vivere, ac audere eas quandoque domi etiam cum uxoribus alere et retinere. Quare, et huic tanto malo Sancta Synodus opportunis remediis provideat, statuit hujusmodi concubinarios, tam solutos quam oxoratos, cujuscunque status, dignitatis et conditionis existant, si, postquam ab Ordinario, etiam ex officio, ter admoniti ea de re fuerint, concubinas non ejecerint, seque ab earum consuetudine non sejunxerint, excommunicatione feriendos esse; a qua non absolvantur, donec reipsa admonitioni factae paruerint. Quod si in concubinatu per annum, censuris neglectis, permanserint, contra eos ab Ordinario severe pro qualitate criminis procedatur. Mulieres, sive conjugatae, sive solutae, quae cum adulteris seu concubinariis publice vivunt, si ter admonitae non paruerint, ab Ordinariis locorum, nullo etiam requirente, ex officio graviter pro modo culpae puniantur . . . , aliis poenis contra adulteros et concubinarios inflictis in suo robore permanentibus."—sess. XXIV, *de ref. matrim.,* c. 8.

state of concubinage. Married men, the Council continued, even dared at times to support and to retain concubines in their homes with their wives. Wherefore the Council introduced opportune remedies for this great evil by decreeing that men, both married and single, regardless of their dignity or position, should be excommunicated if, after three *ex officio* administered warnings of the ordinary, they did not eject their concubines or otherwise detach themselves from association with them. Women also, whether married or single, who publicly lived in concubinage with married or unmarried men, and who, after three warnings by the local ordinary, did not obey, were to be punished according to the gravity of their crime. Together with these penalties decreed for the first time against persons who lived in concubinage the Council retained in their full vigor penalties already in effect against adulterers and persons who lived in concubinage.

From the description as here set down it can readily be seen what the Fathers of the Council of Trent understood by concubinage. To live in concubinage was to live in a state worthy of condemnation (*vivere in hoc damnationis statu*). The Council spoke of having, supporting and retaining (*habere, alere, retinere*) a concubine. The state of concubinage was understood to have a certain permanency (*in concubinatu . . . permanent; seque ab earum consuetudine non sejunxerint*). Married persons, both men and women, as well as the unmarried could be guilty parties in concubinage (*homines solutos, uxoratos; mulieres sive conjugatae sive solutae*). Concubinage, then, according to the mind of the Council of Trent, was defined as a continued extra-marital sexual union between a man and a woman, regardless of the condition of either as a married or a single person.

Concubinage implies a relationship that is attended with some measure of stability. This does not mean that a permanent union, such as is necessary for marriage, is postulated, but that some degree of stability, which is lacking even in repeated isolated acts of fornication, be manifest. That is to say that the illicit union must actually continue over a period of time, and there must be a mutual understanding between a man and a woman that the union will have some permanency. This intention of permanency may be manifested explicitly through some positive statement or through some course of action such as that of the parties' cohabitation in the same home, or deducible only from their implicit agreement in the matter. In the former case the permanency postulated for concubinage can of course be established more easily.[45]

Concubinage is an extra-marital union. It is a state somewhat analogous to conjugal life, although there is present no marriage intent or at least the species of marriage is not present.[46] Concubinage differs from prostitution principally in that a prostitute gives her body promiscuously for hire. As Ovid said, a prostitute sets her body for sale to anyone at a price.[47] Furthermore there is lacking in prostitution the permanency and the at least implied agreement postulated for concubinage.[48]

Concubinage also differs from even repeated acts of adultery or fornication if these are indulged in at varying intervals as opportunity presents itself. Such isolated acts do not connote the element of continuity and the intimate community of life that is a part and parcel of the notion of concubinage.[49] The difference between repeated acts of adultery or fornication on the one hand and concubinage on the other may be exemplified in the light of the distinction with respect to legal prescription as applicable to a continued or habitual delict (*delictum continuatum*) on the one hand and to an unremitting or continuous delict (*delictum quod habet tractum successivum*) on the other. In the latter kind of delict legal prescription becomes operative only from the time when the cause from which the delict arises has ceased. In the case of a continued or habitual delict prescription sets in with the time of the perpetration of the last delictual act.[50] Concubinage, like the unremitting or continuous delict, can be considered to cease

---

[45] Noldin-Schmitt, *Summa Theologiae Moralis,* II, n. 579; De Smet, n. 628.

[46] Cf. Gasparri, *Tractatus de Matrimonio,* n. 737; Payen, *De Matrimonio,* I, n. 1540; Coronata, *De Sacramentis,* III, n. 413.

[47] "Stat meretrix certa cuivis mercabilis aere, et miseras iusso corpore quaerit opes."—*Amores,* I, X, 21 and 22.

[48] Noldin-Schmitt, *op. cit., De Sexto Precepto,* qu. VII, n. 16.

[49] Payen, *loc. cit.;* Noldin-Schmitt, *op. cit.,* n. 579.

[50] Cf. canon 1705, § 2 and § 3; Noval, *Commentarium Codicis Iuris Canonici Lib. IV, De Processibus* (2 vols., Augustae Taurinorum-Romae: Marietti, 1920-1932), Pars I, *De Iudiciis,* n. 380.

only when its essential element, namely, a certain stability in the parties' community of life, has ceased.

A man who, for example, frequents a brothel to have carnal intercourse even with the same woman over a period of time cannot be said to live in concubinage. Since the woman in question gives herself to any man who approaches, the postulated exclusiveness which alone can make concubinage analogous to the marital relationship is lacking.[51] It is not, however, postulated for concubinage that the parties live under the same roof.[52] Nor is it necessary that the concubine be retained at the expense of the man. While cohabitation and the retention of one party at the expense of the other are indications that concubinage exists, they are nevertheless not inseparably connected with it.

Thirdly, as stated in the definition, if a union is to constitute concubinage it must be a sexual union. Wouters (1864-1933),[53] as far as the present writer could ascertain the matter, is the only author who holds that carnal intercourse is not an essential element in concubinage. This author argues in support of his view from the analogy which he says concubinage bears to an invalid marriage, which apart from carnal intercourse can give rise to the impediment of public propriety, and to a valid marriage, which likewise can give rise to the impediment of affinity though the union has not become consummated. The analogy, however, is more apparent than real. Sexual intercourse belongs to the essence of concubinage.[54]

The historical concept of concubinage, as initiated in Roman law and continued in canon law, includes the idea of sexual relations. A concubine was always spoken of not as one who entered a mere platonic relationship, but as one who entered either a quasi-marital relationship, or as one who was kept by a man in satisfaction of his lusts. If a sexual relationship is not postulated for the notion of concubinage, one justly wonders what kind of relationship is postulated. Wouters does not furnish any answer.

---

[51] Payen, *loc. cit.;* Cappello, *De Matrimonio,* n. 413; De Smet, n. 628; Wernz-Vidal, *Ius Matrimoniale,* n. 378, note 30.

[52] Conc. Trident., *loc. cit.; Reiffenstuel,* Lib. III, tit. II, n. 14; Schmalzgrueber, Lib. V, tit. XVI, n. 8.

[53] *Manuale Theologiae Moralis* (2 vols., Bruxelles, 1932), II, n. 799.

[54] Payen, *loc. cit.*

Furthermore, the law states explicitly regarding both valid and invalid marriages that, whether consummated or not, they give rise to the impediments of affinity and public propriety respectively.[55] The law makes no such distinction regarding concubinage, although the latter is mentioned in canon 1078 with invalid marriage as a source of the impediment of public propriety. The law itself thus indicates that no such distinction can be invoked.

Finally, it is stated in the definition that concubinage can exist between parties whether married or single. This particularization, however, is not admitted universally. Vlaming[56] held that, inasmuch as concubinage is a union analogous to marriage, the impediment of public propriety does not arise from adulterous concubinage. In further support of his opinion this author appealed to the Roman law, which he contends reprobated adulterous concubinage,[57] so that such unions in consequence lacked all juridic effect. Furthermore, he contended, that in a Christian society it was not likely for any such unions to exist as a challenge for the consideration of public propriety.

For the opinion of Vlaming there is some support in the works of certain pre-Code authors, who seemed to require that in a concubinary union the woman be unmarried.[58] However, the reasons advanced by Vlaming, which also seemed to be the reasons which influenced some pre-Code authors to say that the female party in a concubinary union necessarily had to be an unmarried person, furnish but tenuous support for the doctrine which he held. In the first place, while these pre-Code authors required that the woman be unmarried in order that her illicit relationship with a man could be classified as concubinage, they did not seem to make a similar demand in the case of the male party to the concubinage. That fact in itself must have a debilitating effect on their position.

The argument drawn from the Roman law, which seems to furnish the main support for the view propounded by Vlaming, is

---

[55] Cf. canons 97, § 1, and 1078.

[56] *Praelectiones Iuris Matrimonii,* I, n. 361

[57] Cf. C. (5. 26) 1; *supra,* p. 100.

[58] "Concubinatus est illicitus consuetudinarius concubitus cum aliqua foemina soluta et corrupta in domo sua, vel alibi commorante."—Reiffenstuel, Lib. III, tit. II, n. 13; Schmalzgrueber, Lib. V, tit. XVI, n. 8; Pirhing, Lib. V, tit. XVI, n. 12.

of a very dubious validity. Even if it be admitted that the institution of concubinage as recognized by the Roman law demanded that neither of the parties living in concubinage be married persons, no provision of law precluded parties from living in concubinage, if they had been divorced. If the argument drawn from the Roman law, to the effect namely that married persons could not be parties in concubinage, while divorced persons could, is a valid argument then analogously it could be maintained that divorced persons today can be parties in a concubinary union such as would give rise to the impediment of public propriety, while married persons cannot be parties in such a union. Such a situation would mean that the Church would recognize a civil divorce as a condition which would alter the juridic effect of concubinage. That would be attributing a canonical effect to a merely civil act, which patently cannot be maintained.

Moreover, it is difficult to see how the concept of concubinage in Roman law can have any essential bearing on the present law of the Church. The concept of concubinage was different in ecclesiastical legislation from the concept that obtained in Roman law.[59] It has already been seen[60] that the I Council of Toledo (400) decreed that a married man who had a concubine could not communicate. The Council therefore recognized that there could be adulterous concubinage. That the Church designated even adulterous unions as concubinage is clear also from the other sources cited above and especially from the Council of Trent.[61]

The Council of Trent referred to both the married and the unmarried who attached themselves to concubines as *concubinarii*—persons who lived in concubinage—although it was dealing with penal matters in which the law and consequently the connotation of the word concubinage was subject to a strict interpretation. The Council, while invoking anew the ancient penalties against adulterers, considered the specific nature of concubinage and branded it a protracted libidinous consorting, contrary to the laws of marriage, of persons whose crime was all the more serious because of

---

[59] Cf. *supra*, pp. 102-103; Benedictus XIV, *De Synodo Dioecesana*, Lib. IX, c. XII, n. 5; Reiffenstuel, *ibid.*, n. 18; Schmalzgrueber, *loc. cit.*

[60] Cf. *supra*, p. 103.

[61] Cf. *supra*, p. 106.

the greater perversity and scandal resulting from the adulterous union. Adultery therefore added a new malice to concubinage, but did not change its species in the juridical order.

Although Schmalzgrueber (1663-1735) as already indicated, seemed to require that for concubinage the woman in the case had to be an unmarried person, yet he plainly acknowledged that concubinage could take place between persons who were married, and that in consequence the further malice of adultery was added to the sin of concubinage.[62] In like manner Mascardus (+ 1588) had stated that a man who had a wife but at the same time retained a concubine incurred legal infamy.[63]

Again, contrary to what Vlaming[64] maintained, the fact that the illicit relationship constitutes adultery does not preclude concubinage from having a likeness to true conjugal life. This likeness is found, not in the semblance of a true marriage bond, as in the case of an invalid marriage, for example, but in the reciprocally shared sexual life between the parties, even though it be evident that a juridical bond is lacking.

An adulterous concubinage is surely attended with the note of indecency which furnishes the basis for the impediment of public propriety. Certainly no one can claim that an adulterous concubinage is not a violation equally grave both of the divine and canon law as is the concubinage of the unmarried. In both cases there is an offense against public decency. Indeed, in the common estimation greater indecency attaches to an adulterous concubinage. Accordingly, the distinction between concubinage of the unmarried and concubinage of the married, which seems from the juridical point of view to be more or less arbitrarily drawn, must not be pressed beyond due limits to a point where it determines the presence or absence of the impediment of public propriety.[65]

The notion of concubinage given by the Council of Trent still

---

[62] "Si mulier cum qua hujusmodi consuetudo habetur, sit conjugata . . . vinculo adstricta sit, carnale commercium, inter eos initum, fornicationi et concubinatui superaddit malitiam adulterii."—*loc. cit.*, n. 16.

[63] "Qui uxorem habet et concubinam retinet infamis est."—*Conclusiones probationum omnium quae in utroque foro quotidie versantur* (3 vols., Venetiis, 1593), I, Prob. CCCXL, n. 17.

[64] *Loc. cit.*

[65] Cf. St. Alphonsus, *Theologia Moralis,* Lib. III, n. 435.

obtains under the law of the Code. The Code law did not change the concept of concubinage as it existed under the former law. The legislator in the Code attributed to concubinage the juridic effect of begetting the impediment of public propriety without in any way changing the essential elements by which concubinage was constituted a crime under the pre-Code legislation. Hence, in accordance with the norms of canon 6, 3°, and canon 18, concubinage in the law of the Code must be attributed the same meaning that was given it by the Fathers of the Council of Trent, and that is now attributed to it by approved authors. That is to say that concubinage as mentioned in canon 1078 must be interpreted as including an adulterous concubinage as well as the concubinage of unmarried persons.[66]

The legislator in canon 1078 makes no distinction between adulterous concubinage and concubinage of the unmarried, nor is there any such distinction implied. To inject such a distinction into the law would cause some anomalous situations to arise regarding the impediment of public propriety. For example, the marriage of a son with the concubine of the father would be valid if the son's mother was still alive during the liaison, but invalid, because of the impediment of public propriety, if his mother was dead. Or, again, a man who obtains a civil divorce and cohabits with a woman after contracting a so-called civil marriage with her could marry the daughter of the woman who is actually his concubine, without a dispensation from the impediment of public propriety, after the death of his lawful wife. But if his wife had died before he began to live in concubinage with this woman, he would need a dispensation from the impediment of public propriety to marry the latter's daughter.[67] A situation of that kind would result in putting a premium on adultery.

It seems clear then that a juridic distinction between adulterous concubinage and concubinage of the unmarried is to be found

[66] Cf. S. R. R., *Nullitate Matrimonii,* 29 nov. 1930, coram R. P. D. Andrea Jullien, Decisio LVI, nn. 2-6—*S. R. Rotae Decisiones seu Sententiae, ab anno 1909* (Romae: Typis Polyglottis Vaticanis, 1912-), XXII (1930), 622-626; Payen, *De Matrimonio,* I, n. 1540; Wernz-Vidal, *Ius Matrimoniale,* n. 378, note 28; De Smet, n. 628; note 2; Coronata, *De Sacramentis,* III, n. 413.

[67] Cf. Payen, *loc. cit.*

neither in the text of canon 1078 nor in the purpose of the law nor in the concept of concubinage as accepted in the earlier law and now received into the Code.

In view of all this it is difficult to see how Doheny is led to say that a doubt exists regarding the matter, which doubt warrants the invoking of the legal principle *impedimentum dubium est impedimentum nullum.*[68]

ARTICLE 3. MEANING OF THE TERMS *Public* AND *Notorious* IN CANON 1078

In the Code itself the term *public* is given a twofold meaning. In canon 1037, where there is question of matrimonial impediments, public is given a different meaning from that which it is given in canon 2197, 1°, where there is question of delicts.

Canon 1037 states that an impediment which can be proved in the external forum is considered public.[69] Accordingly, if the term public as used in canon 1078 is to be taken in the sense defined in canon 1037, concubinage to beget the impediment of public propriety need only be provable in the external forum. Such proof could be furnished by two oathbound trustworthy witnesses,[70] who by reason of household duties, for example, or in view of some other close connection with the parties, know of their unlawful association although otherwise it remains entirely hidden. Even private documents,[71] such as private letters exchanged between the parties, would be of much help in making the concubinage public in the sense of canon 1037. The second meaning given by the Code to the term public is to be found in canon 2197, 1° which states that a delict is public when it is already divulged or when in con-

---

[68] "It is indeed to be regretted that most modern writers are silent on this controverted question. . . . In the solution of practical cases cognizance must of necessity be taken of the existing doubt in this matter. Hence the axiom: *impedimentum dubium est nullum impedimentum* may be invoked if circumstances warrant it."—*Formal Procedure,* p. 481.

[69] "Publicum censetur impedimentum quod probare in foro externo potest; secus est occultum."

[70] Cf. canon 1791, § 2.

[71] Cf. canon 1817.

sideration of the circumstances of place and persons it can and must be prudently judged that it will easily be divulged.[72]

In view of the twofold meaning of the term public in the Code, there can hardly be any doubt that to beget the impediment of public propriety the concubinage must be public in the sense of canon 2197, 1°.[73] In the first place, the term public in canon 1078 is applied to concubinage and not to a marriage impediment. But concubinage is specified as a delict.[74] Therefore the term public in canon 1078 must be understood in the sense in which it is applied to delicts; that is, in accordance with canon 2197, 1°. Furthermore, in canon 2357, § 2, which is the only other canon in the Code in which the designation public is used explicitly in connection with concubinage, there can be no doubt that the term must be taken in the sense in which it is applied to delicts.

It is true one may think of an exceptional case in which concubinage is not a delict in the strict definition of canon 2195, § 1. Because of ignorance the concubinage may possibly lack the element of moral imputability which is essential for the constitution of a delict strictly such. For instance, two poorly instructed Catholics may erroneously think that they can contract a valid marriage civilly, and in consequence attempt to contract such a mar-

---

[72] "*Publicum,* si iam divulgatum est aut talibus contigit seu versatur in adiunctis ut prudenter iudicari possit et debeat facile divulgatum iri."

[73] Payen (*De Matrimonio,* I, n. 1541) considered this a certain doctrine, and he cited De Smet, n. 629, note 3, to support his view, although this latter author, while he perhaps implied it, did not explicitly state that it is a certain doctrine. Most of the authors, including Gasparri (*Tractatus de Matrimonio,* I, n. 738), Chelodi (*Ius Matrimoniale,* n. 104), Vlaming (I, n. 361), Bouscaren-Ellis (p. 492), Cappello (*De Matrimonio,* n. 544) and Noldin Schmitt (*Summa Theologia Moralis,* III, n. 597), assert that the word public is to be understood as in canon 2197, without even implying that there is any doubt regarding the matter. Vidal (*Ius Matrimoniale,* n. 378, note 31) and Garcia F. Bayon (*Tractatus Canonico-moralis de Sacramento Matrimonii* 2 vols., Madrid: Editorial del C. de Maria, 1931, I, n. 531) (hereinafter cited *De Matrimonio*) consider the question sufficiently doubtful to warrant an authentic interpretation. Lardone ("Impedimento ex *publico et notorio concubinatu,*" *Perfice Munus* [Torino, 1926-], IX [1934], 514-516) seems to be the only writer to maintain that the term public in canon 1078 must be understood in the sense in which canon 1037 defines that term.

[74] Canon 2357, § 2.

riage. Ignorance of the law, of course, is not presumed (canon 16, § 2). Yet, if their ignorance is not blameworthy, their subsequent cohabitation would lack the formal imputability necessary for constituting it a delict in the strict sense of the term.

There can hardly be any doubt, however, that such cohabitation, even though as concubinage it is not strictly delictual, gives rise to the impediment of public propriety if it is public or notorious.[75] Cohabitation of this kind has all the elements of concubinage.[76] The ignorance of the parties that their liaison is a source from which arises the impediment of public propriety, while it may excuse them from formal sin, cannot be considered as precluding the presence of the impediment.[77]

It is not formal sin that gives rise to the impediment of public propriety—otherwise fornication could be a source of the impediment—but the pseudo-marital relationship which exists between the parties and which is publicly known to be concubinage. Moreover, the Pontifical Commission for the Interpretation of the Code in a reply of March 12, 1929, used the expression "independently of cohabitation" (*independenter a cohabitatione*), and not the expression "independently of concubinage," when it stated that civil marriage of itself does not give rise to the impediment of public propriety.[78] It may be added that the reason for the impediment (*ratio legis*), namely the interests of public decency, is present in the case wherein the parties may be free from formal sin no less than in the case wherein they are formally guilty. In both cases the illicit union is known publicly as concubinage.[79]

Even though the union of the parties in the case is not a delict in the strict sense of the term, their concubinage, to beget the impediment of public propriety, must nevertheless be public in the sense of canon 2197, 1°, and not in the sense of canon 1037. Otherwise the parties would be subjected to a greater disability

---

[75] Cf. Prümmer, *Summa Theologiae Moralis,* III, n. 485; Genicot-Salsmans, *Institutiones Theologiae Moralis,* II, n. 596; Sebastiani, *Summarium Theologiae Moralis,* n. 557.

[76] Cf. *supra,* pp. 107-109.

[77] Cf. canon 16, § 1.

[78] Cf. *supra,* p. 91.

[79] For the case in which the union is not known publicly to be concubinage, cf. *supra,* p. 98.

precisely because of their good faith, for if their concubinage must be public only in the sense of canon 1037, that is, provable in the external forum, the impediment of public propriety would the more easily arise. Moreover, the concubinage of the parties in the case is in and of itself delictual in nature, since it is only in consequence of the incidental element of ignorance that it lacks the formal element of a delict. Therefore, analogously it can be said that their union must be held to be public in the same sense that a delict is regarded as public.

Secondly, in canon 1078 the question is not that of proving in the external forum an impediment that already exists, but rather that of determining the sources from which the impediment of public propriety originates. Thirdly, the nature of the impediment of public propriety presupposes that the concubinage be public, that is, divulged or manifested, according to canon 2197, 1°. If to be public the impediment needs only to yield to the possibility of its proof in the external forum according to canon 1037, then the concubinage can *de facto* be occult in the vicinity or in the greater part of the community. Thus the revulsion of the public sense of decency, which alone can attach to concubinage the stigma of infamy, whether in law or in fact,[80] and which alone can furnish a foundation for the impediment of public propriety, would be lacking.[81]

Fourthly, this interpretation is confirmed from parallel passages in the Code where there is question of public sinners. They are such when their evil life stands divulged according to canon 2197, and not simply when proof of their sinful life can be established in the external forum according to canon 1037. Thus, according to canon 1240, 6°, public and manifest sinners are to be deprived of ecclesiastical burial.[82] Those who are publicly unworthy, such as the excommunicated, the interdicted and manifestly infamous are to be debarred from the reception of the Holy Eucharist.[83] Similarly canon 693, § 1, states that non-Catholics, those who

---

[80] Cf. canon 2293.

[81] Cf. *infra*, pp. 136-137.

[82] "Alii peccatores publici et manifesti."

[83] "Arcendi sunt ab Eucharistia publice indigni, quales sunt excommunicati, interdicti manifestoque infames. . . ."—canon 855, § 1.

belong to condemned sects, those who are notoriously under censure, and also public sinners in general, cannot be admitted into associations of the faithful.[84] Furthermore, the notion of publicity is mentioned in conjunction with the notion of notoriety in canon 1078, as it is also in canon 2197, which implies that in both of these canons the term public must be given a meaning analogous to notorious. On the other hand, there is no other canon in which the notion of notoriety is linked with the notion of publicity with reference to the determining of a matrimonial impediment.

Finally, what appears to be a convincing argument may be drawn from the earlier law, for the words which the legislator employs in canon 2197 to define a notorious delict are the very same that the decretal law and later the canonists used for specifying the crime of concubinage as manifest and notorious. Pope Gregory IX, when speaking of clerical concubinage, presupposed that its notoriety derived either through the sentence of a judge, or through the act of a judicial confession, or through such strong factual evidence that the delict could not be concealed by means of any subterfuge.[85] Pope Innocent III had spoken in similar language with reference to concubinage.[86] Hence, since the Code uses the same words to designate a delict as notorious as the earlier law used to designate concubinage as public or notorious, and since concubinage is a delict in the law of the Code as well as in the pre-Code law, it seems evident that these same words, namely, the words of canon 2197, which are borrowed from the earlier law, must still serve to explain when concubinage may be labeled as public.[87]

---

[84] "Acatholici et damnatae sectae adscripti aut censura notorie irretiti et in genere publici peccatores valide recipi nequeunt."

[85] ". . . nisi peccatum huiusmodi sit notorium per sententiam seu per confessionem factam in iure, aut per evidentiam rei, quae tergiversatione aliqua celari non possit."—c. 10, X, *de cohabitatione clericorum et mulierum,* III, 2.

[86] ". . . quod, si crimen eorum ita publicum est, ut merito debeat appellari notorium, in eo casu nec testis nec accusator est necessarius, cum huiusmodi crimen nulla possit tergiversatione celari."—c. 8, X, *de cohabitatione clericorum et mulierum,* III, 2; cf. also Benedictus XIV, *De Synodo Dioecesana,* Lib. IX, C. XII, n. 5.

[87] S. R. R., *Nullitatis Matrimonii,* 29 nov. 1930, coram R. P. D. Andrea Jullien, Dec. LVI, n. 8—*S. R. Rotae Decisiones seu Sententiae,* XXII (1930), 627. In the earlier law the use of the terms public and notorious was not as precise as it is today in the law of the Code. Hence the specific distinction

Granted, then, that public in reference to concubinage must be taken in the sense in which it is used of delicts in canon 2197, 1°, any delict, including concubinage, is public if it has already been divulged or when the situation and the circumstances are such that one not only can, but prudently must, judge that the delict will easily be divulged.[88] Thus, in canon 2197, 1°, the Code gives the definition of public in its application to crime, and considers it under a twofold classification, namely, actual publicity and virtual publicity.

A crime is public actually and materially (*materialiter*) if the crime itself in the nature of a performed act is known generally. A crime is public actually and formally (*formaliter*) if, moreover, the imputability of the crime is known generally.[89] The Code does not specify how far a crime must be divulged before it can be considered as a public crime. If it is known to the greater part of the community, or if the persons knowing of it will most likely make it known to the greater part of the community, it definitely and certainly appears to be public.[90]

---

between public and notorious, as applied to concubinage in the law of the Code, is not to be found in the earlier law. The *Corpus Iuris Canonici* sometimes used the terms public and notorious indiscriminately and interchangeably. Cf. cc. 7 and 8, X, *de cohabitatione clericorum et mulierum,* III, 2; Reiffenstuel, Lib. V, tit. I, n. 234; D'Annibale, *Summula Theologiae Moralis,* I, n. 242; Augustine, *A Commentary on the New Code of Canon Law* (8 vols., Vol. VIII, *Penal Law,* 3. ed., 1931, St. Louis: Herder), VIII, 16; Wernz, *loc. cit.*

[88] Cf. canon 2197, 1°. The words of this canon are taken almost *verbatim* from Wernz, IV, n. 17, which reads: ". . . delictum publicum quod iam divulgatum fuit aut patratum est in iis adiunctis, vel saltem nunc in iis adiunctis versatur, ut prudenter iudicari possit et debeat facile divulgatum iri."

[89] Murphy, *Suspension ex Informata Conscientia,* The Catholic University of America Canon Law Studies, n. 76 (Washington, D. C.: The Catholic University of America, 1932), p. 64; Ayrinhac-Lydon, *Penal Legislation in the New Code of Canon Law* (New York: Benziger Brothers, Inc., 1944), p. 4; Roberti, *De Delictis et Poenis* (Romae: Apud Aedes Facultatis Iuridicae ad S. Apollinaris, 1 vol. in 2, 1930-1938), I, 44; Coronata, *Institutiones Iuris Canonici,* IV, n. 1645; Woywod, *A Practical Commentary,* II, n. 2029.

[90] Coronata, *loc. cit.;* Claeys-Bouuaert-Simenon, *Manuale Juris Canonici* (3 vols., Vol. I and III, 3. ed., Vol. II, 1. ed., Gandae et Leodii: Dessain, 1930-1931), III, n. 505.

Authors try to define more precisely the amount of publicity postulated for a public crime. In doing so they take into account not only the size of the community but also the garrulousness of the persons who have knowledge of the crime.[91] While these attempts of the authors to clarify the matter are not without value, here, as D'Annibale (1815-1892)[92] pointed out, there is question of a fact concerning which the estimation of upright men in the community should be the criterion.[93]

A crime may be virtually public in either of two sets of circumstances: first, in its perpetration, namely when it is perpetrated under such circumstances that it can and prudently must be judged that it will easily become divulged in a manner sufficient to make it actually public in the sense explained above, and secondly, after its perpetration, namely when at some later time the circumstances have become such that it can and prudently must be judged that the crime will easily become divulged. A crime that is public in this latter sense may have been occult at the time of perpetration but later, due to circumstances, must be judged to be public.[94]

Any crime may indeed be public materially the while it remains occult formally. That is to say, the fact of the crime may be public, but the imputability of the crime may be occult. In this way a public crime differs from a notorious crime. The imputability of a notorious crime cannot be occult, so that whenever a crime is notorious there can no longer be any need of establishing its imputability.[95]

A crime may be notorious by notoriety of law or by notoriety of fact.[96] Moreover, a crime may be notorious by notoriety of law

---

[91] Woywod, *loc. cit.;* Coronata, *loc. cit.;* Lega, *De Delictis et Poenis* (2. ed., Romae, 1910), n. 244; Ayrinhac, *loc. cit.*

[92] *Summula Theologiae Moralis,* I, n. 242, note 49.

[93] Cf. Vermeersch-Creusen, *Epitome,* III, n. 384.

[94] Wernz-Vidal, *Ius Canonicum,* Tom. VII, *Ius Poenale* (Romae: Universitas Gregoriana, 1937), n. 35; Roberti, *De Delictis et Poenis,* I, 44.

[95] Canon 1747, 1°; cf. Roberti, *loc. cit.;* Sole, *De Delictis et Poenis-Praelectiones in Lib. V Codicis Iuris Canonici* (Romae, 1920), n. 11; Blat, *Commentarium Textus Codicis Iuris Canonici* (5 vols. in 6, Liber V, *De Delictis et Poenis,* Romae: ex Typographia Pontificia in Instituto Pii IX, 1924), Lib. V, *De Delictis et Poenis,* n. 9; Augustine *loc. cit.*

[96] Cf. canon 2197, 2° and 3°.

in a twofold manner: either upon the sentence of a competent judge that has become a closed matter (*res iudicata*), or upon the free judicial confession of the guilty party.

According to canon 1902 a judicial cause can become a *res iudicata* in various ways: upon two conformable sentences; upon the single pronouncement of sentence if no appeal is invoked against it within the time granted for such appeal (*tempus utile*); upon desertion of the prosecution of the cause in the court of appeal; or, finally, upon a definitive sentence against which all appeal is precluded.[97] The legal effect of the definitive and final adjudication of a cause is the emergence of a *praesumptio iuris et de iure* that the sentence is true and just, and consequently cannot any longer be directly impugned.[98]

The second way in which a crime becomes notorious by notoriety of law derives from the guilty party's free judicial confession of his crime.[99] A judicial confession is the written or oral admission of guilt against oneself and in favor of the opposing party in the presence of the judge, whether made spontaneously or upon interrogation by the judge.[100]

A crime is notorious by notoriety of fact if it is publicly known and if it was committed under such circumstances that it cannot be concealed by means of any artifice, nor excused by means of any reason or remedy honored as admissible in law.[101]

Hence, to be notorious by notoriety of fact, a crime must be public in fact and certain in its imputability. It is evident that in many crimes these two conditions will rarely coexist. There are so many circumstances to be considered that prudence will dictate a very cautious procedure when it remains to be determined whether a crime is notorious by notoriety of fact.[102]

Thus, for example, homicide committed before a large number

---

[97] Cf. canon 1880.

[98] Canon 1904, § 1.

[99] Canon 2197, 2°.

[100] Canon 1750.

[101] Canon 2197, 3°.

[102] Noval, *Commentarium Codicis Iuris Canonici*, Lib. IV, *De Processibus*, II, n. 757; Claeys Bouuaert-Simenon, *Manuale Juris Canonici*, III, n. 505; Wernz-Vidal, *Ius Poenale*, n. 35.

of people would seem to be a notorious crime. Yet unless the criminal intent was evident in view of the lack of any and all justification, the crime would not be notorious.[103] In the case of concubinage, however, the imputability of the crime seems more readily evident once the fact of concubinage is publicly known.

---

[103] Ayrinhac, *Penal Legislation,* p. 5; Ferreres, *Institutiones Canonicae iuxta Novissimum Codicem* (2. ed., 2 vols., Barcinone, 1920), II, n. 148; Roberti, *De Delictis et Poenis,* I, 44.

CHAPTER VIII

Public Propriety in Relation to the Marriages of the Unbaptized

The question whether, and if so to what extent, an invalid marriage or a public or notorious concubinage on the part of infidels gives rise to the impediment of public propriety is one of the most difficult and controverted questions with reference to this matrimonial impediment, concerning which in general controversy seems to be the rule rather than the exception. The question arises when one or both parties in the invalid marriage or the concubinage become baptized. The question, however, presents another aspect which seems to be ignored by most of the authors, namely, that one of the infidel parties in the invalid marriage or the concubinage may wish later to marry a baptized relative of the other party, though the prospective spouse be related within the degrees which connote the possible presence of the impediment of public propriety. In the treatment of the impediment of public propriety it must be remembered that two sets of unions—an invalid marriage or a public or notorious concubinage on the one hand, and a later marriage on the other—which involve at least three persons, need to be considered. Any one of those three persons may become baptized, and thus becomes a direct subject of the laws of the Church.

With a view towards clarity, it will be helpful to list for consideration the different combinations of circumstances that may be affected by the impediment of public propriety as these may arise from the union of two infidels. Various types of unions in which one or both of the parties are infidels may be considered in their relation to public propriety:

1. All three parties concerned, namely, the two who are partners in the invalid marriage or the public or notorious concubinage and the party which one of these later wishes to marry, remain unbaptized.

2. The two parties in the union become baptized before the union is dissolved.
3. One of the two partners in the union becomes baptized before the union is dissolved.
4. One or both partners in the union become baptized after the union has already been terminated.
5. The third party, the party with whom one of the unbaptized partners of the union wishes to contract marriage, becomes baptized before or after the union has been terminated.

In the first case presented, when all parties concerned remain unbaptized, the solution is obvious. It is universally admitted that the impediment of public propriety is an institution solely of ecclesiastical law. As such the impediment does not bind infidels when they marry among themselves.[1] It is also admitted by all authorities that in the second instance, when both of the infidel partners become baptized and continue to live in the invalid marriage or the public or notorious concubinage after their baptism, the impediment of public propriety arises. From a study of the authors it appears that these are the only two cases outside the pale of controversy. The remaining three cases seem to be considered by one or more authors of repute as involving a doubt of law, so that in consequence of the prescript of canon 15 the impediment does not arise. As already indicated, however, the authors do not seem to consider the question whether the impediment of public propriety arises if both partners of the illicit union remain unbaptized but one of them later wishes to marry the baptized relative of the other party, when the prospective spouse is related within the degree that connotes the possible existence of the impediment.

---

[1] Canon 12; Coronata, *De Sacramentis,* III, n. 416; Gasparri, *Tractatus de Matrimonio,* n. 744; Vermeersch, *Theologiae Moralis, Principia-Responsa-Concilia* (3. ed., 4 vols., Romae: Apud Aedes Universitatis Gregorianae, 1933-1937), III, n. 729; Garcia F. Bayon, *De Matrimonio,* I, n. 533; Regatillo, *Institutiones Iuris Canonici* (2 vols., Santander: Sal Terrae, 1941-1942), II, n. 466; cf. S. C. S. Off., 26 aug. 1891—*Collectanea,* n. 1247. Inasmuch as civil law systems have not established the impediment of public propriety nor an impediment corresponding to it, the question of the binding force of a civil law impediment of public propriety on infidels does not arise. Cf. De Smet, n. 636; Chelodi, *Ius Matrimoniale,* n. 104.

Regarding the third case contemplated, namely when only one of the partners becomes baptized and still continues in the unlawful union, most of the authors[2] hold that the impediment arises. Yet some authors of note[3] regard the impediment in the case as doubtful, and therefore in practice as non-existent.

It seems that, if, with regard to baptism, one takes into consideration the status with respect to baptism of the parties who wish to contract marriage, one can reconcile and harmonize these two opinions. There can hardly be any doubt that a marital union, even though it be only a pseudo-marital union as in the case of an invalid marriage or a public or notorious concubinage, comes under the jurisdiction of the Church and rightly has to yield to its legislation when one of the partners is baptized.[4] In fact, it appears that canon 1078, in making the general statement that an invalid marriage or a public or notorious concubinage gives rise to the impediment of public propriety, must be taken in the sense that it refers also to the invalid marriage or public or notorious concubinage between a baptized and an unbaptized person. Furthermore, to invalidate a marriage or render it unlawful it is sufficient that one of the parties be bound by the impediment.[5]

Accordingly, if the baptized party of an invalid union wishes later to marry the baptized or even the unbaptized relative of the other party, if the prospective spouse be related within the degrees that give rise to the impediment, the impediment of public propriety seems to be present as an invalidating element relative to the contemplated marriage. If, on the other hand, the unbaptized party

---

[2] Merkelbach, *Summa Theologiae Moralis* (3 vols., Parisiis: Typis Desclee, de Brouwer et Soc., Vols. I-II, 3. ed., 1938; Vol. III, 2. ed., 1936), III, n. 916; Aertnys-Damen, *Theologia Moralis,* II, n. 767; Wouters, *Manuale Theologiae Moralis,* II, n. 799; Coronata, *loc. cit.;* Payen, *De Matrimonio,* I, n. 1545, note 1.

[3] Cappello, *De Matrimonio,* n. 522; Regatillo, *loc. cit.*

[4] Cf. canons 1016; 1038, § 1; Benedictus XIV, const. *Singulari,* 9 febr. 1749, § 7—*Fontes,* n. 394; S. C. S. Off. (Yunnan), resp., 20 sept. 1854—*Collectanea,* n. 1104; *Fontes,* n. 928; S. C. de Prop. Fide, 1 apr. 1816—*Collectanea,* n. 711; *Fontes,* n. 4703; Vromant, *Ius Missionariorum de Matrimonio,* nn. 7-9; Ottaviani, *Institutiones Iuris Publici Ecclesiastici,* I, n. 82; Payen, *op. cit.,* I, n. 202; De Smet, n. 412, note 3.

[5] Canon 1036, § 3.

in the invalid marriage or the public or notorious concubinage wishes to marry the unbaptized relative of the baptized party, then the impediment of public propriety appears not to be present. In both cases the union from which the impediment originates, namely, the invalid marriage or the concubinage between a baptized and a non-baptized person, is the same. The difference is that in the former case there is question of a marriage between two persons of whom one or perhaps both have through baptism become subject to the law of the Church. In the latter case there is question of a marriage between two infidels neither of whom is bound by the law of the Church.[6] In this latter case, although the root of the impediment of public propriety exists in the infidel party of a former invalid union with reference to the unbaptized relative of the baptized party of this union, still the impediment itself does not arise, since neither of the parties who wish to marry come under the law of the Church.

The fourth case, namely that in which the invalid marriage or the notorious concubinage existed prior to the baptism of either one or both of the parties, but had been discontinued before the reception of baptism, gives rise to much controversy. Many authors[7] deny that in such a case the impediment of public propriety precludes the marriage of either party with a relative of the other after their baptism, provided that the illicit union had been dissolved before baptism took place. These authors do not consider the question whether or not the person whom one of these former partners of the invalid marriage or the public concubinage wishes to marry is likewise a baptized person.

Other authors,[8] who form a school of thought which rests its

[6] Canon 12.

[7] Coronata, *De Sacramentis,* III, n. 416; Gasparri, *Tractatus de Matrimonio,* I, n. 746; Vermeersch-Creusen, *Epitome,* II, n. 361; Bouscaren-Ellis. *Canon Law,* p. 492; Payen, *loc. cit.*

[8] Wernz-Vidal, *Ius Matrimoniale,* n. 363; Chelodi, *Ius Matrimoniale,* n. 104; Vlaming, I, n. 364. De Smet (nn. 438 bis, note 3, and 632, note 4), while he disagrees with these authors by claiming that an invalid marriage (whether consummated or not) between infidels, provided that the union has been dissolved before their baptism, does not give rise to the impediment of public propriety after baptism, yet holds that, if the parties lived in concubinage and later became baptized, the impediment of public propriety would arise.

position on the pre-Code law, make a distinction. In the pre-Code law the valid non-consummated marriage of pagans did not give rise to the impediment of public propriety even after the conversion of both parties. This seems clear from a response of the Sacred Congregation of the Holy Office dated April 19, 1837.[9] On the other hand, in the pre-Code law the bond that arose between infidels from carnal copulation, whether licit or illicit, gave rise to the impediment of affinity after their baptism.[10] Applying the provisions of the pre-Code law, these authors hold that the impediment of public propriety does not arise from the invalid non-consummated marriage of infidels, whereas it arises from their invalid consummated marriage, with the effect of invalidating the marriage which after their baptism they attempt with the relative of the other party of the earlier union, even though that union was already dissolved when the baptism took place.

As already indicated, the authors seem to omit from their consideration the fifth case listed above. It involves the case in which baptism has been received by the third party, with whom one of the partners to the earlier invalid union may wish later to contract marriage. The already noted diversity of opinion leads to great confusion on the general question of the binding effect of the impediment of public propriety as deriving from an invalid marriage or a public or notorious concubinage of the unbaptized when at least one of the parties later becomes baptized and wishes to marry a relative, even an unbaptized relative, of the other party, or when, though both of the parties have remained unbaptized, one of them seeks later to marry the baptized relative of the other.[11] From

[9] "Matrimonium ratum non consummatum paganorum producitne honestatem publicam vel censeturne impedimentum dirimens post eorum conversionem?"

Resp. "Impedimentum non subsistere."—*Fontes,* n. 875; *Collectanea,* n. 1254; cf. Schmalzgrueber, Lib. IV, tit. I, n. 96; Sanchez, Lib. VII, disp. 68, n. 2; cf. *infra,* p. 131, footnote 17.

[10] S. C. S. Off., instr. (ad Vic. Ap. Nankin.), 26 aug. 1891: ". . . Affinitatem quae in infidelitate naturaliter contrahitur ex copula tum licita tum illicita non esse impedimentum pro matrimoniis quae in infidelitate ineuntur, evadere tamen impedimentum pro matrimoniis quae ineuntur post baptismum, quo suscepto infideles sunt subditi Ecclesiae eiusque proinde legibus subiecti. . . ." —*Fontes,* n. 1145; *Collectanea,* n. 2180.

[11] Cf. Doheny, *Formal Procedure,* pp. 485-487.

the welter of confusion it could naturally be expected that the statement of the law involves much ambiguity. That, however, can hardly be said to be the case. Furthermore, as pointed out by Ojetti (1862-1932),[12] in regard to a similar matter, great caution should be used, for it should not be too readily admitted that the law is doubtful. In point of fact, if the law is understood according to the proper signification of the terms, much if not all of the confusion vanishes. Such an interpretation renders the law more intelligible by eliminating much of the confusion that surrounds it.

Canon 1078 states that the impediment of public propriety arises from an invalid marriage and from a public or notorious concubinage (*ex matrimonio invalido et ex publico vel notorio concubinatu*). The expressions *invalid marriage* and *public or notorious concubinage* are not circumscribed or limited in any way by any qualifying words, so that as they stand these expressions extend to the invalid marriage or the concubinage between any man and woman whether baptized or unbaptized. The basis of the impediment of public propriety is the quasi-marital union between the parties, and there is nothing to prevent the legislator, should he so wish, from making that union, even though it exists between two non-baptized persons, the basis for an impediment.[13]

This statement does not contravene the prescript of canon 12, for in the present connection it is not held that a law of the Church binds the unbaptized, but rather that the legislator may make the bond of union that now exists, or that had existed in the past between the unbaptized, the basis from which arises an impediment of the ecclesiastical law that precludes the marriage of one of those parties with a relative of the other when at least one of the parties later wishing to contract the marriage is baptized.

The words of the Sacred Congregation of the Holy Office as used in a response to the Bishop of Quebec on September 16, 1824, regarding the impediment of affinity, would generally apply with equal aptitude to the impediment of public propriety under the

---

[12] "Ex infidelium matrimonio legitimo an affinitas oriatur?" *Jus Pontificum,* V (1925), 76.

[13] Michiels, "*De vera impedimenti affinitatis natura,*" *Jus Pontificium,* V (1925), 156; Vlaming, I, n. 352.

Code law. The Holy Office stated that affinity in itself and physically considered differed from the impediment of affinity, for affinity considered in itself was contracted by infidels also inasmuch as a man and a woman are constituted one flesh by their carnal union. The difference was that, whereas affinity did not give rise to an impediment when the parties involved were unbaptized, inasmuch as they were not subject to the Church's law, it became an impediment if one of the partners in the carnal union later became baptized and sought to marry the relative of the other partner—even the unbaptized relative, as it would seem, although this was not explicitly stated—since by baptism he became a subject of the Church's law.[14]

It seems a valid deduction from this response of the Holy Office that, if both partners of the carnal union had remained unbaptized and one of them later, while still an infidel, had sought to marry the baptized relative of the other, the impediment of affinity would likewise have arisen. The same conditions are realized in both cases. The bond of carnal union between the two infidels which formed the basis for the impediment is the same, and one of the parties of the subsequent marriage, not however the partner of the carnal intercourse, is a subject of the law of the Church. In like manner there is no reason why, under the present law, the legislator may not make the bond of union that arises from an invalid marriage or from the public or notorious concubinage of two infidels the basis of the impediment of public propriety when one of them later, even while still unbaptized, seeks to marry the baptized relative in the first or second degree of the direct line of the other unbaptized partner. Indeed, it seems reasonable to

---

[14] Ad 2: "Distingui namque debet affinitas, in se et physice spectata, ab impedimento affinitatis. Porro affinitas etiam ab infidelibus contrahitur, quia etiam inter infideles verum est, quod vir et mulier per carnalem copulam una caro efficiuntur. . . . Id tantum est discriminis, quod affinitas ecclesiasticum non parit infidelibus impedimentum; fidelibus autem parit. Quapropter cum per baptismum non tollatur a Balbina eius iam physice contracta cum Paulo affinitas, haec ipsa affinitas radicaliter in ea inhaerens, quae eidem infideli impedimento non erat ad contrahendum, impedimentum evadit post baptismum, quo subdita fit Ecclesia, eiusque proinde legibus subiecta."—*Collectanea*, n. 784; cf. Feije, n. 380; Wernz, IV, n. 430; Gasparri, *De Matrimonio* (1904), n. 794.

expect that he should do so, since the bond from which public propriety arises under the present law is for the greater part identical with the bond that gave rise to affinity in the pre-Code law.[15]

A reply of the Sacred Congregation for the Propagation of the Faith on August 23, 1852, in answer to two questions which were proposed to it, indicates a similar doctrine with regard to the origin of an ecclesiastical impediment in the bond of union which obtained between two unbaptized persons when one of them later received baptism and sought to marry a relative of the other party. The first question concerned the case of an infidel man who had had illicit carnal intercourse with a woman, who may or may not have been a baptized person. Later he received baptism. The question was: could he marry the woman's relative, who was related to him in a degree of affinity which in the law of the Church was a diriment impediment, regardless of whether this relative had received baptism either before or after the carnal intercourse between him and the woman. The answer was in the negative. Here, it will be noted, the impediment of affinity arose from a bond of which the cause, namely, the carnal intercourse, intervened at a time when all three parties in question were unbaptized. Later, it is true, when the marriage was to take place, the two parties of the contemplated marriage were baptized. There seems no reason, however, to doubt that the impediment would also have arisen if only one of the parties seeking to marry had received baptism, for in that case also the Church claims exclusive jurisdiction.[16]

The answer given by the Sacred Congregation to the second question seemed to apply equally to the impediments both of affinity and of public propriety under the earlier law. The question dealt with a case in which there had been a valid marriage. Since it was not specified whether or not the marriage in question had been consummated, the reply seems to apply equally to both impediments. If the marriage had been consummated the reply would have referred to the impediment of affinity arising from licit copulation. If, on the other hand, the marriage had been unconsummated,

---

[15] Cf. *supra,* p. 63.

[16] Cf. *supra,* p. 70.

the reply would have referred to the impediment of public propriety arising from non-consummated marriage. Both the impediment of affinity as deriving from licit copulation and the impediment of public propriety as arising from valid non-consummated marriage extended to the fourth degree, which is the degree that received mention in the reply.[17]

According to the statement of the question both parties of the valid marriage were unbaptized. The wife died. It was only after her death that the widowed husband received baptism. The question was: could the man, within the degrees that connote the impediment, marry a relative of his deceased wife, regardless of whether this relative had or had not been baptized at the time the first marriage was still in existence. This relative of the deceased wife had become baptized before she sought to enter what was the second marriage for the man. The reply was in the negative. Here again it will be noted that all three parties were unbaptized at the time the bonds of union, namely, the licit carnal copulation or non-consummated marriage, from which the respective impediments arose, were cemented. Again the reply contemplated a case in which both of the parties who later wished to intermarry had become baptized. Nevertheless, as in the former case, it must be held that the impediment of affinity, or respectively that of public propriety, would have arisen if only one of the parties who sought to intermarry was actually a baptized person at that time.[18]

---

[17] It is true that the interpretation which comprises in this reply the impediment of public propriety as arising from valid marriage runs counter to the reply given by the Sacred Congregation of the Holy Office some fifteen years earlier, in 1837. (Cf. *supra,* p. 127). It is also true that the context in the reply of the Sacred Congregation for the Propagation of the Faith points rather to the impediment of affinity. However, the possibility of a change in the *praxis curiae* may not be entirely overlooked. At any rate, the argument deducible from the manner in which the impediment of affinity obtained under the former law retains its validity.

[18] "3. Vir infidelis qui adhuc in infidelitate positus cognovit sive publice, sive private, illicite tamen, mulierem quamdam, sive fidelem, sive infidelem, potestne, post susceptum baptismum valide et licite matrimonium contrahere cum consanguinea eiusdem cognitae mulieris, si ista consanguine baptismum susceperit sive ante, sive post copulam de qua agitur? 4. Et quatenus affirmative (de quo valde dubitandum), idem infidelis ad fidem conversus, post mortem legitimae uxoris infidelis, potestne matrimonium contrahere cum consanguinea

Since both the Holy Office and the Sacred Congregation for the Propagation of the Faith held that the bond of natural affinity between infidels gave rise to the impediment of affinity in the pre-Code law if one of the parties in the subsequent marriage was baptized, there seems no reason to think that the Church should regard a similar bond in any other light under the Code law. Nor is there any indication that a change was introduced in the Code. Rather, there seems warranted the conclusion that the bond of invalid marriage or of public or notorious concubinage between infidels under the present discipline gives rise to the impediment of public propriety provided that one of the parties who later wishes to contract marriage is baptized at the time of the marriage. This conclusion does not necessarily mean that the earlier law is used as the norm of interpretation of the present law. It merely means that there is nothing in the present law to indicate that a physical or moral bond between the unbaptized, which formerly was regarded as the basis of the impediment of affinity after the baptism of the parties, may not be still regarded as the basis of a similar impediment after the baptism of the parties.

In fact, the clear statement of the present law includes such a union as a basis of the impediment of public propriety. Canon 1078 states that an invalid marriage—this expression not being restricted to the union of two baptized persons or to the union of a baptized with an unbaptized person—gives rise to the impediment of public propriety. The expression accordingly leaves room for the inclusion of the valid marriage of two unbaptized persons—*matrimonium legitimum*.[19] Therefore the expression as used in canon 1078 should be understood as extending also to the invalid marriage of two unbaptized persons if one of them later seeks to marry the baptized relative of the other.

The laws of the Church do not bind the unbaptized.[20] Therefore,

---

(usque ad 4 gradum inclusive) eiusdem defunctae uxoris, sive ista consanguinea baptismum susceperit ante, sive post mortem praedictae uxoris infidelis?"

Resp. "Ad 3. Negative. Ad 4. Negative."—*Collectanea,* n. 1079; cf. Gasparri, *De Matrionio* (1904), n. 794; Feije, n. 379; Giovine, I, 555.

[19] Canon 1015, § 3.

[20] Canon 12.

as already stated,[21] when all three parties, that is to say, the two parties of the invalid marriage or concubinage and the person with whom one of them wishes later to contract marriage, are unbaptized, the impediment of public propriety does not arise. Neither does the impediment arise if the non-baptized party of the invalid marriage or concubinage wishes to marry a non-baptized relative of the baptized partner, since then there is question of a marriage between two people neither of whom is bound by the laws of the Church.

However, when one of the partners of the invalid marriage or the public or notorious concubinage becomes baptized, even after the union has already been terminated, and wishes to marry a relative of the other partner even though unbaptized, within the degrees that constitute the impediment, the impediment must be held to exist. Furthermore even if both of the partners remain unbaptized but one of them later wishes to marry the baptized relative, in the first or second degree of the direct line, of the other, the impediment of public propriety also must be held to exist even though the baptism of the third party took place after the union was already terminated. This latter is precisely the fifth case proposed for consideration. The necessary condition for the emergence of the impediment exists in both cases, namely, a bond of union, induced by an invalid marriage, or by a public or notorious concubinage, which bond, even though the illicit relationship which induced it may have been terminated, the Church may make and *de facto* according to the wording of the law does make the basis of an impediment.[22] The further postulate for the applicability of the Church's law is also verified: namely, at least one of the two parties in question is subject to the matrimonial impediment as enacted by the Church.[23]

Furthermore, the sense of public decency, which is the underlying basis for the impediment of public propriety,[24] seems to demand this interpretation. Public decency requires that the Cath-

---

[21] Cf. *supra,* p. 124.

[22] Cf. Michiels, "De vera impedimenti affinitatis natura," *Jus Pontificium,* V (1925), 156.

[23] Cf. Canon 1036, § 3; Payen, *De Matrimonio,* I, n. 1555, note 1.

[24] Cf. *infra,* p. 137.

olic daughter of an unbaptized woman be prevented from marrying the infidel man to whom her mother was invalidly married, no less than it demands that the baptized man, if before his baptism or after he became baptized he was the partner of an invalid marriage with an unbaptized woman, be prevented from marrying her infidel daughter. Yet many authors,[25] while they do not present the former case for consideration, seem to admit the existence of the impediment in the latter case.

What appears to be a convincing argument for the view that the impediment of public propriety arises from the invalid marriage of the public or notorious concubinage of two infidels, provided that one of the parties of the subsequent marriage is baptized, may be drawn from the analogy between the impediment of public propriety and the impediment of affinity. Canon 97, § 1, states that the impediment of affinity arises from a valid marriage whether only ratified (*ratum*) or whether ratified and consummated,[26] and canon 1015, § 1, defines what a ratified marriage is when it states that the valid marriage of baptized persons is said to be ratified.[27] Notwithstanding the fact that the law thus states that a ratified marriage gives rise to the impediment of affinity, and defines a ratified marriage as the marriage of baptized persons, many authors of recognized authority[28] hold that there is a foundation for the impediment of affinity in the valid marriage of two unbaptized persons, and that the impediment of affinity arises from

---

[25] Michiels, *"art. cit.," Jus Pontificium, loc. cit.;* Wouters, *Manuale Theologiae Moralis,* II, n. 799; Merkelbach, *Summa Theologiae Moralis,* III, n. 917; Aertnys-Damen, *Theologia Moralis,* II, n. 768.

[26] "Affinitas oritur ex matrimonio valido sive rato tantum sive rato et consummato."

[27] "Matrimonium baptizorum validum dicitur ratum si nondum consummatione completum est. . . ."

[28] Ojetti, *Commentarium in Codicem Iuris Canonici* (4 vols., Romae: Apud Aedes Universitatis Gregorianae, 1927-1931), II, 77-84; Noldin-Schmitt. *Summa Theologiae Moralis,* III, n. 594; Chelodi, *Ius Matrimoniale,* n. 99; Augustine, *A Commentary,* V (3. ed., St. Louis: B. Herder, 1923), 211; Blat, Commentarium Textus Codicis Iuris Canonici (Liber III, De Sacramentis, 2. ed., Romae: Ex Typographia Pontificia in Instituto Pii IX, 1924), III, 593; cf. "Questioni circa l'impedimento di affinita," *Il Monitore Ecclesiastico,* XLIX (1924), 48-49.

such a marriage if later the surviving partner has received baptism and seeks to marry a baptized relative of the other party.[29]

Analogously it may be held that the invalid marriage of two unbaptized persons may give rise to the impediment of public propriety. The reason is that, although on the one hand the terms of the law (canons 97, § 1, and 1015, § 1) state clearly that affinity arises from a valid marriage of baptized persons, the above-mentioned canonists interpret the law as including the valid marriages of unbaptized persons. The result, according to this view, is that, should the marriage of two unbaptized persons be dissolved, by death for example, the surviving unbaptized partner would be prevented, because of the impediment of affinity, from marrying any baptized relative of the deceased partner as long as the relationship furnished a basis for the impediment.

On the other hand, the law (can. 1078) states clearly that public propriety arises from an invalid marriage. This expression in its full scope includes the invalid marriages of the unbaptized. Therefore, *a fortiori,* since in the case of affinity the wording of the law seems to exclude the union of the unbaptized, while in the case of public propriety it includes such a union, it may be said that the impediment of public propriety arises from the invalid marriage of two unbaptized persons, provided that one of the parties who later seeks to marry is a baptized person at the time of this marriage.

That the invalid marriage or concubinary union has already ceased before either of the parties has received baptism creates no insurmountable difficulty. Baptism, while it wipes away all sin and brings about a regeneration in the soul, does not obliterate a past fact. It was not considered to do so in the responses of the Congregations of the Holy Office and for the Propagation of the Faith regarding the impediment of affinity in the pre-Code law, quoted immediately above. Neither should it be considered to do so here regarding the impediment of public propriety. Furthermore, in the opinion of the above cited authors, who hold that the im-

---

[29] While these authors speak of the case wherein both parties of the subsequent marriage have received baptism, it seems necessary only that one of the parties have received baptism, since the Church claims entire jurisdiction in that case also. Cf. canon 1036, § 3; Wahl, p. 64.

pediment of affinity arises from the valid marriage of two unbaptized persons when one of the parties upon baptism wishes later to contract a marriage with a relative of the other party, the fact or relationship of the former valid marriage of the two infidels is not considered obliterated by the subsequent baptism of one or both of the parties.

Even if it were completely accepted,[80] the doctrine in the pre-Code law that the impediment of public propriety did not arise from the valid non-consummated marriages of the unbaptized after they become baptized, does not serve to discredit the view that under the present law the impediment of public propriety arises from the invalid marriage or the public or notorious concubinage of two infidels provided that at least one of the parties of the subsequent marriage has become baptized. In the first place, the nature of the impediment of public propriety has been entirely changed by the Code. There accordingly is excluded the application of the principle of canon 6, 3°.[81] Moreover, even if it were admitted that the argument from the pre-Code law is valid, it would be counterbalanced by the consideration that the pre-Code impediment of affinity, to which the present impediment of public propriety bears similar traits, did arise from the bond both of a licit and an illicit carnal union once the parties had become baptized.

---

[80] Cf. *supra*, p. 131, note 17.

[81] Cf. *supra*, p. 93.

CHAPTER IX

Purpose, Cessation, Multiplication and Extension of Public Propriety

ARTICLE 1. PURPOSE OR REASON FOR THE INSTITUTION OF PUBLIC PROPRIETY

Although the foundation or basis on which the impediment of public propriety rests was changed by the law of the Code, the purpose or reason on account of which the Church instituted the impediment remained the same.

The foundation of the impediment of public propriety in the former law was twofold, namely, betrothal and non-consummated marriage—*sponsalia de futuro* and *sponsalia de praesenti.*[1] In the law of the Code the foundation of the impediment of public propriety is also twofold, but entirely different from what it was in pre-Code law. The present foundation of the impediment is to be found in an invalid marriage and in a public or notorious concubinage.[2]

In both the present law and the pre-Code as well as in the Roman law the same reason is advanced for the institution of public propriety, or quasi-affinity as it was called in Roman law, namely, that when there was question of marriage not only what was lawful but also what was proper had to be taken into account.[3] The impropriety or indecency which, under the present law, the impediment of public propriety seeks to forestall is that which would arise if a partner in an invalid marriage or a public or notorious concubinage were to marry the close blood relation of the other partner. The partners of such unions are closely conjoined in a moral or physical union, or more often in both. Hence, not only is it not fitting, but also it is contrary to the moral sensibilities and the decent mores of a Christian people that one of the parties

---

[1] Cf. *supra,* pp. 35-36.

[2] Cf. *supra,* p. 64.

[3] Cf. *supra,* p. 13.

should marry the close relation of one with whom he was so intimately and publicly united. Accordingly, as the very appellation of the impediment suggests, the Church preserves Christian decency by guarding against such marriages through the institution of the impediment of public propriety.[4]

A further reason for the institution of the impediment of public propriety is to be found in the solicitude of the Church to promote purity of morals among individuals also. The possibility of marriage between a partner of the invalid marriage or the concubinage and the close blood relation of the other party would present a danger of incontinence because of the familiarity that would be apt to exist between them. So it is apparent that, though the bonds of valid marriage from which the impediment of affinity arises are closer than the bonds from which arises the impediment of public propriety, the reason for the institution of the two impediments is fundamentally the same.[5]

ARTICLE 2. DISPENSATION FROM THE IMPEDIMENT OF PUBLIC PROPRIETY

The impediment of public propriety, whether it arises from an invalid marriage or from a public or notorious concubinage, is an institution solely of ecclesiastical law. Hence it can and *de facto* often is dispensed in both the first and second degrees. The faculties to grant this dispensation in both degrees are vouched for in canons 1043-1045 under the extraordinary conditions there considered. Similarly, powers to dispense from the impediment of public propriety as well as from the impediment of affinity in the direct line if it derived from an illicit copulation, which latter partially corresponds to public propriety under the present law, were contained in the ordinary faculties granted by the Sacred Congregation of the Holy Office on February 20, 1888.[6]

[4] Cf. Payen, *De Matrimonio*, I, n. 1537; Wernz-Vidal, *Ius Matrimoniale*, n. 373; Cappello, *De Matrimonio*, n. 546; Vermeersch, *Theologia Moralis*, III, n. 776; Chelodi, *Ius Matrimoniale*, n. 103; Coronata, *De Sacramentis*, III, n. 411.

[5] Cf. Gasparri, *Tractatus de Matrimonio*, n. 729; Payen, *loc. cit.*

[6] Cf. *Collectanea*, n. 1685; Konings, *Commentarium in Facultates Apostolicas* (4. ed., recognita, curante Joseph Pulzer, Neo-Eboraci: Apud Benziger Fratres, 1897), pp. 376, 407 and 410; Wernz-Vidal, *Ius Matrimoniale*, n. 384.

The impediment of public propriety in the second degree is a minor grade (*gradus minor*) impediment.[7] Accordingly any reasonable cause, even though not a canonical cause, suffices, in accordance with the rescript, for the grant of a dispensation.[8] Furthermore, concealing the facts in the petition or alleging a false cause (*subreptio vel obreptio*), even though it is the only motive cause advanced, does not invalidate the dispensation.[9]

The impediment of public propriety in the first degree can be dispensed for a just and grave cause. In both cases, however, great caution must be taken in the petition and in the grant of the dispensation with a view to certifying that the parties who wish to marry are not related in any degree of the direct line of blood relationship. In the former law, for the proper guarding against this danger, dispensations from the impediment of affinity in the direct line when it derived from illicit copulation were granted only with the proviso that one party of the marriage was not the child of the other—*"Dummodo nullum sit dubium, quod coniux sit proles ab altero contrahentium genita."*[10] This danger is sufficiently obviated if the illicit carnal relations between the two parties of whom one wishes to marry the relative of the other party took place at such a time that it remains physically impossible for this relative of the other party to be the product of these relations.[11]

ARTICLE 3. STATUS OF THE IMPEDIMENT OF PUBLIC PROPRIETY IF THE PARTIES CONTRACT A VALID MARRIAGE BETWEEN THEMSELVES

The question whether the impediment of public propriety continues to coexist with the impediment of affinity, or whether it is absorbed into the latter, when the parties of the invalid marriage or the public or notorious concubinage enter a valid marriage is a mooted question under the present law as it was under the pre-Code

[7] Canon 1042, § 2, 3°.

[8] Payen, *De Matrimonio*, I, n. 1547.

[9] Canon 1054. Cf. canons 42 and 43.

[10] Cf. Konings, *loc. cit.;* Wernz-Vidal, *loc. cit.;* Coronata, *De Sacramentis*, III, n. 417.

[11] De Smet, nn. 522 and 533; Payen, *loc. cit.*

law. Now, as then, the side of the controversy which maintains that the impediment of public propriety is of its nature permanent, and continues on even with the impediment of affinity until it is removed by dispensation appears to be the more probably tenable doctrine.[12]

Some authors[13] consider as certain the doctrine that the impediment of public propriety continues on even after affinity arises. The principal arguments to support the view are the following:

1. The law itself presupposes that multiple impediments may exist in the same case.[14]

2. Nowhere does the law recognize that a pre-existing impediment is supplanted or absorbed by a later one, even though the later one may rest on the stronger bond and be more extensive.

3. The fundamental reason for the institution of the impediment of public propriety, namely the demand of public decency, still persists even after the valid marriage of the parties. Since the reason for the impediment persists, the impediment itself must be held to continue.

4. Cappello[15] adds a fourth reason, namely, that the Holy See considers that both the impediments of public propriety and of affinity coexist in such a case, for it continues to grant dispensations from both.

Regatillo,[16] on the other hand, supports the view that the impediment of public propriety ceases to exist in that it is supplanted by the impediment of affinity when the parties contract a valid marriage. This author's opinion is based on two considerations: that which was held as a probable opinion by grave authors in the pre-Code law is still tenable, and the impediment of affinity, arising as it does from a stronger bond and instituted as it was for the

---

[12] Cappello, *De Matrimonio,* n. 533; Wernz-Vidal, *Ius Matrimoniale,* n. 381; Payen, *De Matrimonio,* I, n. 1542; Aerynys-Damen, *Theologia Moralis,* II, n. 766; Ayrinhac, *Marriage Legislation,* p. 183, De Smet, n. 633. Cf. *supra,* p. 59.

[13] Gasparri, *Tractatus de Matrimonio,* I, n. 748; Coronata, *De Sacramentis,* III, n. 416; Vlaming, I, n. 367.

[14] Cf. canons 1049 and 1050.

[15] *Loc. cit.*

[16] *Institutiones Iuris Canonici,* II, n. 467.

same season as the impediment of public propriety, absorbs the latter.

Although these reasons do not seem very cogent, many authors[17] are loath to deny probability to the opinion.

ARTICLE 4. MULTIPLICATION OF THE IMPEDIMENT OF PUBLIC PROPRIETY

The impediment of public propriety is not multiplied numerically if each of the parties who had previously entered an invalid marriage or lived in a public or notorious concubinage wish to contract marriage with a relative of the other within the degrees which imply the presence of the impediment.[18] Nor is public propriety multiplied, as is affinity,[19] by reason of the fact that the parties may be multiple relatives. Consanguinity in the direct line is not multiplied.[20]

There is, however, a grave question whether the impediment of public propriety is multiplied, after the manner of canon 1077, § 2, 2°, when a party has successively contracted an invalid marriage or has lived in concubinage with two different parties whose common relative in the first or the second degree of the direct line he then seeks to marry. The reasons in law adduced on both sides appear to be equally cogent so that the question, in the absence of an authentic interpretation, seems insoluble.

For the negative side, which denies that the impediment of public propriety is ever multiplied, what seems a rather convincing argument may be drawn from the silence of the law. The Code states both that the impediment of consanguinity and also the impediment of affinity are multiplied, but it is silent regarding the potential multiplication of the impediment of public propriety. In view of the well recognized adage, "*Quidquid legislator voluit expressit, quod noluit tacuit,*" this silence of the legislator is a

---

[17] Cappello, *loc. cit.;* Payen, *ibid.,* note 2; Bouscaren-Ellis, *Canon Law,* p. 492; Doheny, *Formal Procedure,* p. 484.

[18] Payen, *De Matrimonio,* I, n. 1548; De Smet, n. 630.

[19] Cf. canon 1077, § 2, 1°.

[20] Canon 1076, § 2.

strong argument on the negative side. Some authors[21] who favor this view deny that there is any reason for the multiplication of the impediment of public propriety that is equal to the reason for the multiplication of the impediments of consanguinity and affinity, since the latter impediments are much more extensive in scope, so that it is not surprising that it should be the mind of the legislator to multiply these latter impediments the while he foregoes doing the same for the former. It may also be added that, because of the strict limitations of the impediment of public propriety, a case of its multiplication would be so little apt to arise that the legislator simply chose not to include it within the scope of the law.

Other authors[22] hold that the impediment of public propriety can be a multiple impediment. These authors allege that the multiplication of impediments, including the impediment of public propriety, is provided for in a general way in canon 1049. Furthermore, so they argue, the Code is silent regarding the multiplication of the impediment of crime, though it may certainly exist as a multiple impediment.[23]

The majority of the authors[24] feel there is a doubt of law in the case, and hence in accordance with the rule of canon 15 they regard the impediment of public propriety as never arising in the nature of a multiple impediment for which a multiple dispensation would be needed in practice.

ARTICLE 5. THE EXTENSION OF THE IMPEDIMENT OF PUBLIC PROPRIETY

Not only has the nature of the impediment of public propriety been changed by the law of the Code, but the impediment, as retained under the same name, is greatly curtailed in its extension.

[21] Garcia F. Bayon, *De Sacramento Matrimonii,* I, n. 537; Vlaming, *Praelectiones Iuris Matrimonii,* I, n. 366; Cappello, *De Matrimonio,* n. 550.

[22] Merkelbach, *Summa Theologiae Moralis,* III, n. 916; Wouters, *Manuale Theologiae Moralis,* II, n. 799; Gasparri (*Tractatus de Matrimonio,* I, n. 740) considered it certain that the impediment of public propriety may be multiplied.

[23] Gasparri, *loc. cit.*

[24] Cappello, *De Matrimonio,* n. 550; Wernz-Vidal, *Ius Matrimoniale,* n. 382; Coronata, *De Sacramentis,* III, n. 416; De Smet, n. 630; Payen, *De Matrimonio,* I, 1547; Doheny, *Formal Procedure,* p. 485.

In the former law the impediment of public propriety arising from betrothal extended to the first degree of the direct and collateral lines. As arising from a valid non-consummated marriage it extended to the fourth degree inclusive of both lines.[25]

In the present law the impediment of public propriety does not at all extend to the collateral line. A man, therefore, may contract marriage with the sister of the woman to whom he was invalidly married or with whom he had lived in public or notorious concubinage. The impediment is limited to the first and second degrees of the direct lines. It thus bars a man from contracting marriage in the descending line with the daughter or granddaughter, and in the ascending line with the mother or grandmother, of the woman to whom he was invalidly married or with whom he had lived in public or notorious concubinage. In like manner the pseudo-wife or concubine is prevented from contracting marriage with the relatives of the man within the first and second degrees of blood relationship in both the ascending and descending line. The impediment extends to the illegitimate as well as the legitimate offspring and ancestry of the other party within the indicated degrees. The impediment is of its nature perpetual. Apart from the consideration of the probability that it may become absorbed by the supervening impediment of affinity if the parties contract a valid marriage, it ceases only in consequence of an act of dispensation.[26]

---

[25] Cf. *supra*, p. 46.

[26] Cf. Davis, *Moral and Pastoral Theology* (4. ed., 4 vols., New York: Sheed and Ward, 1943), IV, 162; Wernz-Vidal, *Ius Matrimoniale*, n. 380; Payen, *De Matrimonio*, I, n. 1537; Gasparri, *Tractatus de Matrimonio*, I, n. 741.

CONCLUSIONS

1. Before the promulgation of the Code of Canon Law the diriment matrimonial impediment of public propriety, to the extent that it arose from betrothal—*sponsalia*—had the same basis that it had in the Roman law. To the extent that it was based on a non-consummated marriage, public propriety differed from the Roman law impediment to marriage. The reason advanced for the institution of the impediment, namely, public decency, was the same in both legal systems.

2. In Germanic law the betrothal constituted the initial stage of marriage. Apart from a single constitution of Emperor Henry II, evidence that betrothal gave rise to an impediment to marriage in Germanic law seems to be lacking.

3. The diriment impediment of public propriety first appeared in ecclesiastical legislation about the twelfth century. Because of the influence of Roman law on Church legislation, and especially because of the similarity of both laws in respect to the impediment, it is likely that the impediment of public propriety, as it appeared in Church law, was derived from the Roman law.

4. The absence of the impediment of public propriety in ecclesiastical law until the twelfth century is explained by the absence of betrothal or the Roman law *sponsalia*. In canon law the betrothal and the non-consummated marriage became identified and gave rise to the impediment of affinity. Therefore, until such time as affinity was considered to arise solely from carnal intercourse, no basis for the impediment of public propriety remained.

5. The doctrine of the *Decretum* of Gratian, though not explicit, was interpreted by the glossators to mean that both *sponsalia de presenti* and *sponsalia de futuro,* that is, both non-consummated marriage and betrothal, begot the impediment of public propriety. Such also was the doctrine of the Decretal law.

6. In the main the Decretal law on the impediment of public propriety obtained until the Code of Canon Law became the law of the Church on May 19, 1918. The Decretal law was somewhat

modified by the law of the Council of Trent, but the latter affected the impediment only in as far as it arose from betrothal. In the period after the Council of Trent, canonists were, for the most part, preoccupied with resolving doubts inherent in the Decretal law. The tendency throughout was to restrict the scope of the impediment, more especially in regard to its origin in betrothal.

7. The impediment of public propriety in the Code of Canon law springs from two sources: invalid marriage and public or notorious concubinage.

8. Public propriety arises only from an invalid marriage which has the appearance of a marriage, but it arises from every invalid marriage which furnishes the semblance of a marriage. So-called civil marriage lacks in canon law the appearance of a marriage.

9. Concubinage, before it can give rise to the impediment of public propriety, must be public not in the same sense as an impediment is public (canon 1037) but in the sense in which a delict is public (canon 2197, 1-3).

10. The invalid marriage or public and notorious concubinage of infidels may form the basis from which the impediment of public propriety will arise upon the subsequent baptism of one of the parties.

11. The impediment of public propriety ceases only through the grant of a dispensation.

12. The impediment of public propriety need not be considered as amenable to multiplication in its nature as an impediment.

BIBLIOGRAPHY

Sources

Acta Apostolicae Sedis, Commentarium Officiale, Romae, 1909-

Acta et Decreta Sacrorum Conciliorum Recentiorum, Collectio Lacensis, 7 vols., Friburgi Brisgoviae: Herder, 1870-1892.

Acta Sanctae Sedis, 41 vols., Romae, 1865-1908.

Bouscaren, T. L., *Canon Law Digest,* 2 vols., Milwaukee: Bruce, 1934-1943.

Bruns, Hermann T., *Canones Apostolorum et Conciliorum Saeculorum, IV, V, VI, VII,* 2 vols., Berolini, 1839.

Bullarum Diplomatum et Privilegiorum Sanctorum Romanorum Pontificum Taurinensis Editio, 24 vols. et Appendix, Augustae Taurinorum, 1857-1872.

Canones et Decreta Sacrosancti Oecumenici Concilii Tridentini, editio novissima et fidem optimorum exemplarium castigate impressa (XIX reimpressio stereotypa), Taurini, 1913.

Codex Iuris Canonici, Pii X Pontificis Maximi iussu digestus Benedicti Papae XV auctoritate promulgatus, ed. Petri Card. Gasparri, Civitate Vaticana: Typis Polyglottis Vaticanis, 1917. Reimpressio, 1934.

Codicis Iuris Canonici Fontes, cura Emi Petri Card. Gasparri editi, 9 vols., Romae (postea Civitate Vaticana): Typis Polyglottis Vaticanis, 1923-1939. (Vols. VII, VIII, IX, ed. cura et studio Emi Iustiniani Card. Serédi.)

Collectanea S. Congregationis de Propaganda Fide, 2 vols., Romae: Typographia Polyglotta S. C. de Propaganda Fide, 1907.

Corpus Iuris Canonici, Editio Lipsiensis II (Richter-Friedberg), 2 vols., Lipsiae, 1879-1881.

Corpus Iuris Civilis, 3 vols., Berolini, 1928-1929. (Vols. I-II, P. Krueger ed.; Vol. III, R. Schoell-G. Kroll ed.)

Decretales D. Gregorii Papae IX suae integritati una cum glossis restitutae, cum privilegio Gregorii XIII, Pont. Max., et aliorum Principum, Romae, 1582.

Decretum Gratiani emendatum et notationibus illustratum una cum glossis, Gregorii XIII, Pont. Max., iussu editum, 2 vols., Romae, 1582.

Department of Commerce and Labor, *Special Reports: Marriage and Divorce,* 2 vols., Washington, D. C.: U. S. Government Printing Office, 1909.

Ecloga, The, A Manual of Roman Law, trans. by Edwin Freshfield, Cambridge: The University Press, 1926.

Ecloga, The, ad Procheiron Mutata, trans. by Edwin Freshfield, Cambridge: The University Press, 1927.

Fontes Iuris Romani Anteiustiniani, ed. Ioannes Baviera, Florentiae, 1909.

Gallemart, Ioannes, *Sacrosanctum et Oecumenicum Concilium Tridentinum, additis declarationibus Cardinalium Concilii interpretum, ex ultima recognitione Ioannis Gallemart, nunc demum hac postrema editione adnotationibus D. Card. de Luca illustratum,* Tridenti, 1737.

Hardouin, Jean, *Acta Conciliorum et Epistolae Decretales ac Constitutiones Summorum Pontificum,* 12 vols., Parisiis, 1714-1715.

Jaffe, Philippus, *Regesta Pontificum Romanorum ab condita Ecclesia ad annum post Christum natum MCXCVIII* (2. ed., correctam et auctam auspiciis Guielmi Wattenbach curaverunt F. Kaltenbrunner, P. Ewald, S. Loewenfeld), 2 vols. in 1, Lipsiae, 1885-1888.

Ius Graeco-romanum, Vol. I, *Novellae et Aureae Bullae Imperatorum post Iustinianum,* ed. K. E. Zacharias von Lingenthal, Athenis, 1931.

Krueger, P., *Codex Theodosianus,* Berolini: apud Weidmannos, 1923-1926.

Lauchert, Friedrich, *Die Kanones der wichtigsten altkirchlichen Concilien nebst den apostolischen Kanones,* Freiburg i. B. und Leipzig, 1896.

Liber Sextus Decretalium D. Bonifatii Papae VIII, una cum Clementinis et Extravagantibus, tum D. Ioannis XXII tum Communibus, una cum earum glossis, Romae, 1582.

Mansi, J. D., *Sacrorum Conciliorum Nova et Amplissima Collectio,* 53 vols. in 60, Paris-Leipzig-Arnhem, 1901-1927.

Martin, Conradus, *Omnium Concilii Vaticani quae ad doctrinam et disciplinam pertinent documentorum collectio,* Paderbornae, 1873.

Monumenta Germaniae Historica (188 vols. incomplete, Hannoverae, 1826-); Leges, 5 vols., Vol. I-IV, ed. G. Pertz; Vol. V, ed. G. Pertz-G. Waitz-H. Brunner, Hannoverae, 1835-1898.

Epistolae, Gregorii VII, Registrum Lib. I-IV, ed. Societas Aperiendis Fontibus Rerum Germanicarum Medii Aevi, 1920.

Epistolae Karolini Aevi, Tom. IV, Berolini: apud Weidmannos, 1925.

Potthast, A., *Regesta Pontificum Romanorum inde ab anno post Christum natum MCXCVIII ad annum MCCCIV,* 2 vols., Berolini, 1874-1875.

S. R. Rotae Decisiones Recentiores, 19 parts in 25 vols., Francofurti-Aureliae-Romae, 1623-1703.

S. R. Rotae Decisiones seu Sententiae, ab anno 1909—, Romae: Typis Polyglottis Vaticanis, 1912-

Thesaurus Resolutionum Sacrae Congregationis Concilii, 167 vols., Romae, 1718-1908.

Wilkins, J., *Concilia Magnae Brittaniae et Hiberniae,* 4 vols., Londini, 1737.

Authors

Aertnys, J.-Damen, C., *Theologia Moralis,* 14. ed., 2 vols., Taurini: Marietti, 1944.

Alberti, Josephus, *Theologia Pastoralis de Sacramento Matrimonii,* Romae, 1904.

Aichner, Simon, *Compendium Iuris Ecclesiastici,* 11. ed., Brixinae, 1911.

Alford, Culver Bernard, *Ius Matrimoniale Comparatum,* Romae: Anonima Libraria Cattolica Italiana-New York: P. J. Kenedy & Sons, 1937.

Alphonsus Maria de Ligorio, S., *Theologia Moralis,* ed. nova cura et studio P. L. Gaude, 4 vols., Romae: Typis Polyglottis Vaticanis, 1905-1912.

Aquinas, St. Thomas, *Summa Theologica,* de novo edita cura et studio Collegii Provinciae Tolosanae Ordinis Praedicatorum, 6 vols., Parisiis: Andreas Blat, 1935.

Augustine, Charles, *A Commentary on the New Code of Canon Law,* 8 vols., Vol. V, 3. ed., 1923; Vol. VIII, 3. ed., 1931; St. Louis: B. Herder.

Ayrinhac, H. A.-Lydon, P. J., *Marriage Legislation in the New Code of Canon Law,* revised and enlarged, New York: Benziger Brothers, 1932.

———, *Penal Legislation in the New Code of Canon Law,* revised edition, New York: Benziger Brothers, Inc., 1944.

Bangen, Ioannes Henricus, *Instructio Practica de Sponsalibus et Matrimonio,* 4 fasc. in 1, Monasterii, 1858-1860.

Barbosa, Augustinus, *Collectanea doctorum, tam veterum quam recentiorum, in ius pontificium universum,* 6 vols. in 5, Venetiis, 1716-1719.

———, *Pastoralis sollicitudinis sive de officio et potestate episcopi tripartita descriptio,* Lugduni, 1716.

Benedictus XIV, *De Synodo Dioecesana,* 2 vols., Romae, 1806.

———, *Institutiones Ecclesiasticae,* Prati, 1844.

Bernardus Papiensis, *Summa Decretalium,* ed. Ern. Ad. T. Laspeyres, Ratisbonae, 1860.

Bishop, William, *New Commentaries on Marriage, Divorce and Separation,* Vol. I, 6. ed., Chicago, 1891.

Blat, Albertus, *Commentarium Textus Codicis Iuris Canonici,* 5 vols. in 6, Lib. III, *De Sacramentis,* 2. ed., 1924; Lib. V, *De Delictis et Poenis,* 1924, Romae: ex Typographia Pontificia in Instituto Pii IX.

Bouscaren, T. Lincoln-Ellis, Adam, *Canon Law, A Text and Commentary,* Milwaukee: The Bruce Publishing Co., 1946.

Buckland, W. W., *A Text Book of Roman Law from Augustus to Justinian,* Cambridge: University Press, 1932.

Cance, Adrien, *Le Code de Droit Canonique,* 6. ed., 3 vols., Paris: J. Cabalda et Fils, 1930.

Cappello, Felix M., *Tractatus Canonico-moralis de Sacramentis,* Vol. V, *De Matrimonio,* Editio quinta emendata et aucta, Romae: Marietti, 1947.

Catholic Encyclopedia, The, 15 vols. with Index and 2 Supplements, New York, 1907-1922.

Cavagnis, F., *Institutiones Iuris Publici Ecclesiastici,* 4. ed., 3 vols., Romae, 1906.

Cerato, Prosdocimus, *Matrimonium a Codice I. C. integre desumptum,* 4. ed., Patavii, 1927.

Chelodi, Ioannes, *Ius Matrimoniale iuxta Codicem Iuris Canonici,* 4. ed., recognita et aucta a Vigilio Dalpiaz, Tridentini: Libreria Moderna Editrice A. Ardesi, 1937.

Cicognani, Amleto G., *Canon Law,* 2. rev. ed., Authorized English Version by J. M. O'Hara and F. Brennan, Philadelphia: Dolphin Press, 1935.

Claeys Bouuaert, F.-Simenon, G., *Manuale Juris Canonici,* 3 vols., Vols. I and III, 3. ed., Vol. II, ed., Gandae et Leodii: Dessain, 1930-1931.

Cooper, Thomas, *Institutes of Justinian,* 3. ed., New York, 1842.

Corbett, Percy Ellwood, *The Roman Law of Marriage,* Oxford: Clarendon Press, 1930.

Coronata, Matthaeus Conte a, *Institutiones Iuris Canonici,* 2. ed., 5 vols., Taurini: Marietti, 1939-1947.

Ferrini, Contardo, *Pandette,* 3. ed., Romae, 1908.

Freisen, Joseph, *Geschichte des canonischen Eherechts bis zum Verfall der Glossenlitteratur,* 2. Ausgabe, Paderborn, 1893.

Garcia, F. Boyou, J., *Tractatus Canonico-Moralis de Sacramento Matrimonii,* 2 vols., Madrid: Editorial del C. de Maria, 1931.

Gasparri, Petrus, *Tractatus Canonicus de Matrimonio,* 3. ed., 2 vols., Paris, 1904. (When this edition is referred to in the text it will bear the date 1904.)

———, *Tractatus Canonicus de Matrimonio* (ed. nova ad mentem Codicis I. C., 2 vols., Typis Polyglottis Vaticanis, 1932).

Genicot, Eduardus-Salsmans, I., *Institutiones Theologiae Moralis,* 10. ed., 2 vols., Bruxellis, 1922.

Giovine, Petrus, *De Dispensationibus Matrimonialibus Consultationes Canonicae,* 2 vols. in 5 parts, Neapoli, 1863-1866.

Goldsmith, J. William, *The Competence of Church and State over Marriage —Disputed Points,* The Catholic University of America Canon Law Studies, n. 197, Washington, D. C.: The Catholic University of America Press, 1944.

Gonzalez-Tellez, Emmanuel, *Commentaria Perpetua in Singulos Textus Quinque Librorum Decretalium Gregorii IX,* 5 vols., Venetiis, 1699.

Grandclaude, E., *Ius Canonicum,* 3 vols., Parisiis, 1883.

Granderath, Theodor, *Histoire du Concile du Vatican.* Edite par C. Kirch, Bruxelles, 1904, Appendices et Documenta, pp. 150-151.

Gury, Joannes Petrus, *Compendium Theologiae Moralis,* ed. in Germania, 4., Ratisbonae, 1868.

Harrigan, Robert J., *The Radical Sanation of Invalid Marriages,* The Catholic University of America Canon Law Studies, n. 116, Washington, D. C.: The Catholic University of America, 1938.

Hinschius, P., *Decretales Pseudo-Isidorianae et Capitula Angilramni,* Lipsiae, 1863.

Hörmann, Walter, *Quasiaffinität,* 2 vols., Innsbruck, Verlag der Wagnerschen Universitätsbuchhandlung, 1897-1906.

Hostiensis (Henricus de Segusio), *Commentaria in Quinque Decretalium Libros,* 5 vols. in 3, Venetiis, 1581.

Huebner, Rudolf, *A History of Germanic Private Law,* translated by Francis S. Phillinck, Boston: Little Brown, and Company, 1918.

Ioannes Andreae, *In Quartum Decretalium Librum Novella Commentaria,* Venetiis, 1581.

Jolowicz, H. F., *Historical Introduction to the Study of Roman Law,* Cambridge: University Press, 1932.

Joyce, G. H., *Christian Marriage, an Historical and Doctrinal Study, Heythrop Series*: 1, New York: Sheed and Ward, 1933.

Knecht, August, *Handbuch des katholischen Eherechts,* Freiburg im Breisgau: Herder, 1928.

Koegel, Otto E., *Common Law and Its Development in the United States.* Washington: John Byrne & Co., 1922.

Konings, A., *Commentarium in Facultates Apostolicas,* 4. ed. recognita, curante Joseph Putzer, Neo-Eboraci: Apud Benziger Fratres, 1897.

Kurtscheid, Bertrandus, *Historia Iuris Canonici, Historia Institutorum,* I (ab Ecclesiae fundatione usque ad Gratianum), Romae: Officium Libri Catholici, 1941.

Lega, M. Card., *De Delictis et Poenis,* 2. ed., Romae, 1910.

Lombardus, Petrus, *Libri IV Sententiarum,* Ed. ad Claras Agnos prope Florentiam: 2. ed., 2 vols., Ex Typographia Collegii S. Bonaventurae, 1916.

Mansella, Iosaphus, *De Impedimentis Matrimonium Dirimentibus ac de Processu Iudiciali in Causis Matrimonialibus Notiones et Disceptationes Canonicae,* Romae, 1881.

Marbach, Joseph Francis, *Marriage Legislation for the Catholics of the Oriental Rites in the United States and Canada,* The Catholic University of America Canon Law Studies, n. 243, Washington, D. C.: The Catholic University of America Press, 1946.

Mascardus, Joseph, *Conclusiones probationesque Omnium,* 3 vols., Venetiis, 1593.

Merkelbach, Benedictus Henricus, *Summa Theologiae Moralis,* 3 vols., Vol. I-II, 3. ed., 1938; Vol. III, 2. ed., 1936, Parisiis: Typis Desclee de Broewer et Soc.

Meyer, Paul, *Der römische Konkubinat,* Leipzig, 1895.

Michiels, Gommarus, *Principia Generalia de Personis in Ecclesia,* Lublin: Universitas Catholica, 1932.

Migne, J. P., *Patrologiae Cursus Completus, Series Graeca,* 161 vols., Parisiis, 1857-1866.

———, *Patrologiae Cursus Completus, Series Latina,* 221 vols., Parisiis, 1844-1864.

Monacelli, F., *Formularium Legale Practicum Fori Ecclesiastici,* nova ed., 4 vols. in 3, Romae, 1844.

Murphy, Edwin J., *Suspension ex Informata Conscientia,* The Catholic University of America Canon Law Studies, n. 76, Washington, D. C.: The Catholic University of America, 1932.

Neuberger, Nicholas J., *Canon 6 or the Relation of the Codex Iuris Canonici to the Preceding Legislation,* The Catholic University of America Canon Law Studies, n. 44, Washington, D. C.: The Catholic University of America, 1927.

Noldin, H., et Schmitt, A., *Summa Theologiae Moralis,* 3 vols., 26. ed., Ratisbonae: Pustet, 1940.

Noval, I., *Commentarium Codicis Iuris Canonici, Lib. IV, De Processibus,* 2 vols., Augustae Taurinorum-Romae: Marietti, 1920-1932.

Ottaviani, Alaphridus, *Institutiones Iuris Publici Ecclesiastici,* 2 vols., 2. ed., Civitate Vaticana: Typis Polyglottis Vaticanis, 1935-1936.

Oesterle, Gerardus, *Consultationes de Jure Matrimoniali,* Romae: Officium Libri Catholici, 1942.

Ojetti, B., *Synopsis Rerum Moralium et Iuris Pontificii Alphabetico Ordine Digesta,* 3. ed., 4 vols., Romae, 1909-1914.

———, *Commentarium in Codicem Iuris Canonici,* 4 vols., Romae: Apud Aedes Universitatis Gregorianae, 1927-1931.

———, *In Ius Antepianum et Pianum ex Decreto Ne temere de forma celebrationis Sponsalium et matrimonii commentarii,* Romae, 1908.

Pallavicino, Pietro Sforza, *Istoria del Concilio di Trento,* 6 vols., Faenza, 1792-1797.

Panormitanus, Abbas (Nicolaus de Tudeschis), *Commentaria super Quinquc Libros Decretalium,* 5 vols. in 7, Venetiis, 1588.

Payen, G., *De Matrimonio in Missionibus ac Potissimum in Sinis Tractatus Practicus et Casus,* 3 vols., 2. ed., Zi-Ka-wei: In Typographia T'ou-ae-we, 1935-1936.

Petrovits, Joseph J. C., *The New Church Law on Matrimony,* 2. ed., Philadelphia: McVey, 1926.

Pighi, Jo. Bapta., *De Sacramento Matrimonii,* 2. ed., Veronae, 1921.

Pirhing, Ernricus, *Ius Canonicum,* 5 vols., Dilingae, 1674-1678.

Pitonius, Franciscus M., *Disceptationes Ecclesiasticae,* Pars II, Romae, 1704.

Pitra, I. B., *Iuris Ecclesiastici Graecorum Historia et Monumenta,* 2 vols., Romae, 1864-1868.

Pöschl, Arnold, *Lehrbuch des katholischen Kirchenrechts,* Graz, 1921.

Prümmer, Dominicus M., *Manuale Theologiae Moralis,* 8. ed., 3 vols., recognita a E. M. Münch, Friburgi Brisgoviae: Herder, 1935-1936.

Regatillo, E., *Institutiones Iuris Canonici,* 2 vols., Santander: Sal Terrae, 1941-1942.

Reiffenstuel, Anacletus, *Ius Canonicum Universum,* ed. noviss., 5 vols. in 6, Romae, 1831-1834.

Roberti, Franciscus, *De Delictus et Poenis,* Romae: Apud Aedes Facultatis Iuridicae ad S. Apollinaris, 1 vol. in 2, 1930-1938.

Rosset, Michael, *De Sacramento Matrimonii Tractatus Dogmaticus, Moralis, Canonicus, Liturgicus et Iudiciarius,* 6 vols., Paris, 1895-1896.

Rufinus, *Summa Decretorum,* ed. H. Singer, Paderborn, 1902.

Sebastiani, Nicolaus, *Summarium Theologiae Moralis,* ed. octavo minor, Taurini: Marietti, 1925.

Sanchez, Thomas, *De Sancto Matrimonii Sacramento Disputationum Tomi Tres,* Lugduni, 1669.

Santi, Franciscus, *Praelectiones Juris Canonici,* 5 vols. in 3, 4. ed., cura M. Leitner, Ratisbonae-Romae: Pustet, 1903-1905.

Scavini, Petrus, *Theologia Moralis Universa ad Mentem S. Alphonsi M. de Ligorio,* 9. ed., 4 vols., Mediolani, 1869.

Scherer, Rudolf Ritter von, *Handbuch des Kirchenrechtes,* 2 vols., Graz, 1886-1898.

Schmalzgrueber, F., *Ius Ecclesiasticum Universum,* 5 vols. in 12, Romae, 1843-1845.

Schroeder, H. J., *Disciplinary Decrees of the General Councils,* St. Louis: Herder, 1941.

Sherman, Charles P., *Roman Law in the Modern World,* 2. ed., 3 vols., New York: Baker, Voorhis & Company, 1924.

Smith, Charles Edward, *Papal Enforcement of Some Medieval Marriage Laws,* Louisiana State University Press, 1940.

Sole, Iacobus, *De Delictis et Poenis-Praelectiones in Lib. V. Codicis Iuris Canonici,* Romae, 1920.

Van Hove, A., *Commentarium Lovaniense in Codicem Iuris Canonici,* Vol. I, Tom. I (*Prolegomena ad Codicem Iuris Canonici*), 2. ed., Mechliniae-Romae: H. Dessain, 1945.

Vermeersch, A., *Theologiae Moralis, Principia-Responsa-Concilia,* 3. ed., 4 vols., Romae: Apud Aedes Universitatis Gregorianae, 1933-1937.

Vermeersch, A.-Creusen, J., *Epitome Iuris Canonici,* 3 vols., Vol. I, 6. ed., Vols. II & III, 5. ed., 1934-1937.

Vlaming, Th. M., *Praelectiones Iuris Matrimonii ad Normam Codicis Iuris Canonici,* 3. ed., 2 vols., Bussum in Hollandia, 1919-1921.

Vromant, G., *Ius Missionariorum,* Tom. V, *De Matrimonio,* Lovanii: Museum Lessianum, 1931.

Wahl, Francis X., *The Matrimonial Impediments of Consanguinity and Affinity,* The Catholic University Canon Law Studies, n. 90, Washington, D. C.: The Catholic University of America, 1934.

Wernz, F. X., *Ius Decretalium,* 3. ed., 6 vols., Prati, 1913-1915.

Wernz, F. X.-Vidal, P., *Ius Canonicum,* Tom. V, *Ius Matrimoniale,* 3. ed., Romae: Universitas Gregoriana, 1946; Tom. VII, *Ius Poenale,* 1937, Romae, Universitas Gregoriana.

Wouters, Ludovicus, *Manuale Theologiae Moralis,* 2 vols., Bruxelles: Beyaert, 1932.

Woywod, S., *A Practical Commentary on the Code of Canon Law,* 2 vols., 10. printing, revised by C. Smith, New York: Wagner, Inc., 1946.

Zitelli, Zephyrinus, *Apparatus Iuris Ecclesiastici,* Romae, 1888.

ARTICLES

Gearin, M. A., "The Matrimonial Law according to the New Code," *The Ecclesiastical Review,* LVIII (1918), 473-495.

Grandclaude, E., "Competence de l'etat touchant le mariage des infideles," *Le Canoniste Contemporain,* X (1887), 241-257.

Lardone, G., "Impedimento ex publico et notorio concubinatu," *Perfice Munus,* IX (1934), 514-516.

Maroto, "Le Ulterior risposte della Commissione interprete del Codice su l'impedimento di publica onesta," *Studi il Monitore Ecclesiastico,* Maratea, 1876-1881; Conversano, 1882-1898; Roma, 1899, XLI (1929), 181-182.

———, "Quaestioni civia l'impedimento di affinita," *Il Monitore Ecclesiastico,* XLIX (1924), 48-49.

Michiels, C., "De Vera impedimenti affinitatis natura," *Jus Pontificium,* V (1925), 142-159.

Ojetti, B., "Ex infidelium matrimonio legitimo an affinitas oriatur," *Jus Pontificum,* V (1925), 71-76.

O'Neill, P., "Decisions of the Commission for the Interpretation of the Code," "The Impediment of Public Propriety," *The Irish Ecclesiastical Record,* XXXIII (1929), 524-525.

Seckel, Emil, "Zu den Acten der Triburer Synode (895)"—*Neues Archiv der Gesellschaft für ältere deutsche Geschichtskunde,* XVIII (1893), 365-409.

Slater, T., "The impediment of public propriety," *The Ecclesiastical Review,* LXV (1921), 492-498.

PERIODICALS

American Ecclesiastical Review, The (1905-1943, *The Ecclesiastical Review*), Philadelphia, 1889-1943; Baltimore, 1944-

Analecta Ecclesiastica, Romae, 1893-1911.

Analecta Iuris Pontificii, Romae, 1855-1869; Parisiis, 1872-1891.

Apollinaris, Romae, 1928-

Irish Ecclesiastical Record, The, Dublin, 1864-

Jus Pontificum, Romae, 1921-1940.

Monitore Ecclesiastico, Il, Maratea, 1876-1881; Conversano, 1882-1898; Roma, 1876-

Neues Archiv der Gesellschaft für ältere deutsche Geschichtskunde, Hannover und Leipzig, 1876-1922; Berlin, 1923-

Perfice Munus, Torino, 1926-

ABBREVIATIONS

AAS—*Acta Apostolicae Sedis.*

ASS—*Acta Sanctae Sedis.*

Bruns—*Canones Apostolorum et Conciliorum Saeculorum IV-VII.*

Bull. Rom.—*Bullarum Diplomatum et Privilegiorum Sanctorum Pontificum Taurinensis Editio.*

Collectanea—*Collectanea S. Congregationis de Propaganda Fide.*

Fontes—*Codicis Iuris Canonici Fontes cura . . . Gasparri editi.*

Hardouin—*Acta Conciliorum, etc.*

Mansi—*Sacrorum Conciliorum Nova et Amplissima Collectio.*

MGH—Monumenta Germaniae Historica.

MPG—Migne, *Patrologia Graeca.*

MPL—Migne, *Patrologia Latina.*

S. C. C.—Sacra Congregatio Concilii.

S. C. de Prop. Fide—Sacra Congregatio de Propaganda Fide.

S. C. de Sacr.—Sacra Congregatio de Sacramentis.

S. C. S. Off.—Sacra Congregatio Sancti Officii.

Thesaurus—*Thesaurus Resolutionum Sacrae Congregationis Concilii.*

ALPHABETICAL INDEX

BIOGRAPHICAL NOTE

John Francis Gallagher was born October 1, 1908, at Ballina, County Mayo, Ireland. He received his early education at Saint Joseph's National School and Bofield Preparatory School, whence he entered Saint Nathy's College, Ballaghaderreen, County Roscommon, from which he matriculated for Saint Patrick's Seminary, Thurles, County Tipperary, in 1929. Upon completion of the prescribed courses in philosophy and theology he was ordained to the Sacred Priesthood on June 16, 1935, for service in the Diocese of Los Angeles and San Diego in California. In October, 1935, he was appointed to the Church of Our Lady of Angels, San Diego, as assistant pastor, and in April, 1937, he was appointed *defensor vinculi* of the Matrimonial Tribunal of the Diocese of San Diego. In February of 1941 he was appointed pastor of Saint Rita's Church, San Diego. From that time until March, 1943, when he was commissioned in the Army of the United States to serve as chaplain, he exercised the dual functions of pastor and *defensor vinculi*. He was released from active duty with the Army of the United States in April, 1946, and in October of that year enrolled in the School of Canon Law at the Catholic University of America, where he received the degree of Baccalaureate in Canon Law in June, 1947, and the degree of Licentiate in Canon Law in June, 1948.

CANON LAW STUDIES*

1. Freriks, Rev. Celestine A., C.PP.S., J.C.D., Religious Congregations in Their External Relations, 121 pp. 1916.
2. Galliher, Rev. Daniel M., O.P., J.C.D., Canonical Elections, 117 pp., 1917.
3. Borkowski, Rev. Aurelius L., O.F.M., J.C.D., De Confraternibus Ecclesiasticis, 136 pp., 1918.
4. Castillo, Rev. Cayo, J.C.D., Disertacion Historico-Canonica sobre la Potestad del Cabildo en Sede Vacante o Impedida del Vicario Capitular, 99 pp., 1919 (1918).
5. Kubelbeck, Rev. William J., S.T.B., J.C.D., The Sacred Penitentiaria and Its Relation to Faculties of Ordinaries and Priests, 129 pp., 1918.
6. Petrovits, Rev. Joseph, J.C., S.T.D., J.C.D., The New Church Law on Matrimony, X-461 pp., 1919.
7. Hickey, Rev. John J., S.T.B., J.C.D., Irregularities and Simple Impediments in the New Code of Canon Law, 100 pp., 1920.
8. Klekotka, Rev. Peter J., S.T.B., J.C.D., Diocesan Consultors, 179 pp., 1920.
9. Wanenmacher, Rev. Francis, J.C.D., The Evidence in Ecclesiastical Procedure Affecting the Marriage Bond, 1920 (Printed 1935).
10. Golden, Rev. Henry Francis, J.C.D., Parochial Benefices in the New Code, IV-119 pp., 1921 (Printed 1925).
11. Koudelka, Rev. Charles J., J.C.D., Pastors, Their Rights and Duties According to the New Code of Canon Law, 211 pp., 1921.
12. Melo, Rev. Antonius, O.F.M., J.C.D., De Exemptione Regularium, X-188 pp., 1921
13. Schaaf, Rev. Valentine Theodore, O.F.M., S.T.B., J.C.D., The Cloister, X-180 pp., 1921.
14. Burke, Rev. Thomas Joseph, S.T.D., J.C.D., Competence in Ecclesiastical Tribunals, IV-117 pp., 1922.
15. Leech, Rev. George Leo, J.C.D., A Comparative Study of the Constitution "Apostolicae Sedis" and the "Codex Juris Canonici," 179 pp., 1922.
16. Motry, Rev. Hubert Louis, S.T.D., J.C.D., Diocesan Faculties According to the Code of Canon Law, II-167 pp., 1922.
17. Murphy, Rev. George Lawrence, J.C.D., Delinquencies and Penalties in the Administration and the Reception of the Sacraments, IV-121 pp., 1923.

*All published numbers are available from the Catholic University of America Press, 620 Michigan Avenue, N.E., Washington 17, D. C., except the following: Nos. 1-114 inclusive, 116, 118-123, 128, 136, 144, 153, 162, 166, 175, 178, 182 and 198. But the following numbers, now reissued, are obtainable from *The Jurist*, The Catholic University of America, Washington 17, D. C., namely: Nos. 5, 7, 11, 17, 18, 19, 26, 28, 30, 31, 34, 42, 44, 51, 52 and 61.

18. O'Reilly, Rev. John Anthony, S.T.B., J.C.D., Ecclesiastical Sepulture in the New Code of Canon Law, II-129 pp., 1923.
19. Michalicka, Rev. Wenceslas Cyrill, O.S.B., J.C.D., Judicial Procedure in Dismissal of Clerical Exempt Religious, 107 pp., 1923.
20. Dargin, Rev. Edward Vincent, S.T.B., J.C.D., Reserved Cases According to the Code of Canon Law, IV-103 pp., 1924.
21. Godfrey, Rev. John A., S.T.B., J.C.D., The Right of Patronage According to the Code of Canon Law, 153 pp., 1924.
22. Hagedorn, Rev. Francis Edward, J.C.D., General Legislation on Indulgences, II-154 pp., 1924.
23. King, Rev. James Ignatius, J.C.D., The Administration of the Sacraments to Dying Non-Catholics, V-141 pp., 1924.
24. Winslow, Rev. Francis Joseph, O.F.M., J.C.D., Vicars and Prefects Apostolic, IV-149 pp., 1924.
25. Correa, Rev. Jose Servelion, S.T.L., J.C.D., La Potestad Legislativa de la Iglesia Catolica, IV-127 pp., 1925.
26. Dugan, Rev. Henry Francis, A.M., J.C.D., The Judiciary Department of the Diocesan Curia, 87 pp., 1925.
27. Keller, Rev. Charles Frederick, S.T.B., J.C.D., Mass Stipends, 167 pp., 1925.
28. Paschang, Rev. John Linus, J.C.D., The Sacramentals According to the Code of Canon Law, 129 pp., 1925.
29. Piontek, Rev. Cyrillus, O.F.M., S.T.B., J.C.D., De Indulto Exclaustrationis necnon Saecularizationis, XIII-289 pp., 1925.
30. Kearney, Rev. Richard Joseph, S.T.B., J.C.D., Sponsors at Baptism According to the Code of Canon Law, IV-127 pp., 1925.
31. Bartlett, Rev. Chester Joseph, A.M., LL.B., J.C.D., The Tenure of Parochial Property in the United States of America, V-108 pp., 1926.
32. Kilker, Rev. Adrian Jerome, J.C.D., Extreme Unction, V-425 pp., 1926.
33. McCormick, Rev. Robert Emmett, J.C.D., Confessors of Religious, VIII-266 pp., 1926.
34. Miller, Rev. Newton Thomas, J.C.D., Founded Masses According to the Code of Canon Law, VII-93 pp., 1926.
35. Roelker, Rev. Edward G., S.T.D., J.C.D., Principles of Privilege According to the Code of Canon Law, XI-166 pp., 1926.
36. Bakalarczyk, Rev. Richardus, M.I.C., J.U.D., De Novitiatu, VIII-208 pp., 1927.
37. Pizzuti, Rev. Lawrence, O.F.M., J.U.L., De Parochis Religiosis, 1927. (Not Printed.)
38. Bliley, Rev. Nicholas Martin, O.S.B., J.C.D., Altars According to the Code of Canon Law, XIX-132 pp., 1927.
39. Brown, Mr. Brendan Francis, A.B., LL.M., J.U.D., The Canonical Juristic Personality with Special Reference to its Status in the United States of America, V-212 pp., 1927.

40. Cavanaugh, Rev. William Thomas, C.P., J.U.D., The Reservation of the Blessed Sacrament, VIII-101 pp., 1927.
41. Doheny, Rev. William J., C.S.C., A.B., J.C.D., Church Property: Modes of Acquisition, X-118 pp., 1927.
42. Feldhaus, Rev. Aloysius H., C.PP.S., J.C.D., Oratories, IV-141 pp., 1927.
43. Kelly, Rev. James Patrick, A.B., J.C.D., The Jurisdiction of the Simple Confessor, X-208 pp., 1927.
44. Neuberger, Rev. Nicholas J., J.C.D., Canon 6 or the Relation of the Codex Iuris Canonici to the Preceding Legislation, V-95 pp., 1927.
45. O'Keefe, Rev. Gerald Michael, J.C.D., Matrimonial Dispensations, Powers of Bishops, Priests, and Confessors, VIII-232 pp., 1927.
46. Quigley, Rev. Joseph A. M., A.B., J.C.D., Condemned Societies, 139 pp., 1927.
47. Zaplotnik, Rev. Johannes Leo, J.C.D., De Vicariis Foraneis, X-142 pp., 1927.
48. Duskie, Rev. John Aloysius, A.B., J.C.D., The Canonical Status of the Orientals in the United States, VIII-196 pp., 1928.
49. Hyland, Rev. Francis Edward, J.C.D., Excommunication, Its Nature, Historical Development and Effects, VIII-181 pp., 1928.
50. Reimann, Rev. Gerald Joseph, O.M.C., J.C.D., The Third Order Secular of Saint Francis, 201 pp., 1928.
51. Schenk, Rev. Francis J., J.C.D., The Matrimonial Impediments of Mixed Religion and Disparity of Cult, XVI-318 pp., 1929.
52. Coady, Rev. John Joseph, S.T.D., J.U.D., A.M., The Appointment of Pastors, VIII-150 pp., 1929.
53. Kay, Rev. Thomas Henry, J.C.D., Competence in Matrimonial Procedure, VIII-164 pp., 1929.
54. Turner, Rev. Sidney Joseph, C.P., J.U.D., The Vow of Poverty, XLIX-217 pp., 1929.
55. Kearney, Rev. Raymond A., A.B., S.T.D., J.C.D., The Principles of Delegation, VII-149 pp., 1929.
56. Conran, Rev. Edward James, A.B., J.C.D., The Interdict, V-163 pp., 1930.
57. O'Neill, Rev. William H., J.C.D., Papal Rescripts of Favor, VII-218 pp., 1930.
58. Bastnagel, Rev. Clement Vincent, J.U.D., The Appointment of Parochial Adjutants and Assistants, XV-257 pp., 1930.
59. Ferry, Rev. William A., A.B., J.C.D., Stole Fees, V-136 pp., 1930.
60. Costello, Rev. John Michael, A.B., J.C.D., Domicile and Quasi-Domicile, VII-201 pp., 1930.
61. Kremer, Rev. Michael Nicholas, A.B., S.T.B., J.C.D., Church Support in the United States, VI-136 pp., 1930.
62. Angulo, Rev. Luis, C.M., J.C.D., Legislation de la Iglesia sobre la intencion en la application de la Santa Misa, VII-104 pp., 1931.

63. Frey, Rev. Wolfgang Norbert, O.S.B., A.B., J.C.D., The Act of Religious Profession, VIII-174 pp., 1931.
64. Roberts, Rev. James Brendan, A.B., J.C.D., The Banns of Marriage, XIV-140 pp., 1931.
65. Ryder, Rev. Raymond Aloysius, A.B., J.C.D., Simony, IX-151 pp., 1931.
66. Campagna, Rev. Angelo, Ph.D., J.U.D., Il Vicario Generale del Vescovo, VII-205, pp., 1931.
67. Cox, Rev. Joseph Godfrey, A.B., J.C.D., The Administration of Seminaries, VI-124 pp., 1931.
68. Gregory, Rev. Donald J., J.U.D., The Pauline Privilege, XV-165 pp., 1931.
69. Donohue, Rev. John F., J.C.D., The Impediment of Crime, VII-110 pp., 1931.
70. Dooley, Rev. Eugene A., O.M.I., J.C.D., Church Law on Sacred Relics, IX-143 pp., 1931.
71. Orth, Rev. Clement Raymond, O.M.C., J.C.D., The Approbation of Religious Institutes, 171 pp., 1931.
72. Pernicone, Rev. Joseph M., A.B., J.C.D., The Ecclesiastical Prohibition of Books, XII-267 pp., 1932.
73. Clinton, Rev. Connell, A.B., J.C.D., The Paschal Precept, IX-108 pp., 1932.
74. Donnelly, Rev. Francis B., A.M., S.T.L., J.C.D., The Diocesan Synod, VIII-125 pp., 1932.
75. Torrente, Rev. Camilo, C.M.F., J.C.D., Las Procesiones Sagradas, V-145 pp., 1932.
76. Murphy, Rev. Edwin J., C.PP.S., J.C.D., Suspension Ex Informata Conscientia, XI-122 pp., 1932.
77. MacKenzie, Rev. Eric F., A.M., S.T.L., J.C.D., The Delict of Heresy in its Commission, Penalization, Absolution, VII-124 pp., 1932.
78. Lyons, Rev. Avitus E., S.T.B., J.C.D., The Collegiate Tribunal of First Instance, XI-147 pp., 1932.
79. Connolly, Rev. Thomas A., J.C.D., Appeals, XI-195 pp., 1932.
80. Sangmeister, Rev. Joseph V., A.B., J.C.D., Force and Fear as Precluding Matrimonial Consent, V-211 pp., 1932.
81. Jaeger, Rev. Leo A., A.B., J.C.D., The Administration of Vacant and Quasi-Vacant Episcopal Sees in the United States, IX-229 pp., 1932.
82. Rimlinger, Rev. Herbert T., J.C.D., Error Invalidating Matrimonial Consent, VII-79 pp., 1932.
83. Barrett, Rev. John D. M., S.S., J.C.D., A Comparative Study of the Councils of Baltimore and the Code of Canon Law, IX-223 pp., 1932.
84. Carberry, Rev. John J., Ph.D., S.T.D., J.C.D., The Juridical Form of Marriage, X-177 pp., 1934.
85. Dolan, Rev. John L., A.B., J.C.D., The Defensor Vinculi, XII-157 pp., 1934.

86. Hannan, Rev. Jerome D., A.M., S.T.D., LL.B., J.C.D., The Canon Law of Wills, IX-517 pp., 1934.
87. Lemieux, Rev. Delise A., A.M., J.C.D., The Sentence in Ecclesiastical Procedure, IX-131 pp., 1934.
88. O'Rourke, Rev. James J., A.B., J.C.D., Parish Registers, VII-109 pp., 1934.
89. Timlin, Rev. Bartholomew, O.F.M., A.M., J.C.D., Conditional Matrimonial Consent, X-381 pp., 1934.
90. Wahl, Rev. Francis X., A.B., J.C.D., The Matrimonial Impediments of Consanguinity and Affinity, VI-125 pp., 1934.
91. White, Rev. Robert J., A.B., LL.B., S.T.B., J.C.D., Canonical Ante-Nuptial Promises and the Civil Law, VI-152 pp., 1934.
92. Herrera, Rev. Antonio Parra, O.C.D., J.C.D., Legislacion Ecclesiastica sobra el Ayuno y la Abstinencia, XI-191 pp., 1935.
93. Kennedy, Rev. Edwin J., J.C.D., The Special Matrimonial Process in Cases of Evident Nullity, X-165 pp., 1935.
94. Manning, Rev. John J., A.B., J.C.D., Presumption of Law in Matrimonial Procedure, XI-111 pp., 1935.
95. Moeder, Rev. John M., J.C.D., The Proper Bishop for Ordination and Dismissorial Letters, VII-135 pp., 1935.
96. O'Mara, Rev. William A., A.B., J.C.D., Canonical Causes for Matrimonial Dispensations, IX-155 pp., 1935.
97. Reilly, Rev. Peter, J.C.D., Residence of Pastors, IX-81 pp., 1935.
98. Smith, Rev. Mariner T., O.P., S.T.Lr., J.C.D., The Penal Law for Religious, VIII-169 pp., 1935.
99. Whalen, Rev. Donald W., A.M., J.C.D., The Value of Testimonial Evidence in Matrimonial Procedure, XIII-297 pp., 1935.
100. Cleary, Rev. Joseph F., J.C.D., Canonical Limitations on the Alienation of Church Property, VIII-141 pp., 1936.
.01. Glynn, Rev. John C., J.C.D., The Promoter of Justice, XX-337 pp.. 1936.
102. Brennan, Rev. James H., S.S., M.A., S.T.B., J.C.D., The Simple Convalidation of Marriage, VI-135 pp., 1937.
103. Brunini, Rev. Joseph Bernard, J.C.D., The Clerical Obligations of Canons 139 and 142, X-121 pp., 1937.
104. Connor, Rev. Maurice, A.B., J.C.D., The Administrative Removal of Pastors, VIII-159 pp., 1937.
105. Guilfoyle, Rev. Merlin Joseph, J.C.D., Custom, XI-144 pp., 1937.
106. Hughes, Rev. James Austin, A.B., A.M., J.C.D., Witnesses in Criminal Trials of Clerics, IX-140 pp., 1937.
107. Jansen, Rev. Raymond J., A.B., S.T.L., J.C.D., Canonical Provisions for Catechetical Instruction, VII-153 pp., 1937.
108. Kealy, Rev. John James, A.B., J.C.D., The Introductory Libellus in Church Court Procedure, XI-121 pp., 1937.
109. McManus, Rev. James Edward, C.SS.R., J.C.D., The Administration of Temporal Goods in Religious Institutes, XVI-196 pp., 1937.

110. Moriarty, Rev. Eugene James, J.C.D., Oaths in Ecclesiastical Courts, X-115 pp., 1937.
111. Rainer, Reg. Eligius George, C.SS.R., J.C.D., Suspension of Clerics, XVII-249 pp., 1937.
112. Reilly, Rev. Thomas F., C.SS.R., J.C.D., Visitation of Religious, VI-195 pp., 1938.
113. Moriarty, Rev. Francis E., C.SS.R., J.C.D., The Extraordinary Absolution from Censures, XV-334 pp., 1938.
114. Connolly, Rev. Nicholas P., J.C.D., The Canonical Erection of Parishes, X-132 pp., 1938.
115. Donovan, Rev. James Joseph, J.C.D., The Pastor's Obligation in Prenuptial Investigation, XII-322 pp., 1938.
116. Harrigan, Rev. Robert J., M.A., S.T.B., J.C.D., The Radical Sanation of Invalid Marriages, VIII-208 pp., 1938.
117. Boffa, Rev. Conrad Humbert, J.C.D., Canonical Provisions for Catholic Schools, VII-211 pp., 1939.
118. Parsons, Rev. Anscar John, O.M.Cap., J.C.D., Canonical Elections, XII-236 pp., 1939.
119. Reilly, Rev. Edward Michael, A.B., J.C.D., The General Norms of Dispensation, XII-156 pp., 1939.
120. Ryan, Rev. Gerald Aloysius, A.B., J.C.D., Principles of Episcopal Jurisdiction, XII-172 pp., 1939.
121. Burton, Rev. Francis James, C.S.C., A.B., J.C.D., A Commentary on Canon 1125, X-222 pp., 1940.
122. Miaskiewicz, Rev. Francis Sigismund, J.C.D., Supplied Jurisdiction According to Canon 209, XII-340 pp., 1940.
123. Rice, Rev. Patrick William, A.B., J.C.D., Proof of Death in Prenuptial Investigation, VIII-156 pp., 1940.
124. Anglin, Rev. Thomas Francis, M.S., J.C.D., The Eucharistic Fast, VIII-183 pp., 1941.
125. Coleman, Rev. John Jerome, J.C.D., The Minister of Confirmation, VI-153 pp., 1941.
126. Downs, Rev. John Emmanuel, A.B., J.C.D., The Concept of Clerical Immunity, XI-163 pp., 1941.
127. Esswein, Rev. Anthony Albert, J.C.D., Extrajudicial Penal Powers of Ecclesiastical Superiors, X-144 pp., 1941.
128. Farrell, Rev. Benjamin Francis, M.A., S.T.L., J.C.D., The Rights and Duties of the Local Ordinary Regarding Congregations of Women Religious of Pontifical Approval, V-195 pp., 1941.
129. Feeney, Rev. Thomas John, A.B., S.T.L., J.C.D., Restitutio in Integrum, VI-169 pp., 1941.
130. Findlay, Rev. Stephen William, O.S.B., A.B., J.C.D., Canonical Norms Governing the Deposition and Degradation of Clerics, XVII-279 pp., 1941.
131. Goodwine, Rev. John, A.B., S.T.L., J.C.D., The Right of the Church to Acquire Property, VIII-119 pp., 1941.

132. HESTON, REV. EDWARD LOUIS, C.S.C., PH.D., S.T.D., J.C.D., The Alienation of Church Property in the United States, XII-222 pp., 1941.
133. HOGAN, REV. JAMES JOHN, A.B., S.T.L., J.C.D., Judicial Advocates and Procurators, XIII-200 pp., 1941.
134. KEALY, REV. THOMAS M., A.B., LITT.B., J.C.D., Dowry of Women Religious, IX-152 pp., 1941.
135. KEENE, REV. MICHAEL JAMES, O.S.B., J.C.D., Religious Ordinaries and Canon 198, V-164 pp., 1941 (printed 1942).
136. KERIN, REV. CHARLES A., S.S., M.A., S.T.B., J.C.D., The Privation of Christian Burial, XVI-279 pp., 1941.
137. LOUIS, REV. WILLIAM FRANCIS, M.A., J.C.D., Diocesan Archives, X-101 pp., 1941.
138. MCDEVITT, REV. GILBERT JOSEPH, A.B., J.C.D., Legitimacy and Legitimation, X-247 pp., 1941.
139. MCDONOUGH, REV. THOMAS JOSEPH, A.B., J.C.D., Apostolic Administrators, X-217 pp., 1941.
140. MEIER, REV. CARL ANTHONY, A.B., J.C.D., Penal Administrative Procedure Against Negligent Pastors, XI-240 pp., 1941.
141. SCHMIDT, REV. JOHN ROGG, A.B., J.C.D., The Principles of Authentic Interpretation in Canon 17 of the Code of Canon Law, XII-331 pp., 1941.
142. SLAFKOSKY, REV. ANDREW LEONARD, A.B., J.C.D., The Canonical Episcopal Visitation of the Diocese, X-197 pp., 1941.
143. SWOBODA, REV. INNOCENT ROBERT, O.F.M., J.C.D., Ignorance in Relation to the Imputability of Delicts, IX-271 pp., 1941.
144. DUBÉ, REV. ARTHUR JOSEPH, A.B., J.C.D., The General Principles for the Reckoning of Time in Canon Law, VIII-299 pp., 1941.
145. MCBRIDE, REV. JAMES T., A.B., J.C.D., Incardination and Excardination of Seculars, XX-585 pp., 1941.
146. KRÓL, REV. JOHN T., J.C.D., The Defendant in Ecclesiastical Trials, XII-207 pp., 1942.
147. COMYNS, REV. JOSEPH J., C.SS.R., A.B., J.C.D., Papal and Episcopal Administration of Church Property, XIV-155 pp., 1942.
148. BARRY, REV. GARRETT FRANCIS, O.M.I., J.C.D., Violation of the Cloister, XII-260 pp., 1942.
149. BOLDUC, REV. GATIEN, C.S.V., A.B., S.T.L., J.C.D., Les Études dans les Religious Cléricales, VIII-155 pp., 1942.
150. BOYLE, REV. DAVID JOHN, M.A., J.C.D., The Juridic Effects of Moral Certitude on Pre-Nuptial Guarantees, XII-188 pp., 1942.
151. CANAVAN, REV. WALTER JOSEPH, M.A., LITT.D., J.C.D., The Profession of Faith, XII-143 pp., 1942.
152. DESROCHERS, REV. BRUNO, A.B., PH.L., S.T.B., J.C.D., Le Premier Concile Plénier de Québec et le Code de Droit Canonique, XIV-186 pp., 1942.
153. DILLON, REV. ROBERT EDWARD, A.B., J.C.D., Common Law Marriage, X-148 pp., 1942.

154. Dodwell, Rev. Edward John, Ph.D., S.T.B., J.C.D., The Time and Place for the Celebration of Marriage, X-156 pp., 1942.
155. Donnellan, Rev. Thomas Andrew, A.B., J.C.D., The Obligation of the Missa pro Populo, VII-131 pp., 1942.
156. Eltz, Rev. Louis Anthony, A.B., J.C.D., Cooperation in Crime, XII-208 pp., 1942.
157. Gass, Rev. Sylvester Francis, M.A., J.C.D., Ecclesiastical Pensions, XI-206 pp., 1942.
158. Guiniven, Rev. John Joseph, C.SS.R., J.C.D., The Precept of Hearing Mass, XIV-188 pp., 1942.
159. Gulczynski, Rev. John Theophilus, J.C.D., The Desecration and Violation of Churches, X-126 pp., 1942.
160. Hammill, Rev. John Leo, M.A., J.C.D., The Obligations of the Traveler According to Canon 14, VIII-204 pp., 1942.
161. Haydt, Rev. John Joseph, A.B., J.C.D., Reserved Benefices, XI-148 pp., 1942.
162. Huser, Rev. Roger John, O.F.M., A.B., J.C.D., The Crime of Abortion in Canon Law, XII-187 pp., 1942.
163. Kearney, Rev. Francis Patrick, A.B., S.T.L., J.C.D., The Principles of Canon Law 1127, X-162 pp., 1942.
164. Linahen, Rev. Leo James, S.T.L., J.C.D., De Absolutione Complicis in Peccato Turpi, V-114 pp., 1942.
165. McCloskey, Rev. Joseph Aloysius, A.B., J.C.D., The Subject of Ecclesiastical Law According to Canon 12, XVII-246 pp., 1942 (printed 1943).
166. O'Neill, Rev. Francis Joseph, C.SS.R., J.C.D., The Dismissal of Religious in Temporary Vows, XIII-220 pp., 1942.
167. Prince, Rev. John Edward, A.B., S.T.B., J.C.D., The Diocesan Chancellor, X-136 pp., 1942.
168. Riesner, Rev. Albert Joseph, C.SS.R., J.C.D., Apostates and Fugitives from Religious Institutes, IX-168 pp., 1942.
169. Stenger, Rev. Joseph Bernard, J.C.D., The Mortgaging of Church Property, 186 pp., 1942.
170. Waldron, Rev. Joseph Francis, A.B., J.C.D., The Minister of Baptism, XII-197 pp., 1942.
171. Willett, Rev. Robert Albert, J.C.D., The Probative Value of Documents in Ecclesiastical Trials, X-124 pp., 1942.
172. Woeber, Rev. Edward Martin, M.A., J.C.D., The Interpellations, XII-161 pp., 1942.
173. Benko, Rev. Matthew Aloysius, O.S.B., M.A., J.C.D., The Abbot *Nullius*, XVI-148 pp., 1943.
174. Christ, Rev. Joseph James, M.A., S.T.L., J.C.D., Dispensation from Vindicative Penalties, XIV-285 pp., 1943.
175. Clancy, Rev. Patrick M. J., O.P., A.B., S.T.Lr., J.C.D., The Local Religious Superior, X-229 pp., 1943.
176. Clarke, Rev. Thomas James, J.C.D., Parish Societies, XII-147 pp., 1943.

177. CONNOLLY, REV. JOHN PATRICK, S.T.L., J.C.D., Synodical Examiners and Parish Priest Consultors, X-223 pp., 1943.
178. DRUMM, REV. WILLIAM MARTIN, A.B., J.C.D., Hospital Chaplains, XII-175 pp., 1943.
179. FLANAGAN, REV. BERNARD JOSEPH, A.B., S.T.L., J.C.D., The Canonical Erection of Religious Houses, X-147 pp., 1943.
180. KELLEHER, REV. STEPHEN JOSEPH, A.B., S.T.B., J.C.D., Discussions with Non-Catholics: Canonical Legislation, X-93 pp., 1943.
181. LEWIS, REV. GORDIAN, C.P., J.C.D., Chapters in Religious Institutes, XII-169 pp., 1943.
182. MARX, REV. ADOLPH, J.C.D., The Declaration of Nullity of Marriages Contracted Outside the Church, X-151 pp., 1943.
183. MATULENAS, REV. RAYMOND ANTHONY, O.S.B., A.B., J.C.D., Communication, a Source of Privileges, VII-225 pp., 1943.
184. O'LEARY, REV. CHARLES GERARD, C.SS.R., J.C.D., Religious Dismissed After Perpetual Profession, X-213 pp., 1943.
185. POWER, REV. CORNELIUS MICHAEL, J.C.D., The Blessing of Cemeteries, XII-231 pp., 1943.
186. SHUHLER, REV. RALPH VINCENT, O.S.A., J.C.D., Privileges of Religious to Absolve and Dispense, XII-195 pp., 1943.
187. ZIOLKOWSKI, REV. THADDEUS STANISLAUS, A.B., J.C.D., The Consecration and Blessing of Churches, XII-151 pp., 1943.
188. HENEGHAN, REV. JOHN JOSEPH, S.T.D., J.C.D., The Marriages of Unworthy Catholics: Canons 1065 and 1066, XVI-213 pp., 1944.
189. CARROLL, REV. COLEMAN FRANCIS, M.A., S.T.L., J.C.L., Charitable Institutions.
190. CIESLUK, REV. JOSEPH EDWARD, PH.B., S.T.L., J.C.D., National Parishes in the United States, VI-178 pp., 1944.
191. COBURN, REV. VINCENT PAUL, A.B., J.C.D., Marriages of Conscience, XII-172 pp., 1944.
192. CONNORS, REV. CHARLES PAUL, C.S.SP., A.B., J.C.D., Extra-Judicial Procurators in the Code of Canon Law, X-94 pp., 1944.
193. COYLE, REV. PAUL RAYMOND, A.B., J.C.D., Judicial Exceptions, X-142 pp., 1944.
194. FAIR, REV. BARTHOLOMEW FRANCIS, A.B., S.T.L., J.C.D., The Impediment of Abduction, XII-122 pp., 1944.
195. GALLAGHER, REV. THOMAS RAPHAEL, O.P., A.B., S.T.LR., J.C.D., The Examination of the Qualities of the Ordinand, X-166 pp., 1944.
196. GANNON, REV. JOHN MARK, S.T.L., J.C.D., The Interstices Required for the Promotion to Orders, XII-100 pp., 1944.
197. GOLDSMITH, REV. J. WILLIAM, B.C.S., S.T.L., J.C.D., The Competence of Church and State Over Marriages—Disputed Points, X-128 pp., 1944.
198. GOODWINE, REV. JOSEPH GERARD, A.B., S.T.B., J.C.D., The Reception of Converts, XIV-326 pp., 1944.

199. KOWALSKI, REV. ROMUALD EUGENE, O.F.M., A.B., J.C.D., Sustenance of Religious Houses of Regulars, X-174 pp., 1944.
200. McCOY, REV. ALAN EDWARD, O.F.M., J.C.D., Force and Fear in Relation to Delictual Imputability and Penal Responsibility, XII-160 pp., 1944.
201. McDEVITT, REV. VINCENT JOHN, PH.B., S.T.L., J.C.L., Perjury.
202. MARTIN, REV. THOMAS OWEN, PH.D., S.T.D., J.C.D., Adverse Possession, Prescription and Limitation of Actions: The Canonical "Praescriptio," XX-208 pp., 1944.
203. MIKLOSOVIC, REV. PAUL JOHN, A.B., J.C.L., Attempted Marriages and Their Consequent Juridic Effects.
204. MUNDY, REV. THOMAS MAURICE, A.B., S.T.L., J.C.D., The Union of Parishes, X-164 pp. 1944.
205. O'DEA, REV. JOHN COYLE, A.B., J.C.D., The Matrimonial Impediment of Nonage, VIII-126 pp., 1944.
206. OLALIA, REV. ALEXANDER AYSON, S.T.L., J.C.D., A Comparative Study of the Christian Constitution of States and the Constitution of the Philippine Commonwealth, XII-136 pp., 1944.
207. POISSON, REV. PIERRE-MARIE, C.S.C., A.B., PH.L., TH.L., J.C.L., Droits Patrimoniaux des Maisons et des Eglises Religieuses.
208. STADALNIKAS, REV. CASIMIR JOSEPH, M.I.C., J.C.D., Reservation of Censures, X-141 pp., 1944.
209. SULLIVAN, REV. EUGENE HENRY, S.T.L., J.C.D., Proof of the Reception of the Sacraments, X-165 pp., 1944.
210. VAUGHAN, REV. WILLIAM EDWARD, J.C.D., Constitutions for Diocesan Courts, X-200 pp., 1944.
211. PARO, REV. GINO, S.T.D., J.C.D., The Right of Papal Legation, X-221 pp., 1944 (printed 1947).
212. BALZER, REV. RALPH FRANCIS, C.P., J.C.D., The Computation of Time in a Canonical Novitiate, X-227 pp., 1945.
213. DOUGHERTY, REV. JOHN WHELAN, A.B., S.T.L., J.C.D., De Inquisitione Speciali, XII-195 pp., 1945.
214. DZIOB, REV. MICHAEL WALTER, J.C.D., The Sacred Congregation for the Oriental Church, XII-181 pp., 1945.
215. EIDENSCHINK, REV. JOHN ALBERT, O.S.B., B.A., J.C.D., The Election of Bishops in the Letters of Pope Gregory the Great, VIII-200 pp., 1945.
216. GILL, REV. NICHOLAS, C.P., J.C.D., The Spiritual Prefect in Clerical Religious Houses of Study, X-140 pp., 1945.
217. HYNES, REV. HARRY GERARD, S.T.L., J.C.D., The Privileges of Cardinals, XII-183 pp., 1945.
218. McDEVITT, REV. GERALD VINCENT, S.T.L., J.C.D., The Renunciation of an Ecclesiastical Office, XIV-179 pp., 1945.
219. MANNING, REV. JOSEPH LEROY, J.C.D., The Free Conferral of Offices, VII-116 pp., 1945.

220. Meyer, Rev. Louis G., O.S.B., A.B., S.T.B., J.C.D., Alms-gathering by Religious, XII-163 pp., 1945.
221. O'Donnell, Rev. Cletus Francis, M.A., J.C.D., The Marriage of Minors, XII-268 pp., 1945.
222. Prunskis, Rev. Joseph, J.C.D., Comparative Law, Ecclesiastical and Civil, in Lithuanian Concordat, X-161 pp., 1945.
223. Sweeney, Rev. Francis Patrick, C.SS.R., J.C.D., The Reduction of Clerics to the Lay State, X-199 pp., 1945.
224. Vogelpohl, Rev. Henry John, J.C.D., The Simple Impediments to Holy Orders, XVI-190 pp., 1945.
225. Brockhaus, Rev. Thomas Aquinas, O.S.B., J.C.D., Religious who are known as *Conversi*, X-127 pp., 1945.
226. Griese, Rev. Orville Nicholas, S.T.D., J.C.D., The Marriage Contract and the Procreation of Offspring, XVI-224 pp., 1946.
227. Boudreaux, Rev. Warren Louis, J.C.D., The *"ab acatholicis nati"* of Canon 1099, § 2, XII-110 pp., 1946.
228. Bowe, Rev. Thomas Joseph, A.B., J.C.D., Religious Superioresses, VIII-206 pp., 1946.
229. Diederichs, Rev. Michael Ferdinand, S.C.J., J.C.D., The Jurisdiction of the Latin Ordinaries over their Oriental Subjects, XIV-153 pp., 1946.
230. Dingman, Rev. Maurice John, A.B., S.T.L., J.C.L., The Plaintiff in Contentious Trials.
231. Frison, Rev. Basil, C.M.F., M.Mus., J.C.D., The Retroactivity of Law, X-221 pp., 1946.
232. Galvin, Rev. William Anthony, M.A., J.C.D., The Administrative Transfer of Pastors, XII-288 pp., 1946.
233. Goracy, Rev. Joseph C., J.C.L., The Diriment Matrimonial Impediment of Major Orders.
234. Hale, Rev. Joseph Francis, M.A., S.T.L., J.C.D., The Pastor of Burial, X-247 pp., 1946 (printed 1949).
235. Henry, Rev. Joseph Arthur, A.B., J.C.D., The Mass and Holy Communion: Interritual Law, XII-138 pp., 1946.
236. Linenberger, Rev. Herbert, C.PP.S., J.C.D., The False Denunciation of an Innocent Confessor, VIII-205 pp., 1946 (1949).
237. Lowry, Rev. James Martin, A.B., J.C.D., Dispensation from Private Vows, XII-266 pp., 1946.
238. Lynch, Rev. George Edward, A.B., S.T.L., J.C.D., Coadjutors and Auxiliaries of Bishops, X-107 pp., 1946 (printed 1947).
239. Lynch, Rev. Timothy, M.S.SS.T., J.C.D., Contracts between Bishops and Religious Congregations, XIII-232 pp., 1946.
240. McClunn, Rev. Justin David, A.B., S.T.L., J.C.D., Administrative Recourse, VII-142 pp., 1946.
241. Lohmuller, Rev. Martin Nicholas, A.B., J.C.D., The Promulgation of Law, XII-140 pp., 1947.

242. McGrath, Rev. James, A.B., J.C.D., The Privilege of the Canon, XII-156 pp., 1946.
243. Marbach, Rev. Joseph Francis, A.B., J.C.D., Marriage Legislation for the Catholics of the Oriental Rites in the United States and Canada, XIV-314 pp., 1946.
244. Shimkus, Rev. Bernard Aloysius, A.B., J.C.L., The Determination and Transfer of Rite.
245. Smith, Rev. Vincent Michael, A.B., S.T.L., J.C.D., Ignorance Affecting Matrimonial Consent, X-118 pp., 1946 (printed 1950).
246. Wachtrle, Rev. Paul Anthony, A.B., J.C.L., The Baptism of the Children of Non-Catholics.
247. Crotty, Rev. Matthew Michael, J.C.D., The Recipient of First Holy Communion, X-142 pp., 1947.
248. Eagleton, Rev. George, J.C.D., The Quinquennial Faculties, Formula IV, XIV-199 pp., 1947 (printed 1948).
249. Gibbons, Rev. Marion Leo, C.M., J.C.L., Domicile of the Wife Unlawfully Separated from Her Husband, XIV-171 pp., 1947.
250. Kelly, Rev. Bernard M., S.T.L., J.C.D., The Functions Reserved to Pastors, XII-141 pp., 1947.
251. Kilcullen, Rev. Thomas J., LL.M., J.C.D., The Collegiate Moral Person as Party Litigant, X-150 pp., 1947.
252. Lafontaine, Rev. Germaine Joseph, W.F., J.C.D., Relations Canoniques entre le Missionaire et Ses Superieurs, X-117 pp., 1947.
253. Lane, Rev. Loras Thomas, A.B., S.T.L., J.C.D., Matrimonial Procedure in the Ordinary Court of Second Instance, XVI-184 pp., 1947.
254. Lover, Rev. James Francis, C.Ss.R., J.C.D., The Master of Novices, X-168 pp., 1947.
255. McNicholas, Rev. Timothy Joseph, J.C.D., The *Septimae Manus* Witness, XII-133 pp., 1947 (printed 1949).
256. Marositz, Rev. Joseph John, M.S.C., J.C.D., Obligations and Privileges of Religious Promoted to the Episcopal or Cardinalitial Dignities, XII-180 pp., 1947.
257. Murphy, Rev. Francis Joseph, J.C.D., Legislative Powers of the Provincial Council, XII-158 pp., 1947.
258. O'Brien, Rev. Romaeus William, O.Carm., J.C.D., The Provincial Superior in Religious Orders of Men, X-294 pp., 1947.
259. Pfaller, Rev. Benedict Anthony, O.S.B., J.C.D., *The ipso facto* Effected Dismissal of Religious, XII-225 pp., 1947.
260. Popek, Rev. Alphonse Sylvester, J.C.D., The Rights and Obligations of Metropolitans, XX-460 pp., 1947.
261. Ristuccia, Rev. Bernard Joseph, C.M., J.C.D., Quasi-Religious, XVI-318 pp., 1947 (printed 1949).
262. Sonntag, Rev. Nathaniel Louis, O.F.M.Cap., J.C.D., Censorship of Special Classes of Books, XII-147 pp., 1947.
263. Stadler, Rev. Joseph Nicholas, J.C.D., Frequent Holy Communion, X-158 pp., 1947.

264. SZAL, REV. IGNATIUS JOSEPH, J.C.D., The Communication of Catholics with Schismatics, XII-217 pp., 1947.
265. WAGNER, REV. URBAN S., O.F.M., CONV., J.C.D., Parochial Substitute Vicars and Supplying Priests, IX-126 pp., 1947.
266. QUINN, REV. JOSEPH, M.A., J.C.D., Documents Required for the Reception of Orders, XIV-207 pp., 1948.
267. BENNINGTON, REV. JAMES CLEMENT, A.B., J.C.L., The Recipient of Confirmation.
268. BLAHER, REV. DAMIAN JOSEPH, O.F.M., A.B., J.C.D., The Ordinary Processes in Causes of Beatification and Canonization, XVI-290 pp., 1948 (printed 1949).
269. CLUNE, REV. ROBERT BELL, B.A., J.C.D., The Judicial Interrogation of the Parties, XII-142 pp., 1948.
270. COURTEMANCHE, REV. BASIL F., B.A., J.C.D., The Total Simulation of Matrimonial Consent, XX-120 pp., 1948.
271. DLOUHY, REV. MAUR JOHN, O.S.B., A.B., J.C.L., The Ordination of Exempt Religious.
272. DONOVAN, REV. JOHN THOMAS, PH.B., S.T.L., J.C.D., The Clerical Obligation of Canons 138 and 140, XII-209 pp., 1948.
273. FREKING, REV. FREDERICK W., A.B., S.T.B., J.C.D., The Canonical Installation of Pastors, XII-210 pp., 1948.
274. FULTON, REV. THOMAS B., J.C.D., Prenuptial Investigation, XII-190 pp., 1948.
275. GODLEY, REV. JAMES P., J.C.D., Time and Place for the Celebration of Mass, X-206 pp., 1948 (printed 1949).
276. KANE, REV. THOMAS A., A.B., B.S., J.C.D., Jurisdiction of the Patriarchs of the Major Sees in Antiquity and in the Middle Ages, XII-111 pp., 1948 (printed 1949).
277. KENNEDY, REV. ANDREW A., J.C.L., The Annual Pastoral Report to the Local Ordinary.
278. KONRAD, REV. JOSEPH GEORGE, J.C.D., Transfer of Religious to Another Community, VIII-284 pp., 1948 (printed 1949).
279. KRESS, REV. ALPHONSE, J.C.L., Contumacy in Ecclesiastical Trials.
280. MCCARTNEY, REV. MARCELLUS ANTHONY, O.F.M., M.A., J.C.D., Faculties of Regular Confessors, XII-164 pp., 1948 (printed 1949).
281. MCCASLIN, REV. EDWARD PATRICK, M.A., S.T.L., J.C.L., The Division of Parishes.
282. MCELROY, REV. FRANCIS J., A.B., J.C.D., The Privileges of Bishops, XII-142 pp., 1948 (printed 1951).
283. QUINN, REV. STEPHEN, M.S.SS.T., J.C.D., Relation Between the Local Ordinary and Religious of Diocesan Approval, XII-153 pp., 1948 (printed 1949).
284. SCHNEIDER, REV. EDELHARD LOUIS, S.D.S., B.A., J.C.L., The Status of Secularized Ex-Religious Clerics, X-155 pp., 1948..
285. THOMPSON, CHESTER J., A.B., J.C.D., The Simple Removal from Office, XII-141 pp., 1948 (printed 1951).

286. O'BRIEN, REV. KENNETH R., A.B., J.C.D., The Nature of Support of Diocesan Priests in the United States, XVI-162 pp., 1949.
287. METZ, REV. JOHN E., S.T.L., J.C.D., The Recording Judge in the Ecclesiastical Collegiate Tribunal, X-130 pp., 1949.
288. REINHARDT, REV. MARION J., S.T.L., J.C.D., The Rogatory Commission, XIII-182 pp., 1949.
289. ORTEGA UHIUK, REV. JUAN, S.J., J.C.L., De Delicto Sollicitationis.
290. CASEY, REV. JAMES V., J.C.D., A Study of Canon 2222 § 1, XII-127 pp., 1949.
291. ALLGEIER, REV. JOSEPH L., J.C.D., The Canonical Obligation of Preaching in Parish Churches, X-115 pp., 1949 (printed 1950).
292. CAHILL, REV. DANIEL R., J.C.D., The Custody of the Holy Eucharist, XVI-178 pp., 1949 (printed 1950).
293. CARR, REV. AIDEN, O.F.M., CARM., S.T.D., J.C.L., Vocation to the Priesthood: Its Canonical Concept.
294. KNOPKE, REV. ROCH F., O.F.M., J.C.D., Reverential Fear in Matrimonial Cases in Asiatic Countries: Rota Cases, XII-112 pp., 1949.
295. LAVELLE, REV. HOWARD D., J.C.D., The Obligation of Holding Sacred Missions in Parishes, XVI-142 pp., 1949.
296. MICKELLS, REV. ANTHONY B., J.C.L., The Constitutive Elements of Parishes.
297. NOONE, REV. JOHN J., J.C.D., Nullity in Judicial Acts, X-147 pp., 1949 (printed 1950).
298. SHEEHAN, REV. DANIEL E., J.C.L., The Minister of Holy Communion.
299. STATKUS, REV. FRANCIS J., J.C.L., The Minister of the Last Sacraments.
300. COOK, REV. JOHN P., J.C.D., Ecclesiastical Communities and Their Ability to Induce Legal Customs, XII-152 pp., 1949 (printed 1950).
301. FAZZALARO, REV. FRANCIS J., J.C.D., The Place for the Hearing of Confessions, X-150 pp., 1949 (printed 1950).
302. HANNAN, REV. PHILIP M., J.C.D., The Canonical Concept of *congrua sustentatio* for the Secular Clergy, XII-237 pp., 1949 (printed 1950).
303. QUINN, REV. HUGH G., S.T.L., J.C.L., The Particular Penal Precept.
304. GALLAGHER, JOHN F., J.C.L., The Matrimonial Impediment of Public Propriety.

www.ingramcontent.com/pod-product-compliance
Lightning Source LLC
LaVergne TN
LVHW050232080826
844660LV00012B/519

9780813224800